ELITE COMMUNICATION IN SAMOA
A STUDY OF LEADERSHIP

This study has been done under the joint auspices of the Department of Anthropology (formerly the Department of Sociology and Anthropology) of Stanford University and the Center for International Studies, Massachusetts Institute of Technology. It is one of a series of studies sponsored by the Research Program in International Communication of the latter institution.

STANFORD ANTHROPOLOGICAL SERIES
NUMBER THREE

Elite Communication in Samoa
A Study of Leadership

FELIX M. KEESING
MARIE M. KEESING

OCTAGON BOOKS

A DIVISION OF FARRAR, STRAUS AND GIROUX

New York   1973

Reprinted 1973
by special arrangement with Stanford University Press

OCTAGON BOOKS

A DIVISION OF FARRAR, STRAUS & GIROUX, INC.

19 Union Square West

New York, N. Y. 10003

Library of Congress Cataloging in Publication Data

Keesing, Felix Maxwell, 1902-1961.
  Elite communication in Samoa.

  Reprint of the ed. published by Stanford University Press,
which was issued as no. 3 of Stanford anthropological series.

  Bibliography: p.
  1. Elite (Social sciences) 2. Acculturation. 3. Samoan Islands—Civilization. I. Keesing, Marie Margaret (Martin) joint
author. II. Title. III. Series.
[GN492.4.K43   1973]   301.44′92′099613   73-7716
ISBN 0-374-94532-2

Printed in USA by
Thomson-Shore, Inc.
Dexter, Michigan

PREFACE

This study took its impetus from a discussion of communication research problems held in 1953 between interested Stanford University staff members and some representatives of the newly established International Communications Research Program of the Center for International Studies at the Massachusetts Institute of Technology.

One of the writers was incautious enough to remark in an informal conversation that phenomena he had observed relevant to elite communication during some two decades of intermittent field work in Samoa bore strong resemblances to experiences he was having in conducting since 1948 certain diplomatic level operations as a member of an international Commission. At the suggestion of Dr. Ithiel Pool, of the M. I. T. Center, he jotted down privately a number of general propositions which seemed to show common elements between these two apparently vastly different areas of human behavior: one among a people popularly thought of as "primitive," the other in the sophisticated modern arena of "international relations." Out of this came, in due course, a modest financial grant from the M. I. T. Center to the writers to follow up these leads by way of their joint field studies on Samoa.

Acknowledgments to Samoan co-workers and informants of past and recent times would have to be far too numerous to list here; and, Samoan-style, none of any eliteness could be omitted without offense. As symbolizing them honorifically, the authors may acknowledge their special indebtedness to the two highest ranking chiefs, the Honorable <u>Fautua</u> (High Advisers) Tamasese and Malietoa, of Western Samoa, and to the Honorable M. Tuiasosopo, for long the leader of the legislature of American Samoa. They also acknowledge both official and personal aid given by Captain T. F. Darden, U. S. N., the last Naval Governor of American Samoa, and the Hon. G. R. Powles, New Zealand High Commissioner for Western Samoa. This can also be symbolic of the extensive help afforded by government personnel and also by private "European" residents of Samoa in past and present. Thanks are also due to the Center for International Studies at the Massachusetts Institute of Technology, which sponsored the study.

Stanford University   F. M. K.
Stanford, California   M. M. K.

TABLE OF CONTENTS

I. THE PROBLEM

This case study is an experiment in analyzing communication in a society very different from that of the West, though one which is now experiencing urgent need for increased contact with the West. It is a study of "elite communication," i.e., of messages to, from, and among persons who wield influence in negotiation, public-opinion formation, and decision-making.[1] Its focus is predominantly that of social anthropology, with its emphasis on intimate, long-term observation and on viewing problems within the total-culture context.

Samoa, the locale for the study, is very much off the beaten track in terms of priorities ordinarily set for such research, e.g., weight in international affairs, strategic importance, accessibility of written sources, at least reasonably valid statistics, and other data to which modern techniques for quantification can be applied. Over against this, the very value of taking a case from among the many smaller, less known population groups is that it may indicate something of the extreme range in world-wide elite behavior and also the variety of problems involved in research technique. It will be recalled that years ago Dr. Margaret Mead's comparisons between this same Samoan setting and Western-oriented societies had revolutionizing effects on theory and practice relating to adolescent behavior. Furthermore, the compactness and isolation of such an ocean-bound island area gives it something of the characteristics of a laboratory microcosm. It may offer better opportunities for controlled observation and sampling than larger, more diversified societies with greater variability both in internal sociocultural forms and in external contacts.

The Samoans will be seen to have well-defined leadership and mechanisms of decision-making and public opinion formation. Their traditional forms of these are undergoing dynamic modification in the modern period, during which members of the elite group must also interact with representatives in Samoa of the outside world, particularly officials of the countries which are in political control: the United States in American Samoa, and New Zealand in the Trust Territory of Western Samoa. Furthermore, Samoa is being increasingly pervaded by the newer media of "mass" communication— the written word and, especially, radio and motion pictures.

Subject to the sharp local mold of custom and historical detail, the Samoans are in much the same general situation as numerous

---

1 The concept of elite communication as used here follows that delineated in the report of the Planning Committee for the M. I. T. project (see Research in International Communication: An Advisory Report of the Planning Committee. Center for International Studies. Cambridge, 1953, pp. 4-7).

1

other ethnically bounded, village-living peoples, not only in the
Pacific area but along the other frontiers of modern culture contact. Somewhat generalized, the phenomena revealed in this study
may occur frequently in cross-cultural communication widely over
the world. Broad resemblances may also appear between communication phenomena in this case situation and in our own Western
societies; for example, the intergroup processes of negotiation will
evoke parallels with diplomatic procedures in international communication.

    In this latter connection it has not been possible, because of
governmental proprieties, to record directly the diplomatic communication experiences which one of the writers has had, serving
in this case by Presidential appointment and as a private citizen,
as Senior Commissioner of the United States on the South Pacific
Commission. This independent regional commission is an advisory
and consultative body set up by the six metropolitan countries with
territories in the area to promote economic and social welfare and
development among the South Pacific populations; it includes the
two Samoan territories within its scope. In developing propositions
on elite communication for the present study, however, this latter
setting of modern diplomatic behavior has been kept always in mind.
This is particularly so in chapters V and VI, where procedures of
negotiation, public opinion formation, and decision-making are dealt
with most sharply. Every proposition, indeed, has been stated in
general terms (and underlined for emphasis), unless distinctions
are made specifically setting off Samoan communication behavior
or communication behavior in societies at a comparable level of
development. The implication is that these propositions might be
worth testing as working hypotheses for further research even within a range as wide as that of both Samoan and Western communication. It should be understood, however, that they emerged in the
course of this study rather than being superimposed from theory.
Their position in the text is governed by their importance in the
Samoan setting, so that for cross-cultural analysis they might need
to be consolidated and regrouped.

    As examples of the type of proposition referred to here a
small selection of generalized statements may be quoted from various sections of the study:

    Conventional behavior involving location and space position
plays an important part in the context of elite communication, being
immediately visible and recognizable (p. 69).

    Elite decisions tend to involve group responsibility rather than
individual responsibility (p. 97).

    Where elite persons are forced, either by pressure of circum-
stances or by external compulsion from higher authority, to render
"spot" decisions, such decisions can have a purely tentative character, until group reaction is forthcoming (p. 124).

Elite negotiations are likely to be strongly oriented toward producing a public show of at least immediate unanimity (p. 114).

Elite deliberation and decision-making tends to be marked by a balance of the power forces which have to be consolidated through political techniques to achieve unanimity (p. 112).

To be effective, the views of an elite person or a decision made by an elite group must have marshaled behind them a weight of support from the adherent, the peer, and the superior groups involved (p. 97).

Elite deliberation tends to be staccato and chronologically segmented, with relatively short interaction periods, and breaks for intragroup or individual review, planning, and relaxation of tension. Both unduly foreshortened and unduly prolonged interaction make for inefficiency (p. 138).

Elite decisions tend to be undertaken only after problems have been brought into sharpest possible focus, usually in multiple consultations at a variety of hierarchical levels (p. 97).

Elite decisions tend to be verbalized in sparse or minimal statements of explicit semantic character (p. 149).

An understanding of elite decisions calls for analysis of all the "voices" involved, with their inherent rights and responsibilities (p. 97).

To what degree deliberation should best be public or private is probably always a tension area in elite communication (p. 139).

Communication between elites across cultural boundaries is shaped vitally by the particular goals being promoted in the groups concerned; it tends to be facilitated or retarded according to how far the goals involved are congruent or otherwise (p. 215).

On a racial frontier, members of a part-indigenous group play a vital role as mediators. The status afforded to them shapes the kind and content of mediation they provide (p. 197).

In many instances the spotlight of analysis is rather on contrasts between the Samoan setting and our own which may be important for comparative research. An example is the problem of mass-opinion polling, discussed on page 128. In the Samoan milieu a wall of inhibition will be seen to exist against expressing opinion outside the correct elite communication channels on issues of elite concern. As a result, random sampling techniques on most public questions would fail to find pay dirt or would only turn up fool's gold. An investigator would obviously need to go to the persons who not only command significant information but also have the right to impart it, i.e. he would need to employ a purposive type of sampling. Again, in contrast to the Western elite person, who is expected to have significant answers on any public issue, a Samoan leader is deliberately shielded from "message" interaction inappropriate to his status (p. 126).

Still another zone of comparison relates to matters which may be widely characteristic of small, ethnocentrically oriented groups, but not so characteristic of the impersonal mass settings of modern national units. An outsider asking questions may legitimately be "fair game" for deception, tricks, jokes, and general falsification of information by members of an in-group (p. 145). Habits of statistical and other semantic accuracy are likely to be rare outside the societies which batter the citizen from childhood with registration forms, census questionnaires, tax returns, and other public documents carrying penalties for false returns. As regards in-group behavior, the small social unit may be most resistant to factors which endanger its stability by aligning its members in a public majority-minority stand; this is in contrast to the basic expectation of decision-making in the "democratic" mass society (p. 115). Again, a small community in which most problems, at least prior to modern contacts, have long since been faced and structured in terms of solutions, may have its elite communication behavior oriented not toward expeditious decision-making in the business-like Western manner, but rather toward expert and leisurely enjoyment of the processes and contexts of deliberation (p. 91).

The format of the study does not follow any arbitrary preconceptions. It developed entirely from the materials themselves, step by step, as a "natural" organization, starting from initial jottings on one sheet of paper. It grew, in fact, alarmingly in size as the significant data and categories gradually emerged and fell into place out of field notes and other sources. The writers are not aware of any study which has a comparable form and coverage for any sociocultural milieu. The following is a quick guide to the format:

1. Chapters II and III give the essential background facts about the Samoan "setting" and especially the "actors and audiences." As the outline cited in footnote 1 above says: "Only when the persons who make the decisions are identified can research explore the influences of communication upon those decisions."

2. Chapter IV gives the important wider cultural context of "symbol, ceremony, and sanction," which a study of Samoan elite communication brings out vividly but which tends to be neglected by students of communication behavior in western settings.

3. Chapters V and VI contain the central analysis of elite roles in negotiation, public opinion formation, and decision-making, in both the traditional and the modern settings. As noted

above, the Samoan data is set within a framework of propositions
(underlined in the text) which could be a basis for comparative
study and theory building.

4. Chapter VII shows the elite roles in relation to the spread
of modern mass media in Samoa—the written word, visual media,
radio, etc.

5. Chapters VIII and IX have their emphasis on elite communication at the "national" level: on what top leaders are saying
and doing today. They focus on "cross-cultural" or "international"
communication as Samoans interact with other population elements,
particularly with the part-Samoan "Europeans, " with the metropolitan governments controlling the territories, and with the modern
world at large. The nature of the "images" and "goals" influencing
elite behavior is examined, together with the special mediators who
carry the main "message" interaction.

6. Chapter X essays a brief over-all analysis of the significance of the experimental case materials presented. It will also
be noted that an annex offers a further general assessment of the
potential contributions of the anthropologist in elite communication
research.

While the main emphasis of the study is theoretical, its
practical or "applied anthropology" significance may also be recognized. In such places as Samoa the strengths and weaknesses of
"dependency" government by a "metropolitan" authority, and also
the rate at which the usually discrete (even warring) political elements are consolidating into a "self-governing" whole in modern
political terms, tend to be conditioned by success or failure in
communication processes, especially at elite levels. This study
will present some of the contrasts between Samoan—United States
interaction on the one hand and Samoan—New Zealand interaction
on the other. The long-term educative processes by which such
hitherto isolated peoples are being consolidated into the modern
world community are essentially dependent on communication
techniques and resources, and their manipulation by persons in a
position to exercise influence or control.

II. ELITE COMMUNICATION: THE SETTING

1. Communication Behavior

The Samoans have a talking, orally transmitted culture. These tall, brown-skinned, Polynesian people of the South Pacific are highly communication conscious. This shows in their linguistic materials, their social structure, their etiquette and ceremony, indeed in all contexts of behavior.

Children from their earliest years hear and participate nimbly in this orally communicated way of life. Talking well and talking appropriately are essential parts of getting along successfully in Samoan society. To a Samoan a telling speech is tapoto, which can also mean an expert stroke with a club. A saying, "O upu matuia," signifies "words with points like a sharp fish spear."

Talking in Samoa is carefully channeled. Everyone, as a matter of course, discusses everyday affairs: the household activities, the catch of fish, the gossip of the neighborhood. But elite, authority-bounded subjects are correctly talked about publicly by the appropriately elite individuals only. No individual could discuss in public without proportionately strong social disapproval topics outside his own range of rights. Such matters, according to their nature and importance, are likely to be treated formally, spoken of in appropriate places and situations to restricted audiences, surrounded by ceremonious behavior, and couched in honorific forms of language with historically rich allusion and other kinds of symbolic reference.

Some traditional topics, such as important genealogies, the more sacred myths, and sources of land titles, are held in strict "security" by a very narrow circle of qualified persons. To talk of them publicly could mean heavy property confiscations, personal banishment, punishment in modern law courts if a complaint is lodged, and, in former days, killing and warfare. By extension, modern communication with government, missions, and other outside elites tends to be reserved to the Samoan elite.

Modern literacy, product of mission and government education, supplements but does not significantly modify the oral tradition. Only a small proportion of Samoans use English fluently or comfortably. All part-Samoans of European status slip easily into Samoan, and most of the few resident Europeans, Asiatics, and other islanders use it freely in their Samoan contacts. Only the incoming official group from the metropolitan countries (New Zealanders and Americans) are shut out from the Samoan speech community, and they rarely learn more than the rudiments of etiquette and odds and ends of word lists.

6

Practically all Samoans are now literate in the Samoan language. Christian missions, at work for more than a century, developed early a reasonably standardized orthography for the hitherto unwritten Samoan language. Teaching of written Samoan has been a required part of the beginning elementary curriculum in both mission and government schools. Reading matter, however, has been on the whole very scanty and selective, being limited almost wholly to mission literature and government publications (of which more later). Samoans still use writing very little within their own system of communication behavior.

Ability to speak and write in English is considerably more advanced in American Samoa than in Western Samoa. The American schooling has stressed the learning of English, and has carried some hundreds of young people in recent years to high school graduation level. A few have gone on to universities. The naval establishment through which the territory was governed until 1951 also stimulated English language use in adult life. In Western Samoa, English has mainly been taught as a subject in higher elementary school grades rather than made a medium of teaching, and high school work is only now being developed. The very exceptional Samoan who can use English with fluency has either gone overseas for schooling, usually as a child of an elite family, or else has been long in government service and has had to learn to communicate with the transient personnel from the metropolitan country. Opportunities for adult participation in English language media have until recently been very limited.

But the situation is now a highly dynamic one. Motion pictures and radio, existent for some time but limited to the urban settings, have spread into the outer communities. English teaching in the schools is being stepped up, especially in Western Samoa by means of "acceleration" schools and central high schools and by a scholarship system for study in New Zealand. Central libraries of sorts have been established. Though written literature continues to be scanty, and verbal contacts few for people away from port towns, the Samoans are clearly on the move toward bilingualism.

The Samoan language, while retaining its basic integrity, has undergone considerable modification to meet modern conditions. As with other Polynesian languages it is in itself both rich and flexible, and much of the wider acculturation experience has been fitted in through manipulation of its existing store of verbal materials. In addition, "word borrowing" from English, and to a very minor extent from other sources, has occurred extensively, subject to incorporation of such verbal materials into the Samoan grammatical and phonetic systems. Where, too, Samoan cultural elements have become obsolete, as in much of the old religion, corresponding linguistic materials have tended to disappear from

use, or to be revised in meaning. The Samoan tradition is a very
lively one, with constant creativity, especially in oratory and
songs, but also as regards drama and other verbal productions.
Linguistic dimensions will be referred to extensively in the study,
and are also the subject of a special annex.

2. Samoan "Character"

To a point, the Polynesian culture and society show broad
"compatibilities" and "congruences" with the European setting—
much more so indeed than do the cultural and social systems of
the Melanesian peoples in the Western Pacific islands. Broad
likenesses show, for instance, between the Samoan way of life and
that delineated in the Old Testament, with its patrilineally oriented
kin groups, hierarchical leadership, and ceremonious behavior.
Resemblances show, too, with early feudal organization in Europe.
But the differences, linguistic and otherwise, are very real.

From the general context of Samoan life and behavior numerous
observers have tried to abstract dominant characteristics. Notably
stressed have been "security, " "conformity, " and "group responsibility" and the symmetrical balancing of social structures, on the
one hand, with "divisiveness, " "deviousness, " "turbulence, " and
the potential of "violence" on the other. Frequent references are
made to an emphasis on rank and prestige, or "hierarchy, " a
dominant concern with "sociopolitical" values and goals especially
as being par excellence "the preoccupation of the elite. " A consul's
wife, Mrs. Churchill, writing her memoirs in 1901, speaks of
"political intrigue" as "the breath of life. " Also stressed are
"dignity, " involving sensitivity to opinion to the point where some
have called it "vanity" or "pride"; characteristics of "ceremoniousness"; "generosity"; and a flair for the dramatic. Robert Louis
Stevenson, in his vivid portrayals of Samoans, speaks of their
"perpetual" songs, games, journeys, and other "pleasures" as
making them "the gayest and best entertained inhabitants of our
planet. "[1]

Margaret Mead has attempted the most ambitious characterizations, based on her studies of child development and adult behavior in rather isolated Manu'a. Of children and adults she says,
in one brief summary exposition:

----

[1] Churchill, L. P., Samoa Uma (1901); Stevenson, R. L.,
A Footnote to History (1892), Vailima Letters (1895).

Children [in Samoa] learn, not as our children learn:
'If I am to receive reward and escape punishment I
must be good' but 'If I am to be let alone and allowed
to stay where I like, I must keep quiet, sit still, and
conform to the rules.'

The administrative forms of the society are also
congruent with this picture; recalcitrant individuals
are expelled from the household, the village, or the
status which they have attained, and gods are con-
ceived, on the pattern of the formally occupied adults,
as concerned about their own affairs and presiding
graciously over the affairs of men as long as men
keep quiet and conform to the rules. The whole
community is committed to following a way of life,
and to the extent to which the child learns to follow
it, he is permitted to participate in it. Obviously
in such a setting, there is no room for guilt. Trans-
gression and non-transgression are matters of expediency. The ties between parents and children
are attenuated by the existence of large households,
by the use of child nurses, by the system of household government through which it is the head of the
household, whether he be father, uncle, grandfather,
or cousin, who has the authority over the children,
and by the extension of dependence behavior to a wide
group of kin. Adults are regarded as persons who,
with varying degrees of facility, follow the cultural
forms better than children. [2]

Mead's picture, as built up here, is of a Samoa as of the
1920's in which the insecurities of war have ceased and Christianity
has reinforced the older values of security and conformity even
while making only a limited impact in many traditional spheres
such as sex conduct, group orientation of responsibilities, or
hierarchical status. The writers have noted over the last two
decades even greater tendencies toward "security": safer methods

---

[2] Mead, M. "Education and Cultural Surrogates," Journal
of Educational Sociology, 14, 2 (1940), pp. 96-97; see also her
other writings on Samoa cited in the bibliography. Other summary
statements on Samoan characteristics are Keesing, Modern Samoa
(1941), especially pp. 24-32; Cook, P.H., "The Application of the
Rorschach Test to a Samoan Group," Rorschach Research Exchange,
6, 2 (1942), pp. 51-60; Stanner, The South Seas in Transition
(1953), especially pp. 305-23.

of handling, feeding, and bedding infants; improved child care generally under European stimulus; and new health, economic, and other benefits available for both children and adults. Over against this, with greater penetration of European values via Christianity and otherwise, the modal personality of the oncoming generations seems by and large to be becoming considerably more "guilt" motivated and individually oriented. Greater room is developing for individual initiative, for choices among alternative behaviors, and for relaxed and spontaneous activity, as by children and young people, apart from the more ceremonious occasions when public conformity to valued customs of formal group participation is still required. The acculturative process involved here will be considered in later discussions.

A Samoan leader, speaking in a debate as a member of the Legislative Assembly of Western Samoa on the topic of local government, offered a revealing statement as regards motivation in the still dominantly group-responsible, status-oriented, community setting:

> I would like to comment on certain facts which may influence the Samoan to do a thing, or agree to do a thing. Firstly, [he may act] because of the dignity which rests with the Honorable Fautua [i.e., the High Advisers who are 'royal' chiefs], secondly because of the pastors of the villages, as they speak about matters concerning God, and thirdly because of certain witchcraft. The fourth reason is if a person [who wants action] is wealthy and has lots of goods, the fifth reason is if a person is a master of any art such as building boats, and the sixth reason is because of the dignity of the chiefs and orators [i.e., the local elite] of the village. The seventh is because of the wives of the chiefs and orators of the village. [3]

3. Ecological and Demographic Dimensions

The three larger and four smaller islands which make up this central Pacific group have a combined area of somewhat over 1,200 square miles, or about the area of Rhode Island, or one quarter the size of Connecticut.

---

[3] Legislative Assembly Debates, First Session 1949, p. 77.

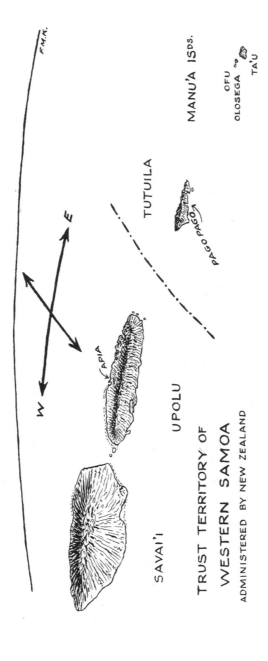

F.M.K.

SAVAI'I

TRUST TERRITORY OF
WESTERN SAMOA
ADMINISTERED BY NEW ZEALAND

APIA

UPOLU

W

E

TUTUILA

PAGO PAGO

MANU'A IS.DS.

OFU
OLOSEGA
TA'U

AMERICAN SAMOA

NOT SHOWN ARE UNINHABITED ROSE ATOLL
TO THE EAST, AND SWAIN'S ISLAND, ADMIN-
ISTERED FROM AMERICAN SAMOA, TO THE
NORTH.

SAMOAN ISLANDS

Western Samoa has a land area of approximately 1,130 square miles. It is comprised of two main islands: Upolu, on which the capital Apia is situated (430 square miles); Savai'i, more isolated and with poor communications (700 square miles); and several very small outliers. Mountainous in the center, the islands have extensive gentle slopes and coastal flats.

American Samoa has a land area of approximately 76 square miles only, nearly all rugged and mountainous. It is made up of one fair-sized island, Tutuila, locale of the capital in Pago Pago (Pango Pango) harbor; an outlying cluster of three small islands (Ta'u, 'Ofu, Olosenga), called collectively the Manu'a group; and two isolated tiny atolls of which Swains Island is inhabited.

A Western Samoa census of 1951 showed 79,588 Samoans, 4,142 part-Samoans of "European" status, 450 white Europeans, 565 immigrant islanders from the Tokelaus and other South Pacific groups, and 164 Chinese. By 1954 the official estimate shows a rise in the Samoan total to 89,201, with 4,927 others. The white European population consists principally of official, mission, and commercial personnel; permanent white residents, once fairly numerous, have dwindled to a few dozen, leaving their properties and other interests usually to part-Samoan descendants. The Chinese comprise a handful of old-settled families, and the remnant of a once large Chinese labor force now almost wholly repatriated.

An American Samoan census of 1950 showed a total population of 18,937, rising to an estimated total of 22,400 by 1954. The census breakdown does not give a clear picture of the constituent ethnic elements. The writers would estimate, however, that approximately 150 were whites, mostly Americans, and nearly all were nonpermanent officials and mission workers and their families. Another 164 were residents of Swains Island, a small United States possession governed from Samoa. Twelve were long resident Asian and Negro settlers, and perhaps 50 were islanders from other South Pacific zones. No legally recognized class of "part-Samoans" exists, but of quite numerous Samoans having some degree of European descent perhaps 300 were identified socially with the white community as traders and otherwise, rather than living within the Samoan social system. American Samoa has never had any sizable non-Samoan population, nor has Western Samoa.

The more than 110,000 persons of Samoan ancestry have the distinction, all the more dubious considering the smallness of their island homes, of being perhaps the most rapidly increasing population of their size in the world. Early estimates of the Samoan population suggest a figure of around 60,000. By 1900, new diseases and other mortality enhancing factors had brought the total for the two territories down to about 40, 000. Subsequent medical, economic, and other ameliorative measures pushed the death rate down progressively, so that an extraordinarily high birth rate characteristic of Samoan sexual and social customs came to dominate the demographic picture.

Crude birth rates per 1, 000 of population for the period 1946-51 totaled 45. 5 for Western Samoa and 42. 9 for American Samoa (cf. New Zealand 25. 2, United States 24. 4, England and Wales 17. 3). For the same period, Western Samoa showed a crude death rate of 9. 6 per 1, 000 and American Samoa a rate of 9. 1 (cf. New Zealand 9. 2, United States 9. 7). The sharp upward trend of recent decades has further produced a remarkably high concentration in the prereproductive and early reproductive age levels: for Western Samoa (1951 census), 46. 9 percent of the population was under 15 years and 73. 6 percent under 30 years, and for American Samoa (1950 census), 46. 3 percent was under 15 and 74. 4 percent under 30; the corresponding percentages for New Zealand were 28. 0 and 49. 5 respectively, and for the United States, 27. 1 and 49. 7.

It is no wonder, therefore, that over the years 1945 to 1951 Western Samoa has had an average annual increase in population of 3. 72 percent, and American Samoa from 1940 to 1950 an average annual increase of 3. 92 percent. In 1953, the New Zealand Government Statistician forecast an increase in the population of Western Samoa as follows: 1955, 97, 000; 1965, 134, 000; 1975, 184, 000. Correspondingly, American Samoa may be expected to double its Samoan population in the next twenty years or so. [4]

---

[4] See the Demographic Yearbook, published by the United Nations Statistical Office, for recent figures on the two territories, and for comparisons with other areas. A fuller analysis of population trends in Western Samoa, including migration data, is given in Stace, V. D. , Economic Survey of Western Samoa (South Pacific Commission, 1955); this includes the forecast by the New Zealand Government Statistician, given as an appendix. More detailed population statistics of American Samoa are obtainable from publications of the U. S. Bureau of the Census and from annual reports. Comparative figures cited from New Zealand are for the white population only; the New Zealand Maoris, a Polynesian group comparable with the Samoans, are currently showing much the same extraordinary rate of increase as the Samoans.

The category "European," as used in Western Samoa, origi-
nated in the settlement of persons of white ancestry. But it has also
come to apply as a legal category to part-Samoan descendants of
white Europeans of legitimate descent on the male side, or legitimized by court process as desiring to hold European status. "European" residents, other than the official, mission, and commercial
class who have their roots outside Samoa, are estimated to be now
over 90 percent of part-Samoan ancestry. The New Zealand government has asked Samoan leaders to agree to abolition of the increasingly artificial distinction between "Europeans" and "Samoans" which
is expressed legally in differential land rights, court procedures,
legislative representation, and other forms. Instead it proposes a
common citizenship for all resident inhabitants of Western Samoa.

American Samoa has not had more than a few non-Samoan
residents, apart from U. S. Navy personnel on temporary assignment, several missionaries, and since 1951 official personnel from
the Department of the Interior. Part-Samoans, quite numerous,
merge without legal distinction into the general milieu. The 1930
census showed 227 Caucasians (179 in the Naval establishment),
11 Asiatics, 6 Negroes, and a few others; as of 1954 there were
about 150 whites, and a few others.

The great bulk of the Samoan population lives in 262 politically
recognized village communities. These units, practically all long
established, range in size from several having somewhat over a
thousand persons to a few with under a hundred persons.

Official census classifications show 192 villages in Western
Samoa and 70 in American Samoa. The American Samoa figure,
here much higher in proportion to the size of the population, is
accounted for by the official recognition of a number of very small
units, most of which have "hived" off from historic communities in
the last few years; the number of older village units is estimated
at 50. In both territories there has been a tendency for new villages
to be established since the coming of peace, and with the population
increase, which in some cases causes a serious pressure of numbers in terms of the available housing and garden space. Even so,
where in 1926 the average number per village was about 210, as of
1950-51 it had risen to about 375.

Two urban port areas have developed in modern times: Apia,
"capital" of Western Samoa, and the Pago Pago harbor area, which
contains the "capital" of American Samoa. Here, government and
mission have their headquarters, and there are trading establish-
ments, banking centers, piers, sports grounds, movies, and other
Western-style facilities which make them, for the Samoans and for
peoples in neighboring small islands, metropolises in miniature.

A small but nevertheless increasing number of Samoans live more
or less permanently in these centers, and nearby villages have
swollen populations. In these areas, too, live nearly all non-Samoan
residents and most of the part-Samoans. A recent official estimate
shows approximately 16, 000 persons living in the Apia area, and
perhaps 3, 000 live in the Pago Pago harbor area. The towns also
draw in many temporary visitors from the outer areas, on official
or mission business, or to shop, look for a job, attend school, call
on relatives, or just "see the sights. "

4.   Travel and Mobility

Physical mobility is on the increase in Samoa in spite of often
rough water channels and rugged terrain. To the older foot tracks
and canoe routes which met traditional needs for travel beyond the
village have been added a limited development of modern types of
transport and communications.

A network of roads now extends from the town areas to nearly
half the villages of Samoa. Bus lines and several taxi companies
are operating, along with government vehicles, private cars, and
bicycles; in 1955, Western Samoa had 210 autos, 100 taxis, 64 buses,
397 trucks and vans, and 31 motorcycles. Launches provide contact with strategic landing points along the coast, and a small vessel services the isolated Manu'a islands. Ocean-going vessels call
every two or three weeks on the average at the two main ports, and
each territory has an air strip served by commercial land planes.
Postal service networks and telephone services are centered mainly
on the two port areas. A local broadcasting station in each capital
center, with many village outlets, especially in Western Samoa,
rounds out the communication picture.

Use of modern facilities by Samoans is highly selective. Bus
and local boat services are always likely to be filled; in the modern
setting of peace the people like to call on relatives, visit the port
areas, and otherwise move around from time to time. Whereas two
decades ago men did most of the travel, women passengers are now
perhaps as numerous. Postal and radio facilities are used increasingly. But taxi travel, telephones, and sea and air transport beyond
Samoa, tend to be limited to exceptional persons mostly of higher
elite status.

A visitor or returning person becomes a major channel through
which news and ideas are disseminated within the dominantly oral
milieu. Samoans, as with comparable peoples, have a great attach-
ment to their home places, and it is the exceptional person who
goes long distances frequently or stays away for long. At present

perhaps 1,100 American Samoans are living abroad, as in Hawaii and on the American mainland, a considerable proportion being U.S. Navy personnel and their families: the Navy has recruited in recent years several hundred young Samoan men for service in Hawaii and elsewhere. About a thousand Samoans and part-Samoans from Western Samoa are in New Zealand, including a considerable number of young people in educational institutions.[5] Members of the elite are likely to have need to travel locally under government auspices or to transact official business, as well as in relation to family and other private affairs. A broad proposition might be stated as follows: <u>elite persons tend to have greater space mobility than non-elite persons, and their relative mobility tends to increase with their rank.</u>

5. Samoan Socio-Political Organization

The elite communication context in Samoa may best be seen in terms of three major socio-political dimensions:
    (a) The local community or "village";
    (b) Traditional "district" structures;
    (c) A traditional "all Samoa" structure of rudimentary "national" character.
In modern times Western-style "governments" have been superimposed upon this Samoan body politic.

a. The Samoan Village

The Samoan village (<u>nu'u</u>) consists in physical terms of a set of thatched houses of two types: superior long or round "guest houses," and less elaborately built family houses, with outdoor cooking shelters. Houses may be strung along a trail or coastal strip, but usually they are in a roughly semicircular group around an open place of grass or sand. This is the ceremonial center (<u>malae</u>) essential to every village, and facing upon it are the "guest houses" of the important families and nowadays often the church or churches. An occasional trade store is located within a village or between adjacent villages.

---

[5] The Annual Report of Western Samoa for 1954 shows an out-migration during that year of 5,090 Samoans, of whom 4,138 crossed the international boundary into American Samoa, and 668 went to New Zealand, 132 to Fiji, and 152 to "other countries." In-migration totaled 4,923, of whom most came correspondingly from American Samoa.

Such a living unit has a basically self-sustaining economy. Within and around it are groves and gardens with quite a rich range of fruit and root crops (coconut, banana, breadfruit, taro, etc.); pigs and chickens, brought by the original migrants, may now be supplemented by cattle, horses (for transport), and ducks; canoe-shelters are indicative of ocean fishing, which along with the reef fisheries provide the main flesh foods; and forest hinterlands supply timber, fibers, and even some wild game, in rounding out the economy. Goods and services which pass beyond the village are virtually wholly ceremonial, pertaining to elite interaction, such as supplying pigs and other "feast foods" or "gift exchanges" of finely woven mats. Even selective and increasing penetration of the modern commercial economy, in which wanted trade goods and money are obtained mainly by selling copra (dried flesh of the coconut) and sometimes bananas, and by temporary wage earning in low-skill jobs, has not disturbed this essential pattern. Economic usages and motivations here are exceedingly complex, as in multiple "authority" and "use" rights in property, and group and individual incentives to "work."

The "John Doe" of Samoa has his roles defined, apart from the general categories of sex and age, primarily in terms of the house group in which he lives, which in turn implies a position within his kin. Socially the community is made up of a series of households of "extended family" or "multiple family" type, each under the authority of a "head" or matai. Kinship ties based on strongly bilateral principles, but with patrilineal-patrilocal emphasis, crisscross the village, and extend beyond it. Neighborliness is also important in social interaction. For a range of economic and ceremonial activities the community as a whole acts as a unit under direction of a "village council."

The most actively divisive force in modern times at the village level is religious denominationalism. Yet on important secular matters ranks are likely to be closed in the general community interest.[6] Further along in the study, certain other disintegrative forces will be seen at work, typical of modern acculturative processes in such areas. But the general picture is of great stability, based on shared traditions, ancestral associations (the dead are

---

[6] More than a century of mission work has submerged the old religion, through it survives selectively. Most Samoans are adherents of the London Missionary Society, which has become an indigenous church with almost fully Samoan personnel in leadership. There are minorities of Roman Catholics, Methodists, Seventh Day Adventists, Latter Day Saints, and a few others, including a local church developed in American Samoa.

still sometimes buried within the village and seem seldom to be far
away from the minds of the living), face-to-face interaction usually
for lifetimes, and notably the elite leadership with which this study
is concerned.

Modern Western (or as it is usually called locally, "European") government has reinforced the integrity of the village community unit. In each territory a system of village officials has
existed for decades: a mayor (Pulen'u, or "authority of the village"), often a secretary to help him with records, and in American Samoa a magistrate and a policeman, all with very limited
training and circumscribed powers. In more recent times the schoolteacher has been added to the roster as well as more itinerant
health, sanitary, agricultural extension, and other personnel. The
indigenous elite, as will be seen, are at work with varying success
on a wide range of governmental enterprises. The modern church
too, with its village pastor, catechist, or other local leader, and
its lay leadership, supports community life with religious sanctions.
A village for weeks or months may not be visited by a white official
or mission worker, and carries on with reasonable efficiency the
combination of Samoan and European activities which enter into its
largely "self-governing" way of life.

The Samoan village, in sum, approximates in miniature an
independent state. It also approaches in microcosm the model of
what the political scientist Deutsch, discussing "political communities," has called a "security community." Here the criteria
which he summarizes in the terms "integration" and "interaction"
approach maximum effectiveness. [7]

b. District Structures

The migrant Polynesian families which settled Samoa, although spreading out over the islands, preserved memories and
tended to retain contacts, especially as regarded their senior lines
of descent and intermarriage, and intricate networks and hierarchies
of "great family" relationship became spun widely over Samoa.
These superlocal kin groups were the lodgment for the leadership
titles which provide the higher ranking elite in Samoan society.

The particular communities and localities with which the
higher seniority descent lines and higher elite titles were associated

---

[7] See Deutsch, K. W. Political Community at the International
Level: Problems of Definition and Measurement. Foreign Policy
Analysis Series No. 2. Princeton University, 1953.

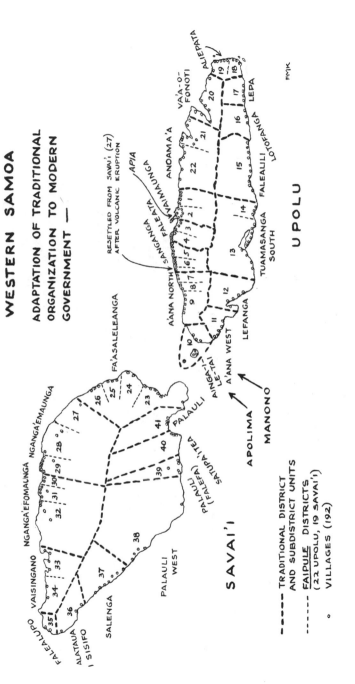

WESTERN SAMOA

ADAPTATION OF TRADITIONAL
ORGANIZATION TO MODERN
GOVERNMENT —

RESETTLED FROM SAVAI'I (27)
AFTER VOLCANIC ERUPTION

APIA

SANGANGA FALEATA VAIMAUNGA
AANA NORTH
ANOAMA'A
VA'A-O-
FONOTI
ALIEPATA
LEPA
LOTOFANGA
FALEALILI
TUAMASANGA
SOUTH
LEFANGA
A'ANA WEST
AINGA-'I-
LE-TAI

UPOLU

APOLIMA
MANONO

FA'ASALELEANGA
NGANGA'EFOMAUNGA NGANGA'EMAUNGA
VAISINGANO
FALEALUPO
ALATAUA
I SISIFO
SALENGA
PALAULI
WEST
PALAULI
(FALEFA)'ITEA
SATUPA'ITEA
PALAULI

SAVAI'I

- - - - - TRADITIONAL DISTRICT
          AND SUBDISTRICT UNITS

- - - - - FAIPULE DISTRICTS
          (22 UPOLU, 19 SAVAI'I)

    o   VILLAGES (192)

FMK

20

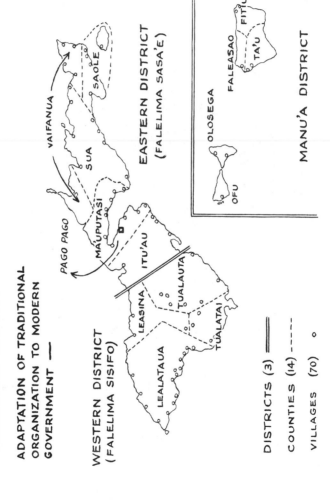

AMERICAN SAMOA

ADAPTATION OF TRADITIONAL
ORGANIZATION TO MODERN
GOVERNMENT ━

WESTERN DISTRICT
(FALELIMA SISIFO)

EASTERN DISTRICT
(FALELIMA SASA'E)

MANU'A DISTRICT

VAIFANUA

SAOLE

SUA

PAGO PAGO

MA'UPUTASI

ITU'AU

LEASINA

TUALAUTA

TUALATAI

LEALATAUA

OLOSEGA

FALEASAO

FITIUTA

TA'U

OFU

F.M.K.

DISTRICTS (3) ≣

COUNTIES (14) ----

VILLAGES (70) ○

residentially tended to become most important. Out of this emerged
a recognized series of district and subdistrict alignments in a complex hierarchy of power, ceremonial, and other relationships.
Each unit came to have a name, its ceremonial center or centers,
its regional lore, and its particular status and role in political
affairs. Such groupings also have had in them divisive tendencies
of factionalism, rivalry, intrigue, and, until the enforced peace of
recent decades, quite destructive war.

The modern governments have sought to use the traditional
subdistrict and district divisions and their appropriate elite groupings, as a basis for their regional authority. Western Samoa has
various types of "district" divisions for administrative, educational,
health, and other purposes compounded from the 11 principal districts and their 41 more important subdivisions. Authority is legally vested, as regards the appropriate spheres, in a Samoan district
representative called a Faipule, acting with the regional leaders
"in council, " and in certain other Samoan officials (e. g., judge,
health personnel, school inspector) mainly on itinerant visits. In
American Samoa the situation is more specific, with three Districts,
each under a Samoan District Governor, and 14 constituent subdis-
tricts or "Counties, " each under a County Chief. As will be seen,
problems of elite communication vis-a-vis Western-style government operations at this level have been difficult, not least of all because of the divisive tendencies mentioned above.

c. The "All Samoa" "National" Structure

As the ethnologist picks his way upward through these kinship
and locality hierarchies he climbs to a rarified atmosphere where
several senior lines with a small number of exalted titles stand
out, together with their locality bases. Topping these he finds three
peaks which in modern European terminology have been called
"royalty, " but which in old Samoa would have been thought of more
in supernatural terms as "god-descended" through the most directly
senior lines. Two of these are based in Western Samoa: one, called
the Samalietoa, heads up in the "royal" title "the Malietoa, " and
commands one great series of kin and district alignments; the other,
called the Satupua, heads up into three top titles which vie for supremacy,—the "Tamasese, " the "Mata'afa, " and the "Tuimaleali'-
ifano, '—and commands another great series of kin and district
alignments. A third and largely independent peak is based in American Samoa on the three little and geographically isolated islands
called Manu'a, and heads up in the title "Tuimanu'a" (Tui being now
translated "king"). Samoan mythology suggests Manu'a as the initial

22

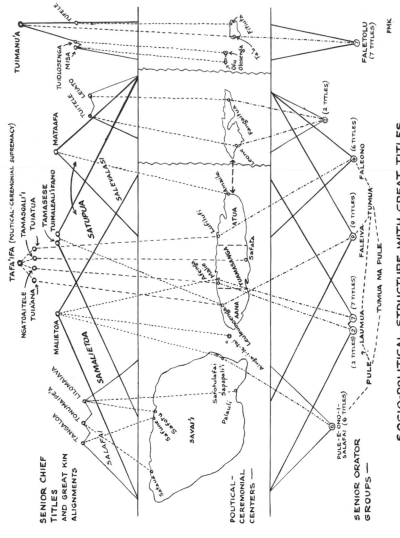

SOCIO-POLITICAL STRUCTURE, WITH GREAT TITLES

SENIOR CHIEF
TITLES
AND GREAT KIN
ALIGNMENTS

POLITICAL-
CEREMONIAL
CENTERS ——

SENIOR ORATOR
GROUPS ——

TUIMANU'A

TUFELE

TUIOLOSENGA
MISA
LEIATO

TUITELE

MATAAFA

TAFA'IFA (POLITICAL-CEREMONIAL SUPREMACY)

TAMASOALI'I
TUIATUA
TAMASESE
TUIMALEALI'IFANO

SATUPUA

SALEVALASI

NGATOAITELE
TUIAANA

MALIETOA

SAMALIETOA

LILOMAIAVA

TONUMAIPE'A

TANGALOA

SALAFAI

Fititi

Oiu
Olosenga

Ta'u

FALETOLU
(7 TITLES)

Fangaloa

(2 TITLES)

Leone

(6 TITLES)

FALEONO

ATUA

Lufilufi

Safata

TUMASANGA

Salani

Male
Fasi

Lepea
AANA

Leulumoenga

Aleipata-Lotofanga

SAVAI'I

Saohulafai
Sappapli'i

Palauli

Safotu
Safune
Safotulafai

Sasi

FALEVA
(9 TITLES)

TUMUA

LAUMUA

FALEVA
(7 TITLES)

PULE

(2 TITLES)

TUMUA MA PULE

PULE = E: ONO = I:
SALAFAI (6 TITLES)

FMK

settlement point and dispersal place, so that it has held a kind of ceremonial seniority.

Feuding and warfare throughout Samoan history have been primarily (a) struggles within kin groups for control of their larger elite titles, (b) struggles among kin and locality groups to enhance their power and prestige position, and (c) a seesaw rivalry between the two great power systems of the Samalietoa and Satupua, which at crisis points could engulf all Samoa except perhaps Manu'a in war and devastation until one side or the other temporarily gained control.

A Samoan term, Malo, applied in later times to the modern Western government, had in the Samoan language the connotation of "the party holding the power (for the time being)." The Malo control became in turn a focal point for elite elaboration. One series of kin and locality alignments became capped by a ceremonial organization or orator leadership called Tumua, and involved the right to bestow two political-ceremonial titles which could be taken by the "royal" elite individual of the Malo party. Correspondingly, a second series had a somewhat parallel orator leadership called Pule, with authority over two similar titles. [8] The Everest-like supreme peak in the Samoan elite system, though indeed a precarious one, was reached by one or other of the "royal chiefs" (Malietoa, Tamasese, or other) if, by way of Malo party dominance, he gained control of all four of these political-ceremonial titles, symbolic of "all Samoa" (except Manu'a), and so received a paramount title Tafa'ifa,—literally, "holder of four."

The missionaries and other early European visitors report on such struggles, with war parties, destroyed villages and gardens,

---

[8] The political character of "Tumua and Pule" has been subject to historic changes based on power balances and other factors and is subject to somewhat different interpretations by Samoan informants within the power structure. The Tumua "voices" appear to comprise (a) fifteen "voices" representative in general of the Satupua kin groupings, that is, the A'ana and Atua districts of Upolu island, and (b) nine representative of the Upolu island sections of the Samalietoa kin groups, i. e., the Tuamasanga district. Pule is made up of six "voices" of leading districts in Savaii, and is associated with the Samalietoa, hence with (b) above. Back of each "voice" is a hierarchy of district and local representation, and the interplay among them out of which a united "voice" might be welded on an appropriate "all Samoan" issue is politically and ceremonially complicated.

and an ultimate control of the Malo by a Malietoa. Much of the subsequent nineteenth-century history is concerned with attempts to
build on the Malietoa succession a stable European style kingship,
and on the Samoan body politic in general a centralized Samoan
government. Inevitably, however, the traditional divisive forces
erupted into periodic wars focused on succession to the king position. This situation became compounded when rivalries among the
Great Powers interested in this section of the Pacific were meshed
in with such factionalism, with the United States and Great Britain
generally supporting the Samalietoa aspirants to the king position
and Germany the Satupua titleholders.

In 1900 Samoa was brought under Western political control to
stop the constant threat of an international crisis. Germany assumed control of the large western islands. As a result of much disturbance and a major rebellion, it declared void the political structure connected with the kingship and Tumua and Pule. The "royal"
contenders for the paramountcy were given a new political-ceremonial
title called Fautua or "High Adviser" in order to channel off and
balance their competitiveness, and this system was continued when
New Zealand took over in 1914. In their new guises, however,
these titleholders continued to hold in Samoan eyes the dignity,
sacredness, and power of their old positions as heading the two
great family hierarchies. By now Tumua and Pule, together with
the kingship, have tended to fade into the somewhat vague and idealized memories of a "Golden Age" with which the serious political
stresses of government today are compared with emotional overtones.

Somewhat similar trends mark American Samoa, following
the establishment of United States control in 1900. In 1906 the
Naval authorities administering the territory, in the face of conflicts with the traditional Tuimanu'a authority and of internal family
dissensions over succession, officially abolished this "royal" title.
It has never been allowed to revive subsequently in spite of attempts
by certain family factions to have this exalted position restored.
A marked trend has shown here for the elite group (other than in
Manu'a), who held what were rather lowly titles by the hierarchy
of old Samoa, to have their status greatly enhanced as being the
top leaders and participants in government of the new territory.
Internally, too, leaders whose districts and communities have happened to be accessible to the port center and seat of government
have tended to rise in status comparatively in relation to those of
remoter zones.

Supravillage relationships at all these levels correspond in
many ways to the relations among states rather than to the internal

organization of a state. What Deutsch calls "integrational" and
"interactional" forces tend to thin out, giving place to more formal
relations of power and ceremony, which are highly fissionable.
As an anthropologist, Stanner, puts it:

> Samoan polity [above the village level]...was
> highly because inherently unstable. Inter-
> village co-operation in large scale political
> matters was evidently possible only under a
> despotic malo. Failing that, faction was the
> condition of life (The South Seas in Transition,
> p. 269).

As the study proceeds, newer tendencies will be seen making for
greater consolidation of the Samoan body politic. Meantime,
rivalries and other divisive forces die hard; the possibilities of
conflict are rarely far below the surface. Communication in this
setting tends to approximate, in an increasing degree as one moves
up in the hierarchy of groups and titled individuals, to diplomatic
processes among state units.

Under influence from the United States, Great Britain, and
Germany, together with mission and other private interests, the
Samoan "Kingdom" developed in the nineteenth century enabled
selective elements of Western-type government to become considerably indigenized, e.g., Samoan judges, village mayors. In
1900, after prolonged attempts at tripartite supervision by the
three powers mentioned, Samoa was partitioned between the United
States and Germany (the later New Zealand—controlled area).

The governmental structures built up in these respective
jurisdictions have inevitably represented an overarching hierarchy
of alien-sponsored power and eliteness, even though attempts have
been made to integrate them with the indigenous political institutions. This political dominance, combined with wider economic
and social behavior expressing European superiority and Samoan
"incompetence" in the face of the larger world, has produced a
series of movements and outbreaks involving Samoans and also
part-Samoans. From crude "rebellion" against German authority
these came to assume more sophisticated "nationalist" or "self-
government" guises. The modern systems of government, together
with current programs attempting to advance self-determination
and make the resident populations feel that the Governments are
their governments rather than alien superstructures, will be briefly described here. The elite communication networks as relating
to interaction between Samoans and representatives of these larger

systems of political authority are particularly significant for this study. On the Samoan side, especially in Western Samoa, they are dominated by factors which are thought of in political theory as characteristic of "nationalism".

6.   Modern Governmental Structures

a.   Western Samoa

Western Samoa is governed today by New Zealand as a United Nations Trust Territory (formerly a League of Nations Mandate). The New Zealand government recognizes certain overarching international responsibilities which this involves. Formal reports are made to the Trusteeship Council; U.N. representatives visit the territory; and the local inhabitants have the right to petition the United Nations. Internal constitutional authority is defined by legislation of the New Zealand Parliament, and is executed by the government of New Zealand through a Ministry and Department of Island Territories. [9]

The territory is supervised by a New Zealand High Commissioner. A range of executive departments draw their senior personnel from New Zealand, but also employ local personnel increasingly in the higher posts within a Samoan Public (Civil) Service. A High Court system, with a New Zealand chief justice and Samoan associate judges, includes the right to appeal to higher British courts. Officially sponsored district and village government organization is rudimentary, apart from Samoan-nominated district representatives (Faipule) and village mayors (Pulenu'u), as described below: Samoans in this territory will be seen as much more resistant than their neighbors in American Samoa to governmental attempts to integrate the traditional regional and local political institutions with the central authority in formal ways. A Samoan constabulary force, with almost exclusively Samoan personnel, is responsible for law and order.

The New Zealand authorities, facing the major front of Samoan-style political power, fell foul of a series of non-co-operation and "self-government" movements—notably from 1927 to 1936, in a so-called Mau or "Opinion" movement which will be referred to from time to time in the further study. In 1947, a "self-government" petition to the United Nations Trusteeship Council led to the

---

[9] For greater detail on these and subsequent matters relating to the modern political situation see the Annual Reports of the Territory.

visit of a United Nations Mission.   The recommendations of this
mission, and co-ordinate action by the New Zealand government,
set the contemporary patterns of Western-style administration in
this territory.

As of 1955, the New Zealand High Commissioner exercises
responsibility for executive affairs, and also presides over a
Council of State, an Executive Council, and a Legislative Council,
all of which had both Samoan and European membership.   A purely
Samoan Fono of Faipule ("Council of Representatives") advises
the High Commissioner.   The following is a brief description of
these bodies:

Council of State.——This consists of the High Commissioner
as presiding officer, with the "royal" Fautua (High Advisers) as
representatives of the "dignity" of Samoa, currently two in number.
The High Commissioner "consults" this body on outstanding legislation and welfare problems, including "matters closely relating
to Samoan custom. "

Executive Council.——This consists of the High Commissioner
as presiding officer; the Fautua (High Advisers); three official
members appointed by the High Commissioner; three Samoan members of the Legislative Assembly nominated by the Samoan members
of that Assembly and appointed by the High Commissioner; and one
European member of the Legislative Assembly named by the European members in a parallel manner.   Its functions are to "confer
with and advise the High Commissioner on the forming, determining
and implementing of the policy of the Government of Western Samoa. "
The four members from the Legislative Assembly have been given
a quasi-Ministerial status in relation to Executive Departments, so
as to gain governmental experience, and are called "Associate
Members. "

Legislative Assembly.——This consists of the High Commissioner as presiding officer, with a casting but not a deliberative
vote; the two Fautua as the other members of the Council of State;
12 Samoan members "elected" for a period of three years by the
Fono of Faipule, with one normally representing each of the 11
major district divisions, and one named at large to fill a position
opened out by the death of an original third Fautua; five European
members elected for a similar period by adult franchise of the
resident European (mainly part-Samoan) population; and not more
than six official members appointed on indefinite terms by the High
Commissioners.   This body has the unusual feature for such a
territory of having a clear Samoan majority (14 members out of 26).
It has authority to initiate and pass legislation, subject to certain
financial and other final powers requiring the approval of the High

28

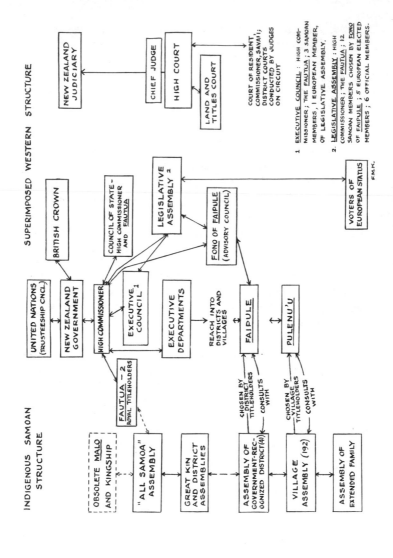

GOVERNMENT OF WESTERN SAMOA : 1954

INDIGENOUS SAMOAN STRUCTURE

SUPERIMPOSED WESTERN STRUCTURE

NEW ZEALAND JUDICIARY

CHIEF JUDGE

HIGH COURT

LAND AND TITLES COURT

COURT OF RESIDENT COMMISSIONER, SAVAI'I; DISTRICT COURTS CONDUCTED BY JUDGES ON CIRCUIT

1 EXECUTIVE COUNCIL : HIGH COMMISSIONER ; THE FAUTUA ; 3 SAMOAN MEMBERS, 1 EUROPEAN MEMBER, OF LEGISLATIVE ASSEMBLY.

2 LEGISLATIVE ASSEMBLY : HIGH COMMISSIONER ; THE FAUTUA ; 12 SAMOAN MEMBERS CHOSEN BY FONO OF FAIPULE ; 5 EUROPEAN ELECTED MEMBERS ; 6 OFFICIAL MEMBERS.

F.M.K.

BRITISH CROWN

COUNCIL OF STATE - HIGH COMMISSIONER AND FAUTUA

LEGISLATIVE ASSEMBLY [2]

FONO OF FAIPULE (ADVISORY COUNCIL)

VOTERS OF EUROPEAN STATUS

UNITED NATIONS (TRUSTEESHIP CNCL.)

NEW ZEALAND GOVERNMENT

HIGH COMMISSIONER

EXECUTIVE COUNCIL [1]

EXECUTIVE DEPARTMENTS

REACH INTO DISTRICTS AND VILLAGES

FAIPULE

PULENU'U

FAUTUA — 2 ROYAL TITLEHOLDERS

CHOSEN BY DISTRICT TITLEHOLDERS / CONSULTS WITH

CHOSEN BY VILLAGE TITLEHOLDERS / CONSULTS WITH

OBSOLETE MALO AND KINGSHIP

"ALL SAMOA" ASSEMBLY

GREAT KIN AND DISTRICT ASSEMBLIES

ASSEMBLY OF GOVERNMENT-RECOGNIZED DISTRICT(A)

VILLAGE ASSEMBLY (192)

ASSEMBLY OF EXTENDED FAMILY

Commissioner. Two sessions are held yearly, and work is done
particularly through five standing committees on Education and
Broadcasting, Finance, Health, Public Works, and Agriculture
and Cooperatives.

Fono of Faipule.——This Council of Samoan Representatives
has existed since 1905 and consists of 41 members, each representative of a traditional district (or subdistrict). Its deliberations
are normally limited to Samoan affairs. It has advisory powers
only, except that it selects the Samoan members of the Legislative
Assembly.

A Western Samoan Public Service fills the responsible and
permanent staff positions in the various executive departments.
Control over this service is still exercised by the New Zealand
government rather than being lodged in the Samoan government.
For major occasions, such as the visit of a United Nations Mission
or a top official from New Zealand, a ceremonious Samoan-style
"Council" representative of "all Samoa" (i.e., Western Samoa)
may also meet, consisting of the highest echelons of the elite, both
traditional and governmental.

The report of the United Nations Mission of 1947 on self-
government in Western Samoa urged that the administration take
steps to develop more effective integration between the district and
village authorities and the central government. Two years later
the Legislative Assembly appointed a special Commission on District and Village Government to investigate the subject. On the
basis of its recommendations, a District and Village Government
Board was set up, consisting of Samoan elite leaders, including the
Fautua, with the High Commissioner as chairman. This board is
empowered to inquire into proposals and prepare "schemes for the
recognition and organization of local authorities, " to give approval
to their form; to consider and approve for recommendation to the
High Commissioner their "proposed regulations and bylaws"; and
generally to advise on local government. The initiative is left essentially to a Samoan community, however, to promote a "local government scheme" for examination and advice by the board: that is,
participation is voluntary. At the time of writing it is not clear
whether developing local authorities will sweep Samoa like a fad
or be quietly allowed to lie dormant as opening the way to possible
external encroachment on Samoan-style local autonomy. Fitting
the many types of local structure into common molds may prove as
confining and frustrating as would fitting the Samoan woman into a
corset.

As of March 19, 1953, the Prime Minister of New Zealand
outlined a new "Development Plan" to advance the body politic toward

"self-government." New Zealand's objectives, he stated, are to assist Western Samoa to develop:

(1) A strong, responsible and representative central government whose authority is accepted by the community, and which is Samoan in outlook, personnel and in the bases of its power.

(2) A united population comprising all Samoan citizens regardless of race.

(3) The administrative machinery, the institutions, and the knowledge necessary for the solution of the political, social and economic problems that will come during the next generation.

To carry out these objectives, it was proposed in the political field that a Constitutional Convention representative of all sections of the Samoan community be held to consider a constitutional plan for the future State of Western Samoa. The New Zealand government suggested that it should include provision for (a) a common citizenship for all residents; (b) a single "House of Representatives" to replace the present Legislative Assembly and Fono of Faipule, with the 11 principal political districts as the constituencies, and one member for each 2,000 to 2,500 population; (c) direct election in secret ballot of members, with "the widest suffrage the Samoan people feel able to accept"; (d) the method of appointment and tenure of office of the Head of the State; (e) executive government through a Premier and Cabinet Ministers, to be members of, and responsible to, the House of Representatives; and (f) the special relation between New Zealand and the future self-governing State.

This Constitutional Convention met from November 10 to December 22, 1954, with 170 delegates, under the chairmanship of one of the two Fautua, Tamasese. In summary, its proposals were:

1. The special relations with New Zealand should continue indefinitely, and should particularly be concerned with defense, foreign affairs, and "seconded officers," i.e., provision of specialist white officials.

2. A British-type Premier and Cabinet should be responsible to a single Legislature. The latter should consist for the time being of the 41 Samoan representatives corresponding to the existing Fono of Faipule, five European members, and two official members (Ministers of Justice and Finance), i.e., neither the common citizenship nor the new district alignments were immediately acceptable. The Public Service was to be wholly controlled by government.

   3. In the Samoan electoral districts, only titleholders (matai) should have the right to vote or to be nominated as candidates. [This was a complete rejection of New Zealand's hope that suffrage could be carried to the level of the adult individual (see pp. 108-09).] A secret ballot should be held among the titleholders of the district if no candidate were supported by an obvious majority, i. e., the secret ballot would not be a required procedure.

   4. The two present Fautua, Tamasese and Malietoa, should "together be the first Head of State." Their term of office should be for life or until resignation, and they would "act together and with equal power."

   This last recommendation represented perhaps the only answer, whether governmentally realistic or not, which a Samoan assembly of 1954 could give to the top ceremonial leadership problem. Though the issue dominated the convention, no majority opinion could be reached favoring one of these two "royal" chiefs (and their great kin groups) over the other. A further controversial dimension was whether, in addition to these two, the other "royal" titles should be represented: Mata'afa and Tuimaleali'ifano. Powerful older incumbents of these two titles had recently died, and they had been passed on to young, not yet as politically influential figures. Some delegates wanted the long-term balance of power to be allowed for by establishing a quadrumvirate. This question reached a dramatic crisis on the last day of the convention when the youthful Mata'afa rose and strongly protested the disregard of the claims of himself and his family for equal consideration. He declared his intention of withdrawing from participation in any such future government of Samoa. The convention thus closed on bitter controversy at the top elite level.

   The New Zealand government, in an official reply to the Samoan recommendations, stated, as of June 1955, that it would create in 1957 a single legislature. Samoan representation would be on the basis of the 41 districts, with four extra seats for heavily populated ones, or 45 Samoan members in all. With reluctance it accepted "for the time being" the limitation of voting and candidates to titled persons, yet expressed expectations that "the inhabitants will continue to give thought to ways and means of liberalizing the franchise." Further study of the common citizenship problem was urged. Establishment of the Premier and Cabinet system and turning over the Public Service to control by the Western Samoa government would be delayed until Samoan political leaders gained more experience, so that the High Commissioner would remain for the time being the head of the government. This statement withheld comment on the question of making the two Fautua the "Head of State," except for noting that it was a matter "in which the feelings and loyalties of the Samoan people are properly involved." It was recognized that there would be an indefinitely continuing relation with New Zealand and with the U.N. Trusteeship Council.[10]

This statement provoked adverse comment among Samoan leaders to the extent that no recommendations were immediately accepted. They took the occasion of a visit by the New Zealand Minister of Island Territories in 1955 to reiterate those items which were being delayed or were by-passed in the New Zealand reply. This was done in preliminary joint meetings of the Legislative Assembly and Fono of Faipule, and in direct representations to the minister.[11] The latter took occasion to urge going slow—a statement which was poorly received. Later New Zealand set 1960 as the date for development of the Cabinet system. In spite, therefore, of the very extensive concessions and advanced experiments in self-government detailed above, there still persists a major continuing zone of tension and resentment as between Samoan leaders and the New Zealand authorities. As will be seen, indeed, it is perhaps the more acute because what is still being withheld concerns (and impugns) most directly the dignity and authority of the royal titleholders and the other top influential leaders who aspire to political control.

b.   American Samoa

This territory, long of interest to the United States for possible use by the Navy of its excellent harbor at Pago Pago as a coaling station, was ceded by Samoan chiefs in 1900. But Congress delayed action on accepting the cession until 1929. Meantime the Navy, which set up a small establishment at Pago Pago, was authorized by the President in his role as Commander-in-Chief to set up an "Island Government." The commanding officer of the Naval Station served as governor, and the officer and enlisted personnel provided, with several civilian American employees, the non-resident administrative staff.

In July 1951, by Presidential Order, the territory was transferred from Naval supervision to that of the Department of the

---

[10] This reply is set out verbatim in U.N. Trusteeship Council Paper, T/1192, 6 July, 1955.

[11] Papers and Proceedings, Joint Session of the Legislative Assembly and Fono of Faipule and Meeting with Honourable the Minister of Island Territories, Apia, July 1955 (mimeographed).

Interior.   The Naval Station was disbanded, and a civilian establishment of government substituted.

An administrative system, with a working body of law, was
set up from 1900, pending the passing of an Organic Law by Congress.   This has continued to provide the basis of government to
the present.   Besides a High Court and central executive departments, there is a Samoan regional and local establishment under
the Attorney General's department.   The following is a summary
picture of the main instrumentalities.

Central legislature.——From various earlier forms of an advisory council or Fono, the Naval authorities developed a bicameral
legislature of American Samoa.   This consisted of an upper "House
of Ali'i (Chiefs)," composed of the 12 highest titleholders, and a
lower "House of Representatives," with 54 members named by the
constituent communities of the territory.   Though it had formal
power only to recommend legislation to the governor, as the representative of the Washington, D.C., authorities, the governor's
advice usually served to guide its resolutions in directions which
circumvented use of the veto power.   In 1952, with the Department
of the Interior in control, the Samoan leaders proposed a new form
of central government, and this has been implemented as follows:

1.   Formation of a new council of highest chiefs, called suc-
cessively the "Council of Paramount Chiefs," "Council of Ceremonial Chiefs," and "Council of Ali'i," the last being its name in
1956.   This is sometimes referred to as an Executive Council or
Fautua Council, which suggests its origin as a reflection of legislative innovation in Western Samoa.   The membership comprises
the 12 titleholders hitherto forming the "House of Ali'i," and its
practical function is limited to advising the governor.

2.   A change from the former type of upper house to a "Senate," with 15 members named by Samoan custom; each of the three
districts names five in such a way as to give adequate regional
representation.

3.   Revision of the "House of Representatives" so that its
members are "elected by universal suffrage of the residents of
American Samoa," and by secret ballot.   This body at first had
18 members, comprising 5 representatives for each of the three
district divisions, 1 for Swain's Island, and 2 for permanent residents placing themselves on a roll of persons "not living under the
matai [titleholder] system."   In 1954 the number of members was

changed to 17, of whom 3 were elected from the most populous
county (see below) containing the capital center, 2 from another
populous county, and 1 from each of the remaining twelve counties. [12]

District government.—This is based on the three traditional
district divisions. Each is headed by a Samoan district governor
appointed by the governor and usually the senior titleholder of the
district. He is aided by a district clerk and presides over a district council of representatives named by Samoan custom. The
latter is charged with the general supervision of district affairs,
and may recommend laws on these. Each district also has a district court, with a Samoan district judge. The three district
governors attend meetings of the legislature.

County government.—This is based on the traditional 14 sub-
districts, which have been called "counties," and is a subregional
replica of the district government except that there is no clerk or
court.

Village government.—The village council, essentially the
traditional leadership group, nominates annually a Pulenu'u (Village
Chief or Mayor), and this is submitted with approval of the county
and district chiefs to the governor, for confirmation. The Pulenu'u
and the "councilors," together with a village police officer can refer offenders to the village magistrate for trial. The magistrate,
with a clerk, deals with minor village breaches of law, including
civil cases where disputes involve amounts not exceeding $10, and
crimes and offenses where prescribed punishments do not exceed
$10 or one month's imprisonment. These judicial and police of-
ficials receive a percentage of the fines and costs up to the limits
set for their monthly stipends.

The system of district, county, and village government summarized under the last three headings was established in its essen-
tials when the United States took charge of the territory more than
a half century ago. The fact that such a long history exists of
regional and local administration, in which the superimposed

_____

[12] This change eliminated a long-standing system of having,
in addition to representatives from organized Samoan communities,
a separate representative for the small Swain's Island community
(Swain's Island is a United States possession attached administra-
tively to American Samoa), and 2 representatives for the small number of residents living outside the Samoan family system. Those
declaring themselves to be in this latter category have been nearly
all part-Samoans living Western fashion and mostly in business oc-
cupations. Elections for their representatives have always been
by secret ballot.

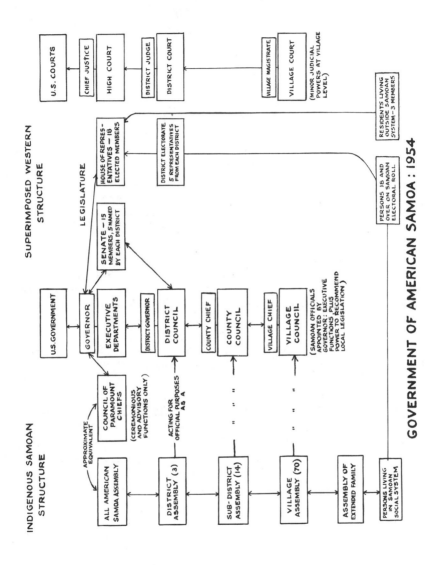

GOVERNMENT OF AMERICAN SAMOA : 1954

INDIGENOUS SAMOAN STRUCTURE

SUPERIMPOSED WESTERN STRUCTURE

U.S. COURTS

CHIEF JUSTICE

HIGH COURT

DISTRICT JUDGE

DISTRICT COURT

VILLAGE MAGISTRATE

VILLAGE COURT

(MINOR JUDICIAL POWERS AT VILLAGE LEVEL)

RESIDENTS LIVING OUTSIDE SAMOAN SYSTEM — 3 MEMBERS

LEGISLATURE

HOUSE OF REPRESENTATIVES — 18 ELECTED MEMBERS

SENATE — 15 MEMBERS, 5 NAMED BY EACH DISTRICT

DISTRICT ELECTORATE 5 REPRESENTATIVES FROM EACH DISTRICT

U.S. GOVERNMENT

GOVERNOR

EXECUTIVE DEPARTMENTS

DISTRICT GOVERNOR

DISTRICT COUNCIL

COUNTY CHIEF

COUNTY COUNCIL

VILLAGE CHIEF

VILLAGE COUNCIL

(SAMOAN OFFICIALS APPOINTED BY GOVERNOR: EXECUTIVE FUNCTIONS PLUS POWER TO RECOMMEND LOCAL LEGISLATION)

COUNCIL OF PARAMOUNT CHIEFS

(CEREMONIOUS AND ADVISORY FUNCTIONS ONLY)

ACTING FOR OFFICIAL PURPOSES AS A

APPROXIMATE EQUIVALENT

ALL AMERICAN SAMOA ASSEMBLY

DISTRICT ASSEMBLY (3)

SUB-DISTRICT ASSEMBLY (14)

VILLAGE ASSEMBLY (70)

ASSEMBLY OF EXTENDED FAMILY

PERSONS LIVING IN SAMOAN SOCIAL SYSTEM

PERSONS 18 AND OVER ON SAMOAN ELECTORAL ROLL

Western authority is well integrated with Samoan organization,
represents one of the major differences between the modern political adjustments in American Samoa and Western Samoa (p. 26).
A United States Congressional group, visiting American Samoa in
November 1954, states in its report:

> Among the important features of this country is the
> Samoans' love for and ability in local government.
> Status within the Samoan society depends largely
> on the acquisition of political knowledge and ability...
> Self-government, as it exists today, is the key to
> the Samoans' ability to adapt themselves to the
> American method of indirect rule through which
> their administration has developed... Because
> the Samoans have always taken an active interest
> in their political affairs, they have attained a
> large degree of local self-government. [13]

Stirrings of non-co-operation have appeared at times in
American Samoa, notably a Mau movement in the 1920's, but not
on the same scale as in Western Samoa. Political ambitions here
are not separatist, but directed toward achieving self-governing
status as a territory within the framework of the United States
polity.

Over the decades many attempts have been made to get drafts
of Organic Acts for American Samoa through the U.S. Congress,
but the territory is still (as of 1956) without such legislation. In
1950, all interested parties appeared to have agreement on a draft.
But this was preceded in Congressional hearings by a draft Organic
Act for the territory of Guam, in which attacks were made upon
provisions giving special protection to Guamanian land and other
customary rights, and these were eliminated by Congressional
action. The Samoan leaders, fearful that the same would occur in
the case of their own organic legislation, immediately took steps
to get action stopped. The Department of the Interior officials,
taking over from the Navy in 1951, found the Samoans adamant
against affording Congress opportunity to consider any bill until
prior assurances were given that protective provisions would be
included.

---

[13] American Samoa. Report of a Special Subcommittee on
Territorial and Insular Affairs of the Committee on Interior and
Insular Affairs, House of Representatives. 84th Congress, 1st
Session, Committee Print, No. 4. p. 7, (Washington, D.C., 1955).

In January 1954, the legislature petitioned to have a Constitutional Committee set up to develop internal constitutional legislation which would be at least in part equivalent to an Organic Act, and overarch the body of territorial law developed in the Code of American Samoa. This committee was established, and consisted of the Samoan president and speaker of the two houses of the legislature, the three district governors, the chief judge, the attorney general, the public defender, and the Samoan affairs officer (as secretary); the speaker of the House of Representatives was to act as chairman. This body was still carrying on active deliberations at the time this study was completed. The committee is vividly illustrative of the modern contexts in which elite communication relative to modern government involves both Samoan and non-Samoan participants.

III. THE PARTICIPANTS: ACTORS AND AUDIENCES

1. What Makes a Person "Elite"?

The principal dramatis personae in elite communication,
both Samoan and non-Samoan, have already been described in broad
characterization. It is essential, however, that their numbers and
roles be made more precise.

Eliteness in the traditional Samoan society is most clearly
possessed by the holders of chiefly "names" or "titles." Such a
title, pertaining to an adherent kin group, is bestowed on a suitable
member, nearly always male, and carries with it both the privileges
and the responsibilities of leadership over the group. Superficially
the graded structure of Samoan titles resembles the officer hierarchy
in the military: individuals come and go, but the status positions
and functions persist. This traditional elite of "titleholders," subject to certain modifications in the modern setting, continues to
operate with integrity and authority.

Derivative eliteness in their spheres also belongs to the wives,
eldest sons, and certain other adherents of titleholders. A more diffused eliteness also derives from membership in the more important
family lines in which the higher titles usually lodge. The elite standing of these family lines is based typically on seniority of descent
within extended kin groups, combined with marriage alignments of
approximately equivalent rank in each generation. Samoan society,
however, has not consolidated a strong class or caste emphasis
along with this individualized leadership system.

Certain new bases of elite status, derived from non-Samoan
sources, either mesh in with the above, or provide new elite roles
for Samoans, e.g., as from government, missions, commerce.
Notable among the modern factors making for eliteness are mastery
of the English language and other skills enabling a person to act in
mediation roles. These often march with some degree of part-
European ancestry, or else with more advanced schooling. Sometimes the old and new are consolidated, that is, the individual in
one of the new elite categories, or else one resigning or retiring
from it, becomes a titleholder.

All Europeans tend to be assigned some degree of elite status
automatically, and also Asians, part-Samoans, and others, to the
extent that they demonstrate affiliation with the "European" status
group and are not in the menial servant occupational role. As will
be seen, Samoans, so elite conscious in their own setting, are particularly sensitive to hierarchical dimensions of other groups. In
the case of the part-Samoans aligned with European status, who

38

now form the great bulk of the resident non-Samoan population, kinship ties with the Samoan group are likely to be maintained quite
actively, and these also help to define the status of individuals.

Beyond the local non-Samoan groups, communication ramifies
outward by way of official hierarchies from the territories themselves to the governing countries. Ultimately, for American Samoa,
this leads symbolically, and even in a warmly personal manner, to
the President of the United States. For Western Samoa it leads in
a more complicated way to two symbolic authorities, the British
Crown, personified in the sovereign, and the United Nations—
"the Father of the World, " as Samoans speak of it in formal oratory. Church affiliations also involve various outside channels of
hierarchical communication—to London (the London Missionary
Society), to Rome, to Salt Lake City, and so on.

Least familiar of these elite groupings, to the Westerner,
will naturally be those of the Samoan society. A very brief exposition of their main characteristics may therefore be given here,
though the ethnographic detail would have to be sought in the standard literature.

2.   The Traditional Samoan Elite

The Samoan, asked to define "eliteness" in his own society,
brings to bear a rich vocabulary centering around two major concepts of pule ("authority, " "power, " "privileges, " "responsibility"),
and mamalu ("dignity, " "respect, " "honor"). These terms have
very high frequency use in Samoan speech.

Authority and dignity have their main human embodiment in
what have been called the "titleholders. " The Samoan name for
such persons, individually or as a class, is matai, popularly translated as "chief. " The whole leadership structure is often spoken
of as "the matai system. "

A census of 1945 in Western Samoa showed 3, 497 matai titleholders in a total Samoan population of 62, 422. This represents
5. 6 percent, or the equivalent of about 40 percent of the males over
30 years old (for age distributions see p. 13). An average of 18
persons are in the group served by one matai, and with approximately
200 village units there are an average of 17 or 18 titleholders to a
village community. These proportions are somewhat different in
American Samoa, where in 1950 there were 828 title-holders in a
total Samoan population of 18, 602. This represents nearly 10 percent, or one matai to 11 or 12 persons, with somewhat under 12 to
a village. While in general the number of titles tends to correspond
to the size of the community, a politically important center is likely

to have a greater concentration of higher titles, and more titleholders, than the less important villages.

Titleholders or <u>matais</u> (as the word is Anglicized) fall into
two great classes: "chiefs" (<u>ali'i</u>) and "talking chiefs" or "orators"
(<u>tulafale</u>). On the same hierarchical level, the chief is the exalted,
ceremonious, supernaturally tinged, ultimately powerful and responsible leader—elite in its full sense—while the talking chief is the
"steward," brain-truster, and executive to the chief and his adherent group, and the mental storehouse for memories and traditions, the custodian of group knowledge, the lawyer-like manipulator
of words. Contrary to much popular thought as to the role of a
"chief," such a leader in Samoa is no mere figurehead. He has to
manage and direct the affairs of his adherent group relating to land
tenure and use, work effort, deaths, marriages and other crises,
negotiation with other groups, and many other problems of importance concerning which his followers share responsiblility. A
higher chief is also caught up in a maze of ceremonious activities
on behalf of the "authority" and "dignity" of his title and his group.

The orator or talking chief, while also providing leadership
in practical matters for his immediate adherents, serves as an aide
to the chief or chiefs with whom his title is associated. A text on
Samoan custom written for Samoan schoolteachers in Western Samoa
by a former director of education gives a somewhat ideally structured
picture of the orator role as follows:

> [The orators] are usually outstanding characters
> and natural leaders. They are an educated class
> and the custodians of history. Orators stand be-
> tween the people and their chiefs. They speak on
> behalf of chiefs at important functions. They also
> place before the chiefs the wishes or the complaints
> of the people whom they represent...
>
> The orators are the men who give the day's
> orders to the whole village and none may disobey.
> Sould an individual be bold enough to disregard
> orders, both he and his family would be punished
> by being fined so many cooked pigs, taro and other
> foods, all of which would have to be served by the
> offenders to the chiefs, orators, and the whole
> village. [1]

---

[1] McKenzie, A., Text on "Samoan Customs" (mimeographed).

An educated American Samoan, Napoleon Tuiteleleapaga, writes of the orator: "The talking chief is at once the mouthpiece of the high chief, and the representative of the people. He is a Jefferson, an Emerson, a Marshall, a Chamberlain, and also a Machiavelli... He is a Doctor Jekyll and Mr. Hyde."[2]

Hierarchies of both chiefs and talking chiefs range from minor titleholders, whose influence barely goes beyond their household and the lowest rungs of the village council, to the exalted or "royal" titleholders overarching the greatest kinship and district alignments. The power of the two groups varies widely in different kin and district groupings, though the long-term trend prior to the coming of Europeans seems to have been for the talking chiefs to build up their practical authority, and the recent trend has been for the chiefs with central government support to edge back authority from the former. Here and there a title carries both chief and talking chief functions, and so becomes a nucleus of high authority. Numerous other elaborations occur, symptomatic of the intense preoccupation of Samoans with hierarchy.

To the extent that an elite has a broad-based "elective" or "achieved" character it tends to be responsible, and responsive to sub-elite opinion, and adaptable to modern needs. Typically, Polynesian groups have an "ascriptive" system and narrow-based leadership in which rank is derived from seniority of descent and fraternal succession, i.e., the eldest in each generation first, then at death to younger brothers in turn, and on in the next generation to the eldest son of the eldest. Marriages of first-borns to spouses of equivalent senior descent held the aristocratic lines within caste-tight breeding channels. Age, fitness, even usurpation by war had only exceptionally any influence on the leadership structure.

In Samoa this is still the normative or ideal pattern as regards succession to significant titles. In practice, however, the leadership system is much more broadly based, and appointment to titles has a largely "achieved" character. Age can play a part, as it is fairly modal for minor titles to go to young or younger middle-aged persons, who then may move up the rank of titles with age as they prove themselves and are chosen for such honor. "Good behavior" by a younger man, as in serving his superiors, leadership qualities, making a "strong" marriage, and accumulating wealth are among many variables which may count in choice of a titleholder besides having a senior line of descent. At lower levels, the pattern in the

---

[2] From a typewritten manuscript on The Legal System of Samoa.

bestowal of a title is fairly clear and standardized. The decision
is made in a family council in which all the adult members of the
kin group over which the title has sway have some voice—the right
to acquiesce or otherwise. Particularly important is the advice of
the incumbent, if he is retiring (as is common in older age) or
dying. Senior male voices take precedence and leadership, as will
become clear later, and the distaff side, the women of the family,
and especially older sisters (usually married and living elsewhere)
have an important negative voice, the right to say "no" and so bar
a candidate. Finally, no title is considered conferred without the
participation of all concerned in a ceremonial feast in which ac-
quiescence is publicly demonstrated. Essential therefore is a
broad base of support and acceptance by the kingroup.

     The adjudicating group for a higher title is highly variable,
though it tends to follow this general pattern at a higher level. It
may, for example, be a gathering of titled representatives of kin
branches from all over Samoa, or a fixed group of talking chiefs
to whom the power has been historically delegated. A kin group
may reach out from the direct line of descent to pick as a titleholder some strong individual in a quite marginal family line,
though this probably has a low frequency of occurrence. Occasionally
a title is given to some very powerful woman. Writers on Samoa
usually attribute this "elective" quality of Samoan leadership to the
historic influence of the talking chiefs, who have maneuvered a
greater say in the choice of titleholders. Certainly it is not a modern development, as it was detailed by the first European observers, and it may be noted that it is congruent with a marked Samoan
characteristic demonstrated throughout their acculturation history—
Samoans "cannot be pushed around." Its main effect is to tend to
fit a title to ability, and to make promotion up the elite ladder sensitive to achievement and popularity. Also it tends to draw into the
title system outstanding individuals and use their energies therein,
instead of leaving them to form an opposition to the "chiefly" class.
The writers over the last twenty years have seen young deviants,
under acculturation influences, later accept titles and rise as leaders
in this elite framework.

     The great body of Samoan titles carry back far in the present
family lines. Their hierarchy has been compared with ranks in the
military service or diplomatic corps. Besides representing statuses
and ceremonial honors they involve utilitarian functions important
in the society: supervision of kin affairs, allotment of land for use,
direction of work parties, conduct of external communication on behalf of the group, in the case of the talking chiefs the management
of much of the property and affairs of the chiefs, and a modern

variety of government services in relation to the central administration, at all levels. Nearly all male Samoans get at least on the bottom rungs of the system by middle age. But those more favored by birth, achievement record, and the drive of ambition, may climb more or less far. Demotion can also come suddenly if appropriate "trusteeship" of the title is not forthcoming; an individual has no vested right in its possession. Old age or other disability will finally bring relegation to some minor or less active title, or to a kind of "retired" status as an "older statesman, " with the right to continue to sit in the community council, so that life can be finished out with honor and dignity. The great bulk of Samoan titleholders are in the age range from 35 to 65.

A variable of obvious importance in supravillage interaction has been force. As shown even far back in folklore themes, seizure of titles from an incumbent was part of the pattern. Kin factions vied to get control of some overarching title and, as indicated already, the great titles were focal points for struggle and "power politics. " As an alternative to hostilities, titles were sometimes split up, with corresponding dissection of land and other perquisites. New titles would also be created, and find their hierarchical place by gradual process. In the modern period, with peace enforced, covert violence is by no means unknown. But the governments from necessity have established by law a court adjudication process in each territory to deal with title disputes not capable of being settled by Samoan-style negotiations. Many of the important titles over the last fifty years have had to be awarded by European judges, sitting with "independent" Samoan judges as assessors, and the same title question may recur periodically as factional disputes re-emerge and are taken to court.

The tendency to split titles between contending kin branches has been considerably accelerated in recent times. An additional stimulus here has undoubtedly come from the rapid expansion of population numbers. Titles have an increasing scarcity value which can aggravate factionalism. In Western Samoa, according to calculations by Grattan (An Introduction to Samoan Custom, pp. 154-56), the proportion of untitled persons per matai rose from 11 in 1921 to 17 by 1945. Even though in this period the total number of titles recorded in census counts rose by 843, or 31.4 percent, this increase has not kept up with population growth. In some instances such increment may represent old or marginal titles which have been revived, or else returns of church pastors or others of the new elite who have come to be treated as titleholders. But the great expansion has undoubtedly come through accelerated title splitting. One important title now has over twenty holders, and titles with

two, three, or four incumbents are becoming common. Though
title splitting has been officially discouraged in American Samoa
until recently, it may be noted that between March 1947 and September 1950 a total of 108 new matai titles were registered, with
the same forces in operation.

The legal code of American Samoa has since early days involved much more control over the authority of the matai and related Samoan custom than has been possible in Western Samoa.
All recognized titles must be registered, and appointment of a new
titleholder must conform to a quite elaborate set of official provisions as to family agreement, residence, and predominantly
Samoan ancestry; a titleholder can also be removed by the governor
at his discretion, upon recommendation of the regional county chief
and district governor after joint investigation of the circumstances,
or by written petition of three-quarters of his adult adherents and an
appropriate court hearing. Section 827 of the code sets a curb on
the authority of chiefs:

> If any Samoan Chief by reason of his rank, or title,
> shall injure, oppress, threaten, subject to indignities,
> or intimidate any person in the free exercise or en-
> joyment of any right or privilege secured to him by
> any law of American Samoa, or because of his having
> so exercised the same, he shall, upon conviction,
> be fined not more than $500.00 or imprisoned not
> more than three years or both.

The American Samoa code also makes illegal one of the major types
of sanction brought to bear under old custom for enforcing matai
authority among adherents, namely "fines" in the form of pigs,
mats, etc. Section 841 reads:

> If any person, or persons, shall impose on any
> other person any "Fa'a Samoa" fine whereby
> anything whatsoever of value is obtained from
> said person on whom said fine is imposed, the
> person or persons, . . . shall be fined not more
> than $300.00. . . or six months or both.

In actual practice these legal provisions have been very rarely
enforced, not least of all because Samoans living within the system
are rarely likely to jeopardize their Samoan-style standing by
lodging formal complaints to an external agency. In both territories, however, the overarching weight of government and also of

mission authority, together with the new economic and social milieu, have in certain respects undermined but in other respects stabilized the title system.

Samoan criteria for the selection of titleholders have in modern times had added to them newer criteria such as ability to command commercial goods through money income, governmental or church leadership, or linguistic and other competence in dealing with Europeans. Even those who may nowadays leave the country as rebels and misfits in their youth are apt to come back with the added prestige of travel and other educative experience, and often with money, and "politic" their way to a desirable title.

It is not surprising that the Samoans with higher titles are usually outstanding personalities, and the matais as a class tend to be an elite in psychological as well as status terms. The quietly dignified, decisive person will tend to be given a chief's title, while the "lawyer-like, " fluent-speaking person will quickly be spotted as a "natural" for a talking chief. Power in Samoa is wielded most fully when a great personality is fitted to a great title. By contrast the greatest title may be relatively unimportant if held by a colorless person, or by one who for any reason is insecure; this has happened today in some cases where individuals, perhaps of impeccable descent, have been awarded a title through court adjudication, much to the unhappiness of kin factions who want to replace them with stronger and more prestige-generating incumbents.

The title system, in sum, tends to channel into itself the dominant and energetic individuals. Functionally such elite status and prestige might be looked at as a form of reward and incentive in a society where the individual economic profit motif—or other personalized kind of gain which might entice the more able to carry group responsibilities—has been absent or marginal. A Samoan member of the Western Samoa Legislative Assembly said:

> We all know that in other countries of the world
> people are only recognized if they are in possession
> of wealth, but this country of Samoa is quite different
> because the wealth of Samoa I think is the... matai
> title. If a matai should travel... even to American
> Samoa with no money in his pocket he will still be
> fed and housed properly and that is because he is
> recognized as a matai. [3]

[3] Legislative Assembly Debates, First Session, 1953, pp. 157-58. The speaker added that the New Zealand plan for introducing universal suffrage would "make this great wealth of no value. "

While Samoans still focus ambition upon the title ladder, there is a growing tendency for higher elite persons to throw their energies additionally into commercial and other pursuits which involve European-style sources of power. A small but increasing number of such leaders run, or participate in, trading ventures, employ paid labor to produce cocoa and other commercial crops, or handicrafts, or organize work squads in their kin or community settings to work on European plantations, do stevedoring at the ports, or carry out governmental roading or other money-producing work.

An increasing tendency is discernible, too, for some of these leaders to move residentially into town for much of the time, to shed their Samoan-style obligations of distributing food and other wealth, along with other onerous and costly duties of leadership. This is one of the nub points in recent social change, and is an almost universal trend along the acculturation frontiers of the world.

In honoring elite statuses in the persons of the current incumbents, the adherent group involved feel that they are honoring themselves. An orator speaking of a "royal" chief will extend this principle to an all-Samoa basis: "You represent," he will say, "the honor and dignity of Samoa."

One of the "royal" chiefs giving an address in a modern political meeting with Europeans, acknowledged the principle in his opening words: "On behalf of [my fellow royal chiefs] and the dignity of Samoa..." Correspondingly, Samoans judge the status of a European or other outsider largely in terms of the group, governmental or otherwise, that stands back of him, and the honor and dignity which his person embodies on its behalf.

People of elite status are shielded as fully as possible from situations that would harm dignity and lower prestige. Such situations may occur today where Samoan elite members fall foul of Western law, with its concepts of impersonal justice regardless of status. The judicial authorities in American Samoa, for example, have been uncertain in spite of all evidence they could gather whether several young men recently convicted of serious offenses were the actual persons who committed these acts or whether they were only "stand-ins" for elite persons really responsible. The writers were present at a judicial session in a village where the American chief judge had the unpleasant duty of dealing with a number of titleholders for head-tax delinquency. When the "court" assembled in the leading guesthouse, women were sitting at most of the posts. As the chief judge called the name of each delinquent in turn, his wife replied with apologies that he had to be away on business but that she was taking his place. She received on his behalf the "bawling out" and the order to pay by a certain deadline. The court then adjourned, and back came all the delinquent titleholders, with friendly smiles, to take their places in the formal Samoan-style reception for honored visitors. Tactfully, no mention was made from either side of the painful court session. This is typical of the many Samoan devices to protect their elite from the impersonal stress of Western law in cases where an "offense" does not evoke equivalent Samoan disapproval; other ways involve treating any elite person under sentence as something of a hero and martyr, his imprisonment as a time for visiting him and sending him gifts, and his release as an occasion for welcoming him with a celebration.

In its baldest sense, "elite communication" in Samoa is the interaction of matais, or else of members of the matai group with Europeans or with others considered to have elite status. When, however, the mechanisms of opinion formation and decision-making are probed it becomes essential to look not only at matai behavior as such, but also back of the matai to the adherent group which he represents. In each sphere there are highly institutionalized types of formal organization, and at the same time room for informal and idiosyncratic variables to have play.

3. Samoan Assemblies

Matters of importance in Samoa are channeled to the appropriate matai status persons or groups in whose sphere they lie, much as they would pass to the appropriate "desk" in a business or government establishment. The titleholders concerned then provide leadership in deliberations at the appropriate level—the household, larger kin grouping, the village community, or the supravillage organizations.

The Samoan language has a rich terminology for group assemblies of various kinds which provide formal or informal opportunities for discussion and the marshaling of opinion (Annex II). Of these the most significant as regards systematic communication is the term fono, usually translated "council."

The fono is a more or less formalized face-to-face consultation group ("the fono") or consultation process ("to meet in fono"). It may involve a general meeting of elite and non-elite persons presided over by a matai titleholder, or more ceremoniously a meeting of titleholders exclusively, at many levels, from the formal village council right up to the official Fono of the territory in both Western and American Samoa. Participation by the appropriate persons in such an institutionalized assembly is at once an expected duty and a valued right, whether they have authority to speak or merely to be present with an audience-supporter relationship.

Individuals come and go, but each type of fono is a continuum; there is cultural transmission of experience in the fono and no break in continuity. The child grows up sitting on the fringes of household, family, and village fono assemblies. The women and young people participate in their own fono assemblies besides taking part in family fono. The young men have the privilege and responsibility of serving as audience to the fono of the village titleholders. The older retired titleholders have a continuing honored place in the village fono, even when eased out of active roles. Supravillage fono are likely to have great continuity of personnel. This is in contrast to our own governmental procedures where there is for most people a considerable hiatus between their own personal experience and governmental processes, apart from voting and paying income tax, unless they grow up in families engaged in governmental activities. Fono procedure at all levels therefore has realism and interest for all Samoans. They know the rules of the game, and are interested in changes in those rules.

Three levels of assembly and deliberation are involved directly or indirectly in elite communication:

(1.) The household and intimate family level—deliberations of the matai with adherents in his immediate residential and local kinship groups.

(2.) The village level—organizations of the matai and also of the untitled men and women on a community basis.

(3.) Supravillage levels—consultations of matai in relation to the larger kin and political structures of Samoan society.

4. The Mass Base: Household and "Family"

A matai consults with his adherents in his role as head of a household or of a close local kin group, thus providing the broadest base for opinion formation and decision-making. A formal meeting of this kind is called fono fa'aleainga, or "family council."

The term matai is frequently translated by its minimum common denominator, "head of a household." Typically, the group a matai heads occupies a single house structure, but it may comprise a close "family" alignment covering more than one house within a community. The household unit may include several nuclear families, e.g., a group of brothers and their wives and children and perhaps families of married sons, with occasionally a married daughter and her husband and children who have elected to throw in their lot here rather than with her husband's people, and also assorted dependent kinsmen and other adherents.

The house group, meeting daily at least for the evening meal
hot from the ovens and for evening prayers, offers constant opportunities for informal discussion. With greater formality it assem-
bles frequently to plan work, discuss household and kin welfare,
share hospitality with visitors, or deliberate upon some current
problem. Formal meetings of the household or close "family"
group are "presided" over by the titleholder or by the senior titleholder if more than one is present.

It is in the family council that sub-elite and elite communication are most intimately intermeshed. The matai is at the same
time the beloved grandfather, father, uncle, or other senior male
relative. In a formal meeting all the characteristics to be observed
in an elite assembly tend to be present, but there is naturally a close
family feeling and a greater measure of informality. This is, above
all others, the "in-group." Women can have their say along with
men; the untitled man or youth may speak; even a child might be
questioned on some appropriate point. Children learn early to sit
as quiet and respectful spectators if they want to be present, thus
laying the groundwork for continuity. From the personal viewpoint,
each individual has affiliation with a number of family groupings and
lines which he may choose to keep active: his ainga (kinsmen) on
his father's side, those on his mother's side, relatives created by
his marriage, his son's wife's relatives, his daughter's husband's
relatives, and so on.

Grattan discusses the significance of such family consultations:

> Such an assembly to discuss family affairs is not
> merely a duty on the part of the members of the
> family, but is a right which is jealously guarded,
> and the matai risks the dissatisfaction and dis-
> pleasure and the possibility (in modern times) of
> a subsequent complaint to the Department of
> (Samoan) Affairs on the part of anyone to whom
> he does not extend the opportunity of attending such
> a meeting or of being represented... A matai,
> dealing with family matters of importance, will
> consider it prudent to report to or consult with
> the members of his family; so also a represent-
> ative of the village approached on important
> matters affecting the village will wish to consult
> with and secure the agreement of his fellow chiefs
> and orators, who, being the representatives of
> their families in the fono, are entitled after dis-
> cussion to commit their families to a course of
> action (op. cit., pp. 10-11, 22).

Grattan is here using the term "family" partly in a wider sense than that of the immediate living group. Gatherings of relatives may involve kin branches from widely scattered points, as seen in the summary of supravillage structure. Matters to be handled could include succession to the higher titles, marriages and funerals of important persons, and disposal of lands. In such larger "family" assemblies, consultation tends to be limited to matai participants acting on behalf of their adherent groups. Non-elite persons become more or less eliminated other than as audiences.

The household and close kin group have institutionalized systems of authority relative to their nontitled members. These untitled persons are the men and youths who have not yet become titleholders, and women and girls who, except in rare cases, are ineligible for titles and so can at best gain derivative power as wives of titleholders.

Nearly all males of competence and repute can aspire to getting at least a very minor matai title by middle age in the role of head of a household or otherwise. In the meantime this numerically large and vigorous younger group of youths and men who have not, as yet, received titles (called taulele'a, or in the singular, taule-'ale'a) is by no means without influence. A school text prepared by a Samoan official in the American Samoan education department says of the relation of the matai to his male adherents in the family: "The matai... sends the young men to look after the plantations, to cut copra, to fish, to prepare, cook, and serve the food [cooking in Samoa is correctly done by young men], to look after the pigs, and to do all the hard work."[4]

The untitled man or youth, correctly serving his family in such ways, is making an investment in his future career. But he is also in a position to discuss problems directly with his matai and in the family council. He likewise has an important stake in the village organization (see below). A family or community whose untitled men and youths are dissatisfied and move off to serve a matai in some related kin group, or go off to the port center to make their own way, is correspondingly weakened and loses prestige.

No male of elite status or otherwise would venture interference in what are regarded as women's exclusive spheres. Within the household and family the wife of the matai tends to direct the affairs of the other women and the girls. The school text quoted above

_____

[4] Second Book of Samoan Social Culture, by Chief S. Faamausili (1945, mimeographed).

states this perhaps overbaldly: "Respect and obedience are also shown to the matai's wife. She orders the girls and the wives of the taulele'a to make tapa [bark cloth], weave mats, prepare coconut oil, clean the house, pull out the weeds, and do the washing." In the next section the special activities of women and girls will also be seen operating in community organizations.

In affairs outside women's exclusive spheres, the female voice has its main scope in the family setting, both informally and through the formal council. Opinion, however, tends to channel by way of the senior women who are likely to act as the speakers. The modern position of women, a blending of old Samoan and Christian concepts, adds up to a position of general respect and responsibility. Samoan women typically are not subdued females, and in all matters, while recognizing their secondary and reflective position in the prestige hierarchy, they are inclined to be forceful "back-seat drivers." The wife of the matai, in particular, is in a strong position to exercise her full weight—and her prestige often literally correlates with weight—in all family decisions. It is a common Samoan joke that the important thing in any matter is to get the faletua (wife) on your side.

Women exercise, too, highly institutionalized authority rights within kin alignments. While there is in Samoan culture a strict brother and sister avoidance on a sexual basis, the relationship between brother and sister is close and sacred. Persisting from the old religion is a concept that a sister's curse is particularly destructive and potent, and that brothers have a duty to please their sisters, especially their eldest sister and her children. This tie, known as feangainga, carries forward to their recognized descendants, and "permeates the whole of Samoan society, " as Grattan puts it, involving a complex interplay of rights and duties.

The feangainga invests powerful constraints in the "distaff" side of the family by which women and relatives on the female side have a "veto" voice. This puts them in a position of unobtrusive power, especially as they have children and reach older age. Their consent would need to be obtained, for example, in the naming of a new matai. A matai is always likely to consult with the women of the family (both wives and sisters) on important matters and try to ascertain how they react, ahead of the actual family fono, just as he will have informally talked such matters over ahead of time with the other males of any stature in the family group.

The traditional history and genealogies of Samoa record powerful women holding important titles, including a famous "queen" or holder of top ceremonial names, Salamasina. The occasional woman titleholder found today is likely to be a similar "strong"

character. She is also skilled at riding a balance between her status
as a matai and noninterference in the affairs of males with which the
matai group are markedly concerned. Ethnographic information is
scanty on the role of such a "woman leader." The writers have a
marked impression from limited case materials that she participates actively with her fellow matais in general as well as in ceremonial affairs, and also gives the correct leadership to the adherent
group pertaining to the title. She is also likely to exercise dominant
authority within the women's groups.

5. Community Organizations

Each village community has an institutionalized structure of
elites and audiences. As a basis for analysis the following groupings
may be tabulated:
1.   The "village council" (fainganu'u, literally "the doing-
village"), consisting of all the matai titleholders of the community
sitting in a more or less formal fono meeting, with or without a
non-elite spectator audience. A frequently used collective name for
this group is ali'i ma faipule, "the chiefs and talking chiefs." This
is the nuclear center of significant community communication and
decision, and the same participants handle "legislative," "judicial,"
and "executive management" functions. The traditional leadership
of such a council is vested in the senior titles in ways which will
be seen.
2.   The wives of the titleholders, together with any woman
who holds a title in her own right, meeting in more or less formal
council. This group, usually called faletua ma tausi, or "wives of
chiefs and talking chiefs" reflects very directly the elite status of
the titleholder husbands, hence it is spoken of above as a secondary
repository of eliteness. Elite matters in women's spheres center
in this group.
3.   The untitled men and youths (taulele'a), also aligned
status-wise in terms of their relation to the hierarchy of titleholders.
Each individual takes rank essentially according to the status of his
matai, though personal factors of seniority, age, and experience also enter in. Called the 'aumanga, this group is organized on a
village basis for both co-operative work and entertainment, as in
dance and game displays. Sitting as a fono, they have as their
ceremonial head the manaia or "heir apparent" of the senior chief,
normally his eldest son, or his next-eldest brother if this individual
is not already a matai. The 'aumanga has been described as literally
"the strength of the village."
4.   The unmarried and unattached (divorced or widowed)
women and older girls (roughly from the age of puberty), similarly

53

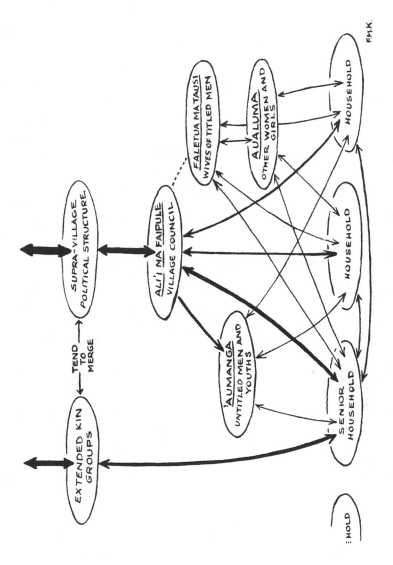

CHANNELS OF COMMUNICATION AND AUTHORITY-RESPONSIBILITY

reflecting derivatively the status of the titleholders, though with
personal factors also entering in. Called aualuma, this group was
organized for work and entertainment. Leadership lay with elderly
women and with the taupou, or "ceremonial hostess" (often referred
to as the "village virgin" or "princess"). The latter is a marriageable young woman of high birth, normally a daughter of the high
ranking chief, and trained in the "hostess" arts. Having a taupou
was one of the many honors which surrounded important chiefly
rank. In former days the aualuma slept as a group, so that unattached marriageable females would not be around the family houses
at night; and even under modern Christian conditions many families
prefer their girls to sleep at the home of the village pastor or catechist.

     The organized village groups listed in these four categories
serve both as significant audiences and as initiators of communication and decision-making in their own spheres. The 'aumanga or
untitled men's group has the right, unless otherwise instructed, to
listen in as auditors at matai village council meetings, thereby
gaining experience and understanding of elite affairs against the
time when most of them normally assume this role, and the same
is true as regards the relations of the aualuma to the senior women's group. It will be noted that all members of the community
are comprehended in one or another of these four groups except
those of roughly prepuberty age. Indeed, the children also are
likely to be around sitting quietly in the margins of all but the most
formal of these groupings, absorbing, learning—an apprenticeship
audience.

     Under modern conditions the nuclear institution of the village
council of titleholders has lost little of its vigor. Rather, in many
ways it has grown in importance through its tougher leadership
tasks in the face of acculturation. Particularly it has assumed new
functions when, presided over by the "mayor," it deals as an official
government body with matters of concern to the central administration of the territory. Again quoting a somewhat moralistic delinea-
tion for children, taken from Chief Faamausili's text on Samoan
social culture: "The matters discussed at the village fono are those
which are important to the whole village: upkeep of roads and plantations, cleanliness of houses and lands; quarrels of people, building
of pig fences, election of (village officials), etc." For Western
Samoa, where in the period since the Mau outbreaks of the 1920's
the central government has not pressed formal organization upon
the village councils, local adaptations for handling official affairs
have varied widely according to local tastes. The 1950 Commission
on District and Village Government says of this:

In some villages there is one general committee;
in others there are several to perform different
duties. In some all the matais are nominally members, whereas in the majority of places the membership of the committee is kept fairly small.
Certain villages have kept the committee as a
body with a traditional structure and confined
membership to the holders of particular orator
titles. In other places membership is much more
open. In many villages there are now taulelea
[untitled persons] serving on village committees
along with matai; and in at least one or two places
representatives of the women also take part in
the work of the general village committees.

The report discusses also the problem of handling village funds in
these days of an accelerating money economy:

District and village authorities are now handling
much larger sums of money than was formerly
the case...a number of districts and villages
have appointed as treasurers, to take charge of
their funds, men who have experience of keeping
accounts, such as traders and school teachers.

The 'aumanga or male work force also tends to hold its identity
intact, though some untitled men leave the village for work or schooling. Furthermore, its role tends to be reinforced as commanding
economic power, including money earnings, and individuals may
emerge to leadership in it as having special skills in high demand,
such as electrical or engineering ability.

By contrast, the women's organizations have tended to change.
The aualuma, comprising the women and girls of lesser status, has
largely passed from the scene or declined in function, though it may
still organize dances and entertainments. The taupou institution is
played down as no longer so important to a chief's prestige, though
even so a temporary taupou will be selected for specific occasions
where the "hostess" role is essential, and any woman in a party is
liable to be treated as the taupou for ceremonial purposes. [5] The

----

[5] See Keesing, F. M. "The Taupou System of Samoa—a Study
in Institutional Change, " Oceania, 8 (1938), pp. 1-14.

faletua ma tausi, on the other hand, has been transformed into a
much more powerful and organized village grouping, especially in
Western Samoa, where it now assumes the name of the "Women's
Committee"; as such it includes unmarried and unattached women
as well as wives.

Village Women's Committees were first formed under medical
department auspices in the 1920's to improve infant care, health,
and sanitation. During the subsequent antigovernment Mau ("Opinion")
movement, men's assemblies above the village level were officially
forbidden, and women for a time assumed the overt exercise of
political functions, with assemblies all the way up to Mau Women's
"Councils of all (Western) Samoa." Subsequently, women's committees withdrew once more into activity mainly concerned with
hospitality, health, child care, village cleanliness, and hygiene,
though with greatly enhanced authority and dignity. The former
aualuma institution has been incorporated as a kind of "junior
league" at the lower rungs of this powerful feminine elite ladder.
Women's Committees in Western Samoa have local uniforms, usually
brilliantly colored, and very recently the idea of building a special
house in each village as a center for their activities has been spreading through Western Samoa. At the same time resistance has been
generated among many of the male titleholders against the enhance-
ment of women's authority. This forms another of the currently
critical areas of conflict in modern Samoan society.

One of the constant threads in the modern legislative settings
of both territories is a discernible desire on the part of the titleholder elite to use governmental authority to bolster and strengthen
their position, especially in the face both of external official pressures and of internal stirrings toward greater egalitarianism and
individualism. Legislative proceedings show requests over many
years for putting governmental authority back of the matai so that
he can control the taulele'a and other untitled adherents, e.g., keep
youths from going off to the ports and so draining away the village
work force; bring earnings of individuals into control of the family;
keep women's groups from encroaching on spheres of titled males.
In general, government authorities have resisted such elite stands.

For Western Samoa a notable documentation of these tendencies
is provided in the report of the recent Commission on District and
Village Government (p. 29). This commission consisted, apart from
the European chairman, of higher elite Samoans, and its consultations were conducted with regional and local elites throughout the
territory. Its recommendations for establishing village administrations have a strong, if probably nonconscious, bias toward reinforcing matai authority. Again and again the commission report

uses the phrase: "In the interests of the ali'i and faipule (chiefs and orators) and of the Government"—but it rarely speaks correspondingly of the people at large. Some of the most revealing passages here relate to the organizations of the untitled males and women, these conforming to patterns of elite opinion manifested generally in the writers' field work materials. Women's committees are given the tribute of being "a highly successful example of effective cooperation between the central government and the villages"; but "it is not necessary for them to receive any statutory recognition, as the ali'i and faipule stand firmly behind them, and their decisions are nearly all of a kind which can be carried out by individual families on a social, rather than a legal basis."[6]

The position of the untitled males is considered by the commission to offer a "more complex problem."

> In Samoan custom, the position of the taulele'a
> is not one of impotence, or unimportance...
> Nearly all the taulele'a in any village stand in
> close family relationship to the matai... In
> addition to the personal links which this gives
> them with those who control village affairs
> [they can be present as observers at fono
> meetings, and have an organized influence
> in the 'aumanga]... In recent times, changed
> conditions have in some respects affected the
> relationship between the taulele'a and other
> sections of the village. There are now other
> opportunities for a taulele'a besides that of
> remaining in his own village... On the other

---

[6] A chief, speaking of Women's Committees in the Legislative Assembly, said:
> The Women's Committees in the villages are a
> source of suffering to the villages concerned,
> because if there is a gathering of the Women's
> Committee...it usually takes a whole day for
> their discussions whereas there are certain
> duties for them to do. If a woman does not
> attend the meeting she is fined...and yet
> there are other useful things for her to do in-
> stead of sitting down all day and talking about
> things. Legislative Assembly Debates, First
> Session 1949, p. 75.

> hand, the composition of the aumaga ['aumanga]
> itself has undergone a change. It is coming to
> include more and more men who have received
> useful experience outside...[or] a good educa-
> tion...[leadership in 'aumanga affairs is being put
> increasingly into their hands, and they are being
> given a greater say in village affairs]... They
> are developments, however, which can best be
> left to come about in response to the gradual
> change in public opinion. They should not be
> imposed on villages by legislative action on the
> part of the Government.

These and other passages indicate firm stands for putting
legal authority into the hands of the elite level organizations only,
thus adding the official stamp to the traditional system. "Control
of the taulele'a" is specifically listed in the report among powers
which should be delegated by statute to local authorities. It is
characteristic that though the commission "discussed thoroughly
every aspect of our inquiry with the ali'i and faipule of every district, " no mention is made of consultations in which these other
groups had any direct part. Critics of the report have raised the
question in this context as to whether indeed it is wise to put a
statutory "strait jacket" upon the local Samoan society just at the
time it needs informal maneuvering room for development and
change. (These problems are discussed further on pp. 259-61).

At this point in the analysis it is possible to discern in a
rounded way how the elite and non-elite groupings are meshed.
The situation may be reviewed as follows:

1. A non-elite and an elite person may interact as individuals
within household, kin, or other settings, subject to rules of respect
and obedience in the case of the former, and rules of authority and
responsibility in the case of the latter.

2. An organized opinion of non-elite men and youths (taulele-
'a) can be marshaled within the family council in relation to their
own matai, and also in the community 'aumanga. Communication
channels in the case of the 'aumanga go directly to the village fono
(alii ma faipule) by way of the matais assigned to supervise 'aumanga
activities.

3. The organized opinion of females other than the very rare
titleholders can be marshaled in the family councils, including the
important feangainga (brother-sister) relations, and in the organizations of women and girls. Formulated views from the female side
are likely to be communicated by way of senior women, usually the

wives of senior chiefs, to and through their elite spouses in or outside the family council; but on a crucial matter a female deputation
may state its views directly to an elite assembly. [7]

The problem of how far weighting is given to the various
"voices" represented in non-elite and elite groupings will be a subject for discussion in chapter IV.

6. Supravillage Communication

Beyond the village level, Samoan style communication and
decision-making is almost wholly carried on by the titleholders of
higher rank. On any matter involving a larger kin or district group
the appropriate senior matais attend from the village concerned;
lesser titleholders drop out automatically. At the higher echelons,
only the more important kin lines, village centers, or districts
are represented. Ultimately, for a Samoan-style "council" or
fono of "all Samoa" the appropriate "royal" titleholders and their
correct alignment of exalted "talking chiefs" would be the active
participants. In their entourages would most likely be the highest
echelons of matai, attending as a spectator-audience, and their
wives, manaia, taupou, and selected 'aumanga and aualuma squads
of dancers and singers.

A vital Samoan concept here is that of proper and authorized
representation. Most usually it is referred to by the term filifili
and its derivatives, variously having the related meanings of a
"representative," "a voice," and an "opinion" or decided position.
A chief said of representation in higher councils:

> According to Samoan custom, when a meeting is held
> there are special chiefs and orators who should attend
> that assembly, as it is not necessary for everyone
> to be present. The districts of course will first
> discuss and decide their representative who will
> represent them in such a meeting. Matters which
> will be of benefit to certain districts, or to the

---

[7] In 1947 the United Nations Mission investigating the self-
government issue, in its first major public reception, was addressed by a delegation of senior women representatives of "all (Western) Samoa" separately from the men; this was headed by the wives
of the three "royal" titleholders holding Fautua positions at the
time.

districts of any person so appointed, will be
prepared by their representative to be placed
before the meeting. Dissatisfaction occurs in
a district if representatives withhold district
opinion and do not put it before the assembly.

Selection of an elite representative to participate in some
higher consultation process is normally carried out by elite members of the group to be represented. It is likely to be a delicate
and sensitive matter proportionately to the extent that "peers" are
involved. Where a group has a clearly defined order of hierarchy,
and representation involves going to a higher level, the norm would
be for the one or more top level persons to go without any question
being raised. In the latter case "selection, " "naming, " "appointment, " "election, " and similar concepts become tenuous terms.

The title concerned, in the person of the current incumbent,
will nearly always have taken its authorized place automatically in
the higher group back as far as living memory goes. Where, however, more than one title carries fairly equivalent authority and
"dignity, " as among heads of family branches or in a subdistrict
assembly, a deliberate selection process may be called for in
naming a representative.

No Samoan equivalent of the "popular franchise" exists
(pp. 104-06). A representative is named in the course of consultation among all the authorized spokesmen, usually in a fono meeting.
There is a tendency for "peers" or near peers to take turns as
representatives in an agreed order which upholds their importance.
In the case of government councils, as with the Samoan members
of the Western Samoa Legislative Assembly and the Fono of Faipule
or "Advisory Council of Representatives, " the resulting turnover
of personnel has been a source of concern to officialdom as it breaks
the continuity of experience. In the three Assembly elections from
1948 to 1955, only two Samoan members have held continuous
office. Occasionally impasses occur in such selective processes
which formerly would have been settled by violence, but which have
to be adjudicated as well as possible by government if it wants an
active representative to be on hand. In much the same way, a
Samoan assembly will name representatives to carry out some unpleasant or downward-oriented duty, under government auspices or
otherwise; it will be assigned to persons at an appropriate hierarchical level, perhaps with turns taken among persons of approximately equivalent rank.

On this Samoan-style elite structure, modern governments
have been building Samoan participation in their central institutions

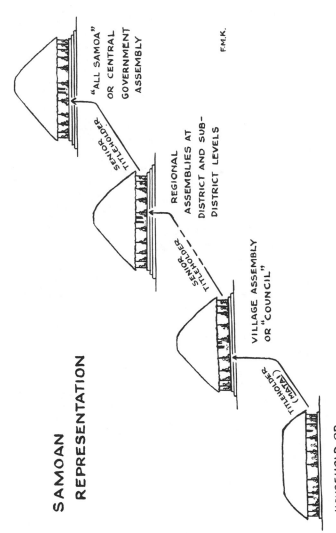

SAMOAN
REPRESENTATION

HOUSEHOLD OR
FAMILY ASSEMBLY

TITLEHOLDER
(MATAI)

VILLAGE ASSEMBLY
OR "COUNCIL"

SENIOR
TITLEHOLDER

REGIONAL
ASSEMBLIES AT
DISTRICT AND SUB-
DISTRICT LEVELS

SENIOR
TITLEHOLDER

"ALL SAMOA"
OR CENTRAL
GOVERNMENT
ASSEMBLY

F.M.K.

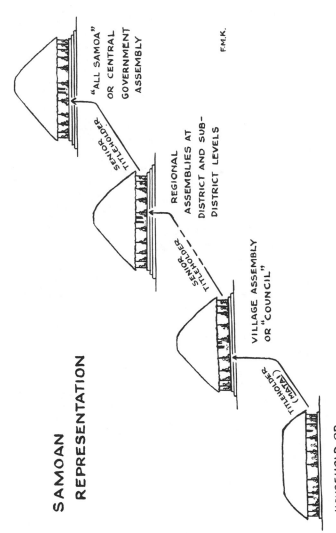

of advisory, executive, and, most recently, partially responsible legislative and judicial authority. At regional levels there are more or less effective district administrations based on the appropriate elites. The 1950 Commission on District and Village Government describes the largely self-generated role of district authorities in Western Samoa, under the leadership of the Faipules, as follows:

> The executive activities of district authorities are, in most cases, on a relatively restricted scale. In certain parts of Samoa, the district fono makes regulations on many subjects and deals with the more serious offences; but to a large extent they leave the carrying out of these decisions to the individual villages. Certain important decisions of a traditional kind—such as those concerning the exclusion of a village from, or its readmission to, district affairs—have executive consequences, (but are mainly social in character)... Executive action by districts...mainly relates to matters such as the raising of money for hospitals, schools, water supplies, local roads or other works, and the construction and maintenance of these works or of the services which they provide. In most cases they will be delegated by the district fono to a committee...the work performed by such committees may be on a considerable scale.

The governmental systems have also involved selective integration of the higher Samoan elite with European dimensions of eliteness both within and beyond Samoa. Problems of representation and other factors relevant to communication processes at all these levels will be noted as the analysis proceeds.

7.   Eliteness Derived from Non-Samoan Authority

To the extent that any of the newer elite roles involve European-style authority and prestige, they have tended to assume a hierarchically superior position to the traditional Samoan roles.

This dimension, characteristic of the "colonial" frontier society, continues to mark personal and to some degree official interaction between Samoans and non-Samoans. It has involved such a self-contained and proud people in very ambivalent attitudes and behavior: on the one hand a great respect for Europeans and

Europeanism and a desire to supply their own Samoan elite with
European prestige symbols; and on the other, a tenacious feeling
of superiority in local matters of custom and knowledge.

As already stated, Europeanism always tends to involve some
degree of eliteness. It puts its historic magic on certain types of
Samoans, titleholders or otherwise, on part-Samoans, and on non-
Samoans. All interaction other than in purely Samoan society and
affairs involves this special eliteness in some degree; the only
exceptions are the small communities of other islanders, the few
Asians of the unskilled labor class, and an indeterminate number
of relatively statusless part-Samoans who move shiftlessly between
the two parent groups.

At the village community level, European-generated eliteness
falls partly on Samoan titled persons, as in the village council when
used as a governmental agency, and partly on persons outside the
traditional title system. The main figures involved are:

1. The "Mayor" or Pulenu'u, literally "authority of the
village." Since the kingship days this post has been the key to
"indirect rule" at the community level. The Samoan titleholders
name, usually from year to year, one of their number, nearly always of comparatively minor rank, to act as the front man and
bear the brunt of interaction with government. Official attempts
to transmute such meager-salaried individuals into efficient government servants run up against the fact that inevitably they are first
and foremost representatives of their communities and gear their
work to local wishes, notably those of the higher titleholders who
avoid entangling themselves in this government-paid position. In
American Samoa, village officialdom also includes a magistrate,
a clerk, and a policeman, none with more than rudimentary training.

2. The pastor or catechist. Only rarely is a village accessible
to a European-staffed mission center, so that religious personnel
at local levels is Samoan. These individuals, who have assumed
in some degree the traditional mantle of the old-time priestly adept,
are counted supreme in matters that touch the spiritual and the
ethical, and also usually exercise strong secular influence. They
have normally received a training in a central mission "college,"
approximating in the case of younger men to lower high school
grades. Age and influence gives them a status much like that of a
matai.

3. The schoolteacher, usually government trained but formerly mostly a mission college product. The teacher is steadily rising
from a generally low status, but still has minor prestige in the village setting except where a strong individual makes an impact.

Female teachers are now quite numerous in both territories where at first they were exclusively male.

Beyond the village level, there are the following regional figures:

1. District representatives. In Western Samoa the Faipule, numbering 41 in all, have long had a dual role of being named by their constituencies (i.e., through elite interconsultation) to act as representatives in the central Samoan assembly (Fono of Faipule), and of being executive heads of their districts for governmental purposes. In American Samoa the executive role is carried by regional "County Chiefs" and by "District Governors," numbering 14 and 3 respectively. Such a prestige post should correctly go to the leading titleholder of the regional unit concerned. Usually, if government tries to place any person of lesser rank in such an office (as has happened at times in American Samoa when incumbents have fallen foul of the law, or proved inefficient) the adherent group offers strong resistance. A minor tendency now shows for the Samoans themselves to put a strong figure into the post regardless of rank, including even part-Samoans living as members of Samoan society. Normally in such cases, however, the situation is made "seemly" by bestowing an appropriate title on such a person. In the rare case where such a leader becomes persona non grata to his people, as has happened in Western Samoa, he will be voted or petitioned out. The government is powerless to interfere significantly, even though it is known that administration may suffer because a secondary chief may be quite unable to command the respect necessary to get things done in the district.

2. The judge or Fa'amasino. Judicial authority over Samoans at the district level is primarily in the hands of Samoan associate judges who make itinerant visits and are empowered to adjudicate minor cases and act as a court of first instance, subject to the superior authority of a European chief justice.

3. The Samoan medical practitioner, with his nursing staff. This now very influential group of health workers carries modern medicine to the community level with extraordinary effectiveness. Samoan medical practitioners in both territories have been nearly all trained in the Suva Medical School in Fiji, with its basic four-year course, and have usually gained supplementary training in the European-staffed government hospitals. These latter institutions also train the nursing cadre. With age and influence, the medical practitioner assumes a status much like that of a matai.

4. The Samoan trader. Occasionally a Samoan manages or even owns one of the trading stores dotted here and there in or between villages. More usually the storekeeper is a part-Samoan of

European status. Samoan owners are nearly always considerably Europeanized higher titleholders; in a few cases the enterprises are group owned as joint stock companies or else co-operatives.

Overarching the regional figures are a considerable range of participants and employees in the central government structures and in private commercial or other non-Samoan settings. Special attention will be given later to the top elite mediators in the legislative bodies, including the "royal" Fautua (see especially chapter VIII). Executive departments of government employ an increasing range and number of Samoans, each group having its particular status and influence: the constabulary, public works personnel, communications technicians, and others. Samoan taxi drivers have acquired many of the characteristic marks of this profession.

Samoans who live in the urban settings tend to acquire automatically some eliteness which is enhanced to the extent that they hold regular governmental or other money-earning posts. Though physically cut off from their Samoan kinship groups, and usually living at a low standard because of the high cost of commercial goods, they are likely to have a stream of relatives coming to stay or otherwise hoping to live off their money income. The urban Samoan is likely to regard rural stay-at-homes as "country bumpkins."

The persons in all these statuses play vital roles in mediation and integration between the traditional Samoan setting and the wider non-Samoan world. All individuals acquiring an official or other outside imprimatur are likely first of all to behave as Samoans, taking their main cues from Samoan public opinion and elite pressures within their own families and other adherent groups. To the extent, however, that they are trained and reasonably paid, also backed up and closely supervised by the government or other non-Samoan authority concerned, they tend to pass outside the Samoan system and assume status as a new and increasingly superior elite. When in the Samoan setting, they receive the equivalent of matai respect according to their age and influence even if they are not of matai status, as with most pastors, catechists, and medical practitioners.

All these figures of the new Samoa, whether well integrated in the Samoan-style elite or not, have their reasonably measurable roles in the total status system of contemporary Samoa. To them are added the considerable complexities of hierarchy in the part-Samoan and non-Samoan groups. The main constituent elements are:

1. Part-Samoans, now increasing rapidly in numbers. Persons legally so recognized have a dual definition of status, first by

their connections, achievements, and wealth in the European society, and second by their kin connections, leadership, popularity, and generosity in the Samoan society. Hierarchically they pyramid up to several families and individuals who have risen high in government, or have become wealthy by way of local business enterprises; usually such outstanding individuals have a thorough western education, and excellent connections in Samoan society.

2. Europeans, once fairly numerous as settlers, but now reduced by death or emigration to a few score except as they may have come recently in official, mission, or commercial posts. To these are added, usually for a day or two only, a small tourist or traveler influx, limited almost wholly to port and airfield zones. Status relationships of the European society are very important in Samoan eyes; they pyramid in secular affairs to the senior official from the metropolitan government in each territory, and in religious matters to the top denominational representatives; also above them to the occasional visiting elite representatives of still higher authorities.

Interaction between Samoans and these European-oriented elites widens the range of communication problems. Modern Samoan history is in many respects a story of misunderstandings and communication inadequacies. These dimensions, and problems of grappling with them, will be brought out particularly in chapters VIII and IX.

8. Less Formal Alignments

The emphasis to this point has been on well-institutionalized social structures into which individuals are fitted according to either traditional or newer usage. But it would be inadequate to accept these ethnologically recorded patterns or "models" as entirely realistic.

As sociologists have noted in theory relating to "formal organizations, "[8] the institutionalized structure tends to serve as a framework in which less formal systems of interaction and power get built up, and are subject to dynamic change from time to time. This shows in folklore and pre-European history just as it does in modern times. Here a strong titleholder or clique of titleholders

---

[8] See especially Selznick, P. "Foundation of the Theory of Organization, " American Sociological Review, Vol. 13 (1948), pp. 25-35.

emerges to exercise special influence or to jockey for power; an important title is taken by a new incumbent, and so loses out in authority for perhaps years until the new titleholder can build up its prestige again; an energetic women's group may force the pace of change in village affairs to a point which angers conservative matais; a well-educated young man without a title becomes essential to a village in mediator relations with Europeans and so breaks out from the conventional taule'ale'a status.

Under such circumstances, the authority and power relations, the goal-values, the controls and constraints represented in the formal structures may break down or change. The modern acculturative situation particularly opens out opportunities for modification of the traditional patterns, with resulting tendencies to increased tension and conflict, as well as possibilities for new forms of integration and cohesion.

Informal alignments among Samoans, part-Samoans, and Europeans in political, economic, and other spheres have been particularly important in influencing the history of modern Samoa.

IV. SYMBOL, CEREMONY, AND SANCTION

1. The Importance of Symbolic and Ceremonial Behavior

Elite communication in Samoa cannot be understood without taking account of its symbolic-ceremonial context, and the social and religious sanctions which validate it.

Important interaction among elite persons is carried on, if at all possible, in a formal setting, and publicly recognized and made memorable by elaborate paraphernalia and ceremonial behavior. These appear to have particular functional significance within an oral tradition as structuring and stabilizing what might otherwise be a precarious continuity. They marshal recognition of and support for elite personalities and their actions within their adherent groups and the community at large. In Samoa, moreover, they appear to have been elaborated into a major preoccupation. Ceremony is one of the main delights of life.

Elite persons may communicate informally, it is true. This occurs particularly in the modern setting where leaders of higher rank, usually with considerable Western education, may don a "European" personality when outside the Samoan milieu. Speaking usually in English, with Western manners, they feel free to do and say things that would be offensive in their Samoan role. In such settings, too, they may conform easily to the elite communication behavior customary in the Western milieu, as in governmental activities or travel overseas. Even among higher elite persons in their own in-group communication there is an increasing tendency to use the less formal procedures of European style if no objection is raised. In public Samoan settings, however, except under wholly emergency conditions, the correct symbolic-ceremonial context is virtually mandatory; lapses would bring shame not only upon the elite persons but on their kinsmen and other adherent groups, and in important matters could be remembered for years.

The chief forms the centerpiece for all such activity: embodiment of the "dignity" of his group, seated in the position of honor, the focus of speeches, a recipient of appropriate services, in the case of "royal" personages invested almost with deity, and all of course meticulously ordered in terms of his precise rank. But the main responsibilities in ceremonious matters are carried by the orators, along with more specialized participants. Notable among the latter are figures already mentioned: the chiefly heir apparent (manaia), the ceremonial hostess (taupou), and senior members of the women's organizations.

In the sections which follow, dealing with various aspects of

68

symbol, ceremony, and sanction, it will be seen that these operate
consistently as validating forces to

   1.   Signalize and lend public support to the particular occasion and its agenda, and provide witnesses to the procedure by
way of making it memorable to many people.

   2.   Recognize and exercise publicly the prestige status of
authorized participants; and by implication admit the right of ex-
cluding non-participants.

   3.   Signalize the status and opinions of the adherent groups
represented by the active participants.

   In such a setting, without written records except as they have
come in very sparsely during modern times, there is great stress
upon what can be immediately seen, clearly heard, or otherwise
directly identified by the senses: space positions, honorific language, distinctive action sequences limited to particular occasions.
The public nature of this symbolic-ceremonial context is also an
essential feature, even where actual elite deliberation may be
strictly private.

   Europeans of elite status engaging in interaction with Samoan
elite persons under circumstances of public Samoan knowledge are
virtually compelled to operate within this context, playing the role
to the best of their ability. A circumstance making this easier
than it would be otherwise is that such a European is inevitably treated as a "chief," so that the active role of talking chief is correctly
filled by a well-chosen Samoan interpreter who manipulates him
through the maze of Samoan custom involved.

2.   Place and Space Position

   Conventional behavior involving location and space position
plays an important part in the context of elite communication, being
immediately visible and recognizable. Only a brief summary is
possible here of the highly elaborate use by the Samoans of such
"space" or "place" factors, which fortunately are discussed extensively in the literature.

   Every village community has a malae or "village square"
recognized as its ceremonial center, where all formal open-air
gatherings pertaining to the community as a whole are held. Each
subdistrict, district, great kin, and other traditionally organized
supracommunity group has its correct malae or malaes, and "all
Samoa" comes together on certain malaes, notably at the old kingship center of Mulinu'u adjacent to the port of Apia. Modern governmental activities at elite levels are properly consummated at the
correct center, including Mulinu'u. The antigovernment Mau

(Opinion) movements of recent times, and the self-government movement of 1947 in Western Samoa, focused their activities upon traditionally exalted malaes which became for them a "capital."

Each malae has on it a key "guesthouse," either "round" or "long," of superior craftsmanship. Here are held indoor ceremonies and meetings. It is an indoor-outdoor structure, a platform with a roof supported on posts, and except when venetian-like storm blinds are let down, it (like all Samoan dwellings) is open on all sides. Correctly it pertains to the senior chiefly title of the group concerned. Other chiefs may have guesthouses on the malae or at their family living site in the community, and here appropriate groups foregather. A visiting party is likely to sleep in one or more of these, or in one of the regular family-type houses, but to eat, rest, and talk in the principal guesthouse. Government and missions maintain the equivalent of such a guesthouse at their centers.

Any house, however, is capable of being used in an elite fashion as regards its internal seating arrangements, and the wall-less architecture insures that all proceedings within these Samoan structures are open to public observance. Definition of status is provided by the sectors of a house, and use of its outer ring of posts as backrests. Buck says of conventional seating positions in the round guesthouse:

> There are set positions to be occupied by the chiefs
> on all ceremonial occasions. The two rounded ends
> are the places of honor: entering from the front,
> that on the right is occupied by the village chiefs;
> that on the left by [visiting chiefs or other guests].
> The middle end posts serve as back rests for the
> chiefs of highest rank on either side... The prin-
> cipal visiting talking chief sits by the middle [post]
> on the front side... About midway between his own
> high chief and the visiting talking chief sits the
> principal talking chief of the village... [A] stranger
> who is unheralded and unknown has the right to
> the stranger's post... If the stranger is of chief's
> rank, he takes the fourth post on the front [on the
> guest side], but if beneath that rank, he takes the
> corresponding fourth post at the back. No matter
> what chief is sitting before it, the stranger can
> demand that he relinquish the position (Samoan
> Material Culture, pp. 96-97, 147).

Elite persons trained in Samoan custom assume more or less automatically their correct positions in terms of the hierarchical status
of the individuals present. Sitting in certain "back" zones of the
house, or between the post backrests, defines the person concerned
as of minor importance, or as ceremonially nonexistent. In formal
elite meetings within an important house, a relatively small number
of the top hierarchy assume these recognized positions, and then
as many subordinates as count themselves entitled to do so may herd
in one spectator-like section or else sit within earshot outside.
Whe're elite and non-elite persons assemble, as in a kin gathering,
or at a meeting of the women or young men, space position is just
as meticulously observed, usually derivative from relation to the
titled persons. It becomes almost axiomatic that any assembly of
elite persons will be able to "structure" itself in terms of publicly
recognized principles of hierarchy pertaining to the status of the
participants.

Disputes are unlikely to occur over space-expressed status
position in the familiar settings of local kin and community. But
elite visiting, especially in the accelerated setting of modern peace
and easier means of communication (roads, buses, etc.) has in it
seeds of dispute regarding precedence which occasionally erupt
into feuding and even open violence. Orators of important traveling
parties, and also government and mission specialists in protocol,
are particularly sensitive to such possibilities.

In settings away from malae and house, Samoans are equally
adept at expressing their status by space position, while meticulously
avoiding stances which might bring the accusation of presuming beyond their station or the taunt of neglecting their rights. At the
airport in Western Samoa, for example, a very distinguished visitor
may be met by "representatives of all Samoa." Almost like a dis-
ciplined drill, the "royal" Fautua are in a knot here, with their
wives, the Faipule or district representatives are lined up in a
given order there, and so on. Under Navy control, in American
Samoa, the expression of hierarchy in space positions by Samoans
fitted with remarkable congruence into that of U.S. Navy personnel.
The main open area of the former naval station served as combined
parade ground and malae of American Samoa.

A frequent remark in Samoan conversation is : "We shall
settle that at the proper place." Except, therefore, under emergency conditions, elite communication involving Samoan custom is
only likely to be advanced effectively after everyone concerned is
seated in his authorized position in the right locality. The one major break in this pattern is where an elite person or persons is involved in private interaction with non-Samoan personnel under mod-

ern conditions.   Usually a higher ranking person with some education, he may take the nearest chair in office or home.   But given
a public situation even in a European setting, he is likely to show
continuing sensitivity to space position.

3.   Rank Order

Rank order systems tend to proliferate in settings of elite
interaction, especially those formations that give public recognition.   Just as space relations demonstrate superordinate-sub-
ordinate relationships, so do sequences involving motion over time,
as in the order of walking, receiving food and drink, presentation
of gifts, speaking, and similar matters which permit this factor to
operate.

As a prime example relating to elite communication, the
Samoans have carried to its greatest elaboration a widely spread
South Pacific cultural element which everywhere tends to demonstrate rank order: the drinking of kava (in Samoan, 'ava).   The
serial distribution of this beverage, which is infused with water
from the roots of a peppery shrub (Piper methysticum) lends itself
ideally to expressing an order of precedence.   At the same time
kava, with its stimulating, astringent, muscle-easing, though non-
alcoholic properties, has, for Samoan diplomacy, something of the
same function as the western cocktail or highball; it relaxes, and
produces an atmosphere of friendliness and in-group association.

All analyses of Samoan culture have stressed the importance
of the kava custom.   No activity involving the assemblage of titled
people, formally or informally, could go forward until kava is
mixed and drunk.   It is antecedent to any formal discussion or
decision-making.   Its preparation is supervised by an orator who
takes responsibility for calling the order of precedence for its distribution.   The modal pattern is for this to express the rank order
from first to last among those entitled to drink.   Repeated constantly
in all kinds of elite constellations it spells out definitively the hierarchy of those present.   An attendant solemnity, the pouring of a
libation on receipt of the cup (coconut shell), the offering of prayer,
the sanctity of the mixing bowl and other gear, provide an atmosphere
of supernatural as well as social sanctions.

Around this basic pattern Samoan creativity has woven an
amazing array of variants.   An orator art is to manipulate the order
of distribution so as to give special honor to individuals without
offending others (or occasionally to perpetrate a deliberate subtle
taunt by placing a person after a rival whom he normally expects

to outrank). Titled individuals have special <u>kava</u> names which the distributor must know. Historical allusions come into the <u>kava</u> ceremonies, with all sorts of side play such as summoning an individual who is entitled to stay away until his name is called.

Normally, <u>kava</u> drinking ceremonially is a male prerogative, but an elite woman may be specially honored by having her name called at a high point in the sequence and partaking of <u>kava</u> seated in the circle of chiefs. In olden days an important <u>taupou</u> of a visiting party was so honored, and nowadays, an elite European woman frequently is, also a woman holding a title in her own right. Elaboration reaches its peak in certain "royal" ceremonies in which high-titled persons replace the usually untitled men and girls who prepare and distribute the <u>kava</u>. In pre-Christian days great <u>kava</u> rituals were part of the Samoan religion. <u>Kava</u> ceremonies may also be conducted in formal gatherings of the women or the untitled men and youths, with distribution based derivatively on relationship to titled persons. New elite personnel such as pastors, school-teachers, and medical practitioners may on occasion join the <u>kava</u> circle. Europeans, at first drinkers in the name of etiquette, usually acquire the taste, and one of the nimblest feats of an orator is to call a hierarchical order which integrates European governmental or other dignitaries with Samoan titleholders.

The <u>kava</u> ceremony has been discussed at some length here as being a high point in what are a whole series of Samoan ceremonious activities involving the rank order principle. In the further analysis this principle will appear indeed as a consistent thread in Samoan elite behavior.

4. Etiquette

<u>Etiquette is greatly elaborated in elite situations, and assumes highly structured forms recognized throughout the particular world of communication involved.</u> Etiquette "oils the wheels" of difficult interaction, regionally and hierarchically. The traditional etiquette system is one of the most persistent facets of Samoan life as being of high "social maintenance" value. Europeans of status find it necessary to fit into it.

Etiquette emphasizes particularly the "respect" elements that go with status. This is well brought out in a text on Samoan social culture for American Samoan schools, prepared in 1941 by a Samoan education official, Chief S. Faamusili; it covers primary and intermediate grades. The outline reads as follows:

September
  1st Week—How children should pay respect to parents.
  2nd Week—How to respect Naval and Island Government officials.
  3rd Week—How to respect the Chiefs and Faifeaus (Pastors).
  4th Week—Review.

October
  1st Week—How to pay respects to the chief's kava ceremony.
  2nd Week—How to show respect for the chief's food.
  3rd Week—How to show respect for the chief's meetings.
  4th Week—Review.

November
  1st Week—Teaching several ways of showing respect and good behavior.
  2nd Week—How to respect visitors.
                    [And so on.]

Orators are traditionally specialists in etiquette. The chief and the European of status may rest on their prestige while the orators hold the stage. An expert orator of high rank should be able to weave his way in many, if not all, Samoan communities without offense to hosts and without mistakes which reflect on the dignity of himself, and hence his own group.

Two illustrations may be given, both important to elite communication. The first concerns a ceremonial type of reference called fa'alupenga, a verbal distillate of history and a "Who's Who" of a community, a district, and even of "all Samoa, " in allegorical language, to be recited on the appropriate occasion. Each village and district has its own fa'alupenga. The orator of a visiting party does well to know it without error. It is another of the numerous institutions which recognize and validate rank, in lieu of written records.

The second, a preliminary to speechmaking, is a kind of competitive talking-down ceremony by orators whose rank and group representation might entitle them to be the "voice" for that occasion. Usually standing in a line and leaning on their staffs, they talk back and forth in conventional phrases, and one by one yield until the final speaker (probably not only agreed on but recognized ahead of time by all as the appropriate person), stands alone. His ensuing speech, perhaps twenty minutes of ceremonious honorifics and traditional allusion, evokes admiration but is likely to say nothing on any practical issue under consideration.

Among the many other persistent etiquette habits which the Westerner in Samoa will observe as still widely practiced are the

crouched or stooped position assumed by persons of lesser rank
when coming into the presence of titled persons, and the act of
touching a gift to the bowed forehead as an acknowledgment of its
receipt. Both gestures are eloquent expressions of a complex of
Samoan values.

Elite persons, steeped as they are in this traditional etiquette,
can usually step out with ready facility and carry on Western forms
of etiquette. A handshake, joking and other relaxed expression, a
witty speech, or dignity when required, come easily. With non-
elite Samoans present, however, such behavior beyond the handshake is likely to be restrained; it is seen behind government doors,
at European-style gatherings, and when groups and individuals of
high status travel abroad.

5. Material Prestige Symbols

Visible material prestige symbols are a mark of elite interaction having high recognition value. For important occasions the
house or other space setting is likely to be furbished and often
elaborately decorated with leaves and flowers, the best matting,
and other indications of ceremonious use.

Clothing and personal adornment provide particularly effective and mobile means of publicly demonstrating status and the
nature of the occasion. In traditional ceremonies the chiefs and
members of their retinues will still almost invariably wear garments of patterned "tapa" bark cloth (siapo) or "fine mats," made
of very finely plaited fiber, or shaggy hand-plaited garments of
white, brown, red, or black, having high symbolic value. The
wearing of a large headdress of human hair, shell, and other materials, and in the old days of tooth and tusk necklaces and other
body ornaments now largely in museums abroad, is appropriate
to certain persons. Distinctive traditional hairdos are still seen
on a few conservative leaders. For high ceremonies the faces of
some participants may be partially blackened. Body tattooing of
superior quality on the thighs and lower back is still almost universal among titled men, though the younger generation is not sub-
mitting to this custom.

On ceremonious occasions the chiefs and orators use distinctive fly whisks, which, hung over a shoulder, are something of
a "badge of office." For standing speeches in the open they will
lean on a wooden staff. Carved wooden clubs may be held in the
hand. Other usages involving material goods will appear in subsequent sections.

In "dress-up" settings not involving traditional ceremony titled persons may now wear waistcloths (lavalava), usually of subdued color perhaps smartly tailored, sometimes with side pockets and belt loops, white shirts well laundered, ties, coats of tailored European style, frequently leather sandals, felt or panama hats, and a cane. (Trousers are almost never worn by the culture-conscious Samoans of Western Samoa, though they are used somewhat more in American Samoa.) An umbrella may be carried by a subordinate. Glasses and a leather briefcase may be favored. Women married to rank or of high family may appear in Samoan community settings in the often brightly colored uniforms of the local Women's Committee, a dress over an appropriately colored long waist-cloth, or in individual variations on this traditional theme. In European settings and especially around the port centers dress and lavalava are often skillfully cut and co-ordinated in color and material to give the effect of a long, shaped suit, and in this form shows signs of becoming a self-conscious "national" costume. For Sunday church attendance, everyone dresses in immaculate white clothes, though darker coats may be worn by the pastor or catechist and by titled men alternative to washable white coats. For these Sunday services all women, following the Pauline doctrine, wear homemade plaited brimmed hats in a great variety of design.

6. Property Accumulation and Exchange

Display and transfer of property in gift-giving ceremonials may become a highly developed form of communication among groups and their elites and an important technique for demonstrating and validating status and for fostering social integration. In Samoa, as in many other places, wealth display and gift exchange for purposes of enhancing prestige is also a potent factor in stimulating work and raising the standard for good living well above the purely subsistence level, hence providing the society with a greater margin of safety for well-being.

The elite are the custodians and the distributors of "display" or "ceremonial" wealth. The property used for such exhibition and exchange includes first of all food, with the pig cooked whole as the centerpiece, fine mats, which are often heirlooms of great value in ceremonial terms, siapo (bark cloth), scented oil, ornaments, fans, carved utensils, large roots of kava, and, not least important in modern days, money.

The adherent groups supporting a chiefly title accumulate this property and surplus food wealth, and their chief, when it is strategic

to use it, calls for contributions to the group effort which he then
fronts. Among the many occasions calling for gift exchange ceremonials, are important political consultations, weddings, funerals,
succession to titles, and visiting or welcoming visitors. The ceremonies concerned take on a great variety of specific forms. When
very important fine mats are involved, for instance, it is customary
to fire off guns, as, held high by proud bearers, the mats are being
carried forward; this is a salute to the honor of the specific mat
and its history. Always there is well-staged and dramatic display:
usually a procession bearing the gifts, a mountain of material goods
and foodstuffs on the malae, the loud proclamation of each gift and
its donors by the "talking chief" of the recipient party, the sharing
of food gifts among all groups present. These are typical procedures, but the range of variation in occasion, detail, and terminology is very great.

Basic to all such gift giving, as will be seen, is a principle
of reciprocity or equivalence. Even so, there is plenty of room for
power manipulation. Students of Samoan custom have speculated
that a factor in bringing about the great elaboration of such ceremonial usages here has been that, though given to honor the chiefs,
the fine mats and other important nonperishable articles are actually
passed over to the custody of talking chiefs. Possession of large
amounts of such wealth redounds to the honor and influence of a
talking chief. However true such a historical hypothesis as to the
role of talking chiefs may be, it is clear that the chief and his re-
tinue become the focal point in a great power and wealth game which
appears as perhaps the dominant "theme" or "value" in Samoan
cultural behavior, with functional significance to everyone from chief
to child.

Writers on Samoa also project the customs concerned into the
older setting in which the rights and obligations generated through
property exchanges could be used to cement alliances or to redress
a balance in case of feuding or war—in this case they could be a
life and death matter. Even under modern conditions of peace,
they are likely to be called upon to repair breaches in social relationships. Reciprocal gift giving can also provide a kind of "insurance" when any group or individual is struck by hardship or
disaster. Gifts, hospitality, and other aid are likely to come from
neighbors and from kinsmen near or far, and in turn, when fortune
is favorable, the recipient will be subject to enormous social pressure to share. The elite person of importance, however, must if
at all possible, keep ahead of the game skillfully. Without seeming
niggardly or ungenerous, he must always command an easy edge
of material goods and today of money, so that when occasions arise

he can support his prestige by giving prodigally from his own personal and family property stores.   This is one of the major pressures that are driving many of the higher Samoan elite into part-
time European style business or plantation enterprise on the side.

The non-elite supporter of an elite title, in giving without
stint, and working industriously so as to have the means to do so,
publicly demonstrates his worth to his leader.   He takes pride in
seeing the ceremonial wealth in front of the chief mount high, gains
identification with him, and participates publicly in the prestige
which the affair brings to the chief, just as later he will participate
in redistribution of reciprocally given gifts.   This constantly run
social drama enforces and reinforces the identification of the matai
and his group, so that even small children are so sensitized to it
that they are apt to show tenseness or glowing pleasure in accordance
with how smoothly the show is running, or shame if the group has
been caught with low resources.

7.   Feasts and Food Presentations

Food, especially that of ceremonially defined character, is
a universal accompaniment of elite contacts; its importance is both
social and symbolic.   Food in Samoa has fundamental symbolic importance in every transaction or communication that is not of an
entirely casual nature.   Every affair of any importance in Samoan
life necessitates "feasting" in the sense of consumption of ceremonious foods, and in the feast, no less than in the kava ceremony,
rank and status are dramatized and demonstrated.

Foodstuffs, unprocessed or cooked as is appropriate, are the
most essential part of all gift presentations.   There are a great
many different kinds of food-giving presentation ceremonies each
appropriate to its own specific occasion and known by its own name.
Some of the principal ones are summarized by Buck:

> The sua ta'i is the ceremonial meal brought in
> to a high chief to honor him (fa'aaloalo).   Four
> bearers bring in a drinking nut, talo taisi (taro
> root cooked in ti leaves), taro root, a fowl, and
> a roasted pig in that order...   If the chief is of
> outstanding rank, he alone is served on a (plaited)
> platter.   The others are served on leaves.   If
> there are other chiefs of high rank, each may
> get a sua...   The laulautasi is a presentation of
> cooked food to visitors by the chiefs (matai) of
> the village...   The taalolo is a presentation of

food to visitors by the village, and is of a more
public character... [The] talinga... is the women's ta'alolo... talo pa'ia is a form of the ta'a-
lolo in which a whole district takes part in presenting food (op. cit., pp. 140-46).

Capping all other food gifts in presentation prestige value is
the pig. Usually brought on a platform of lashed poles, it has been
dressed and cooked whole (though lightly, as the portions after
distribution are recooked at home), and often decked with hibiscus
or other flowers. The prestige of the group making the presentation
is very definitely involved with the size and type of pig. The pig
is essentially a "chiefly" gift. In its cutting up—an almost religious
rite—there is a strict order of prestige portions, each with its
recognized name, due to ranking persons involved. Chickens,
sharks, turtles, and certain other foods also have well-defined
elite portions. In public presentations, however, even one taro
or coconut added to the food pile by a woman or child has its particular symbolic value.

Customs of food distribution are widespread and very functional in the tropic belt where many foods are not readily preserved
and stored by indigenous techniques. Thus the great catch of fish,
the large animal killed, is so distributed that it is used while fresh
and a network of reciprocal rights and obligations brought into
play, creating in effect "living storage." Such distribution also
becomes to a degree an economic leveler. But feasting and food
presentation has further important meaning in the Samoan setting
in terms of communication.

1. As with the kava ceremony, so food distributions, too,
and the feasts that normally follow them, involve strict order sequences and seating positions in terms of rank. Titled people of
appropriate rank eat together. Women and untitled men eat separately, usually later, and children usually last on the remaining
pickings. This status distinction in commensal usages comes to
have deep emotional context. The writers have seen a Samoan
chief ask a younger untitled man to join them and him, in an informal
meal on a modern egalitarian basis as being "all educated people."
The younger man tried again and again to swallow food but it would
not go past his throat so that he almost choked on his respect, and
finally the chief said: "You had better go and finish your meal with
the women and young men."

2. Feasting is a central ingredient in a complex of pleasurable
activities that "spike" community life, lifting it from the ordinary
round, and increasing communication processes. Accompaniments

are almost always formal or informal <u>fono</u> meetings for discussions,
and community dancing and singing involving all age and sex groupings. Its role in social integration cannot be overestimated.
3.   The feast, and the other pleasurable events associated
with it, insure that the occasion and its business purpose are publicly validated and made <u>memorable</u> for the appropriate people.
It insures nearly always a large number of participants and witnesses, a matter of great importance in an oral culture without the
habit of making a written record. A Samoan reaching in memory
for some fact or decision is likely to recall details of the associated
feast, such as what kin group gave the pig, and so to the matter
sought.

Westerners are apt to underestimate the extent to which the
feasting itself and associated ceremonial is important to Samoans.
The European outsider is likely to consider them "wasteful" or
"unnecessary." Such a viewpoint comes out even in official documents, as reports of the United Nations Missions in Samoa. While
interest is expressed in these enjoyable Samoan customs, there is
an anxiety to get ahead with the "serious business." In Samoa
feasting is always serious business, for Samoans "say it with
food."

8.   Hospitality; the Ceremonial Journey

Hospitality, central to ceremonious activity, is a great ce-
menting and validating factor in elite relationships, and a principal
integrative force in community and national life. To a Samoan
practically every village is an inn or lodging place, since in almost
all of them he can with any ingenuity whatever claim a relative by
blood, marriage, or adoption, or at least a person obligated through
friendship or property distribution, and there he may be assured
a welcome. A Samoan keeps tab of his relationship links as an
American businessman keeps track of his bank account; relationships are also kept warm and personal by messages, visits, gifts,
and the like. The elite visitor, especially, is always treated to
"generous" hospitality and becomes the welcome center for leisure
activities, including <u>kava</u> drinking and gossip, feasting and gift
giving, games, dances and singing. The importance of this to the
exchange of ideas—that is as a means of wider communication—
can hardly be overemphasized.

Hospitality operates most constantly through the custom of
"going on <u>malanga</u>" (i. e., "a journey"), usually in a party. <u>The
ceremonial journey, a highly institutionalized part of communication
behavior</u>, facilitates interaction beyond the local setting; the leader

does well to show himself. Very frequently the party is organized
around a senior titleholder. At times virtually whole villages may
go on malanga, visiting other communities at a greater or lesser
distance. The ostensible purpose is frequently to play one of the
prolonged cricket matches (lasting perhaps for days) that are a
favored Samoan activity. Or the malanga party, small or large,
may be on family business, visiting relatives in another area, or
concerned with political, church, school, medical, or other affairs.
A malanga party may go on tour around the island or islands with
a dramatic play that has been worked out in one village, to raise
funds, say, for a new church roof or some such local purpose.
These malanga parties, passing by foot trail or Samoan craft, along
the coast through village after village, sometimes where possible
or necessary journeying nowadays by bus, or using the interisland
launch or other boat service, are the social blood stream of these
otherwise isolated village-dwelling peoples.

Visitors rarely pass a village without a longer or shorter
stay, even if only long enough for a kava-drinking ceremony of
their elite members with the elite of the village through which their
path lies, and an exchange of gossip. Particularly in villages where
they stay overnight there is the excuse and occasion for entertainments, exchange of news, renewal of varied kinship ties, and ro-
mancing on the part of the younger members of the party and their
corresponding host members. The party picks up information as
it travels and passes it on. The titled people in the party will have
contact mainly with their own status group, and the same is true
of the womenfolk and the young people. There is a general quickening
of the community pulse. In function therefore the malanga is a
form of newspaper, theater, sport, and lecture circuit, with political forum included.

The malanga is also most important in stimulating marriages
(at both elite and non-elite levels) out of the village circle, so keeping the web of kinship widespread. Even the largely arranged
marriages of higher elite persons rest on such journeys by "go-
betweens." It is unseemly for brothers and sisters, or their extended kin equivalents, to dance in front of one another, or partake
of any sex-tinged activity;—a so-called "brother and sister avoidance" still important to Samoans. Thus it is in these malanga festivities that romance is least circumscribed, since in affairs within
the village there are so many close relatives to be avoided.

A strong impression is gained that the tendency to structure
the malanga very formally traces back to the earlier days of insecurity and war. Where casual or individual journeying would
ordinarily have been dangerous the organized party, if possible

sending notice in advance, could move with apparent safety if it
kept to the correct procedures. Undoubtedly, however, such
journeying has greatly increased with modern peace, and especially
so for persons of lower status, including women and children traveling informally.

So essential is this malanga technique for doing business of
any kind in Samoa that it is used constantly by the administration.
The official malanga for purposes of health work, school inspection,
radio survey, and the like, and the periodic malanga of the senior
representative of the metropolitan country, are regular activities of
modern government.

One of the irritants that contributed quite considerably to the
Mau (Opinion) resistance movement to the New Zealand administration in the twenties was the attempt of the government to control
malanga-making. Any malanga involving more than a day's journey was supposed to get a written permit. Intended in the first
place to curtail what were regarded as wasteful customs and the
neglect of plantations, and later as a means of suppressing antigovernment assembly, the ordinance roused all the fury and indig-
nation that curtailment of the freedom of the press and of assembly
would arouse in this country.

9. Arts and Sports

Traditional arts and sports can be put to use for recognition
and validation of status as well as for relaxation and pleasure purposes. A formal assemblage of elite persons becomes an occasion
for their adherents to perform music, dance, pageantry, and drama.
The preparation of such spectacles may take weeks of practice.
The occasion gives a charge of social energy that mobilizes the
kin, community, or district group ooncerned. For matters em-
bracing "all Samoa, " talent will be drawn from all the correctly
representative groups.

Such artistic activities comprise both formalized traditional
pageantry, and mobile creative traditions. Examples of the former
are the high ceremonies of "royal" kava, and receptions of distinguished persons by district or village parties headed by regalia-
decked honorific persons, with traditional-style chant and dance.
Some rarely performed ceremonies may still be revived on outstandingly elite occasions such as the visit of a United Nations
Mission or United States Congressional visitor: one such, seen by
one of the writers, involved the burning of "sacred fire" on the
malae (ceremonial "square") to creat the necessary hallowed atmosphere.

Dancing, music, and drama are also living and growing traditions in that here Samoans tolerate and welcome innovation. Dancing parties are always on the alert for new twists to the standard themes, and even in high ceremonies an exalted taupou (ceremonial maiden) may try out along with conventional dancing some variant based on what she has seen in a Hollywood movie at the port center. Dance types are copied from Hawaii, the Tokelaus, and other islands. Costumes have become a riot of (on the whole) pleasing color, by way of cloth, raffia, and other new materials, and the writers have seen an older "joker" woman clowning in the traditional manner, on the fringe of a dance team, with a costume plastered with labels from "bully beef" cans.

Samoans, in taking over the British game of cricket during the nineteenth century, have turned it into a pageant of dancing and song.[1] Elite occasions may also be marked by the staging of plays, both original and adapted from Shakespeare and other Western sources, with dance chorus interweaving. In one remote district a local playwright composed a drama, in honor of a distinguished visiting European party, based on the conflict between the army and navy in ancient Persia, but with train and telephone among the props; the action broke off periodically to allow the chorus to sing and dance the current theme, and each actor at his entrance danced twice around the stage before starting his part. The composers of such dances and songs have elite recognition even where they are not titled people. A young untitled Samoan who accompanied the writers on one trip into an outer area was given considerable honor in each village visited because he was known for the songs he had composed, and they were sung in recognition of him.

Art can also be used effectively to influence public opinion. Pro-and antigovernment political songs were employed during the Mau (Opinion) movements, and the later self-government movement. The writers have seen, as part of the entertainment of a government party by a district, a series of policy allusions made in successive song performances by schoolchildren, the aumanga (untitled men), and other groups, to make clear the views of the district on current problems.

---

[1] Compared with this sport, rugby football, baseball (in American Samoa), tennis, and golf have gained only a very minor place in Samoan leisure activities, though they have been taken up in the part-Samoan group. Boxing has become a popular commercialized sport in Western Samoa.

10. The Linguistic Context

Language is, uniquely and above all others, the rich and
mobile medium through which eliteness is demonstrated and honored; notably this is achieved through a special honorific vocabulary, but also by grammatical forms, intonation, and gesture.
The emphasis upon honorific names and titles has already
been noted. These are extended not only to persons but also to
places and objects: mountains and other geographic localities of
mythological or historical significance, important malaes and
guest houses, kava bowls and cups, fine mats, and other symbols
of special eliteness. Samoan conversation relating to elite subjects
is replete with etiquette and other appropriate allusion, always
with due regard to hierarchy: afioga mai, susunga mai, "your
highness," "your mightiness," and so on.
Much has been written, too, of honorific speech pertaining
to "chiefly" status. Parts of the body, for example, involve special
terms if speaking about or to a chief, much as in Victorian England
"legs" were "limbs" before the ladies or in speaking of a lady.
Such distinctions are so extensive as to have been referred to frequently though erroneously as a "separate" language. They consist
rather, as Grattan says, of

> Specialized vocabularies of courtesy and cere-
> mony for use on appropriate occasions... for
> reference to different groups in society, special
> words for referring to the same things or con-
> ditions as applied to different persons, and often
> special terms, particularly for referring to
> death, in certain distinguished families...
> One of the strictest rules in this matter is
> that which forbids the use by any person, how-
> ever high in rank, of the language of courtesy
> in regard to himself or his own family; but it
> is properly and habitually employed in addres-
> sing or speaking of titled people or any others...
> to whom one wishes to show the forms of
> politeness. In certain circumstances custom
> requires the use of respectful terms or ex-
> pressions in describing animate or inanimate
> things in the presence of chiefs or orators...
> Again there are words the apt choice of which
> defines the rank or social group of the person...,
> or a reference of personal or individual signifi-

cance may involve an explanation reaching far
back into the early traditions of the village or district (An Introduction to Samoan Custom, p. 171).

The place that communication holds in Samoan life is demonstrated by the very rich vocabulary relating to speech and speech
processes, in which the most delicate and subtle nuances are
separated out with special terms. Pratt's Samoan dictionary shows
more than 400 such terms overtly descriptive of speech and speech
techniques. This precision and sensitivity will be brought out in
some specific examples in the subsequent chapters as processes
of elite communication and decision making are seen at work. It
is also discussed in Annex II on the language context.

11. Time and Tempo

Time and tempo are particularly important in elite activities,
and the expectation of conformity to the prevailing culture patterning
in this respect is very strong. Unlike the elite person in Western
settings who may clock his appointments by minutes, the Samoan
world of time gives much more latitude.

By Western standards the ceremonial contexts of elite communication involve a leisurely and measured, as well as correctly
ordered, sequence of events which is likely to tax even the most
patient European. What the latter judge as slow action, repetition,
long intervals, are to the Samoan an essential part of his savoring
of the occasion. It is a reinforcement of the recognition and validation functions of symbol and ceremony. It also adds an appreciated
note of eliteness, unusualness, at times virtual sanctification, to
what otherwise is the rather commonplace familiar round of community and kin affairs. So any speed-up or short cut in the long-
drawn timing and tempo would verge on sin.

Samoans recognize that a European participant, used to his
own timing, is put under a strain. They are likely to provide rest
periods, refreshments, and other aids, and also appreciative acknowledgment of conformity. "Thank you, " the presiding orator
states on one such occasion, "for your quiet patience while we
were engaged in Samoan matters at this time. All the respectful
customs have been accomplished which it is proper to provide.
When you first arrived our respect was not complete. We hope
that you are satisfied with all that has been done with the day to
show our welcome. " [So tonight, all the correct honorifics having
been carried out in proper order and tempo, and everyone recognized
and validated, we can proceed to business.]

In reverse, elite persons who have European contacts, which usually means considerable Western education, move easily into the time and tempo systems of European elite settings on appropriate occasions. Meetings of the former House of <u>Ali'i</u> (Chiefs) in American Samoa moved in brisk fashion in at least rough conformity to "Roberts' rules of order," and looked to an outsider much like a Cabinet or business Board of Directors meeting. Stepping out from the relatively clockless Samoan world, regulated perhaps most by the Christian weekly calendar, headed up into Sundays (a ceremonial day marked by virtually universal churchgoing), the leader may check his appointments by wrist watch and confine or discard honorifics in the interests of European-style business.

12. Reciprocity or Equivalence

A characteristic feature of all such elite interaction may be summed up in the terms "reciprocity" or "equivalence." Whatever is involved—goods, services, participation—a careful balance of give-and-take, of rights and obligations, of "basic compensation" (p. 289) is maintained. Especially when status equals are involved the equilibrium tends to be meticulously observed.

In some ceremonious situations the equivalence is expressed in immediately reciprocal behavior, as in formal "gift" exchanges or back-and-forth speeches. But to the extent that delay is involved, as may occur in compensation for an injury or in returning hospitality, the imbalance is carefully recognized until such time as a return is made. Samoans therefore keep a kind of mental bank account of these matters, and notably so the talking chiefs in relation to the rights and responsibilities of their chiefs. To be on the debit side beyond the proprieties brings shame and loss of prestige to the elite person and his adherent group. The idea of "profiting" out of such interaction, especially among coequals, is foreign except as it might be part of some devious power manipulation among higher elite persons and factions.

The reciprocity factor exercised in such contexts of ceremonious behavior has by no means always been recognized by Western visitors, though if they are being coached by persons familiar with Samoan custom they will learn this among their first rules of induction to the local setting. The outside observer, seeing Samoan pageantry and handling of ceremonial property in action, tends to apply European concepts such as "generosity," even "prodigality," though these are not really apt.

From the Samoan viewpoint, a non-Samoan who receives benefits should make an equivalent return according to his status,

just as a Samoan would. The giving of wealth and services obviously
could not persist as a one-sided affair. To the extent that the person involved claims eliteness, reciprocity becomes essential if
the Samoans are not to write him off as "uncouth" or a "nobody"
to be disregarded. At the same time, it would evoke criticism if
he were to give more than his recognized status calls for, especially if his return puts the Samoans concerned under an undue obliga-
tion. It would also be unfortunate if any reciprocal return were to
be given the semantic context of a Western-type commercial pay-
ment, even when, as is so often appropriately done, the equivalence
is expressed through a money "gift." In modern days Samoans
have come to look upon a gift of kegged beef and canned ship's bis-
cuits as the Western equivalent of higher ceremonial wealth.

Circumspection and proper observance of etiquette is of the
essence here, and the inexperienced person will need advice. The
writers recall the final night of their stay in an isolated village
when the key titleholders came for a last talk; in due course an
equivalence gift of money was passed with appropriate words by
way of the writers' talking chief to the village talking chief—far
more than a professor could really afford from his travel grant.
The talking chief went outside and "shouted" the gift formally into
the darkness of the village. Fron the waiting villagers, sitting
quietly in the lantern-lighted households, came a hand clapping and
exclamations of approving appreciation, and one more ordeal was
over.

In the section on property exchanges emphasis was laid on
derivative functions of reciprocal give-and-take. The binding of
groups and individuals in an equivalent network of mutual rights
and obligations contributes strongly to social integration and provides a kind of "insurance" system in terms of economic and
political securities. Samoans at all levels tend to "keep glowing
the embers" of kinship and friendship by acts of remembrance
usually involving gifts or services. In property matters such equivalence makes for a complex system of multiple rights, interests,
or equities.   The holder of an important piece of property shares
it potentially with a wide circle of others. "Authority" or "prestige" type rights may pyramid upwards hierarchically in terms of
overarching titles, while practical "use" type rights may extend
outward in terms of kinsmen entitled to request use of the item
concerned, or even to take it without asking.

In a later chapter, political repercussions of the equivalence
principle will be seen in relation to the context of the European-
sponsored government, in which differential salary scales and
other inconsistencies as between Samoans and non-Samoans assuming more or less similar responsibilites are a cause of tension.

13. Social and Religious Sanctions

Social sanctions operate strongly in support of the elite structure. This is true even though in the modern setting the traditional rule-and-sanction (legal) aspect of Samoan culture is under pressure and somewhat disintegrated in the face of European law backed by Western-style force.

To a remarkable degree, considering the acculturative processes involved, the Samoan milieu has carried forward the traditional social control systems. Particularly at the village level and within the more intimate kinship constellations conformity reaps the reward of "positive sanctions, " while deviation evokes "negative" reactions of unpopularity, condemnation, or even stronger manifestations. Elite authority, backed by public opinion, may be expressed in "fines" of livestock, taro, or other goods, or even banishment from the group. European laws formally forbidding Samoan-style punishments, such as have been on the books of American Samoan law for many years, can be bypassed when public opinion is strong enough.

On the other side of the legal coin, European law has strongly backed up the authority of the elite provided they are operating within the scope of the European legal code. Titles are officially registered, and if necessary succession to a title is negotiated in the courts between disputing claimants or rival family lines. Any disturbance of an elite assembly would contravene European-style law, and bring to hand the constabulary (now almost wholly Samoan in personnel) if it were to get beyond the control of the village policeman. While the authority of the Samoan leader has undoubtedly been greatly curbed by Western-style codes and enforcement agencies, his security appears certainly to have been enhanced.

Religious symbols and sanctions are utilized markedly in elite communication. In the modern setting of Samoa they are mostly of a generalized character which is supradenominational and validates the total culture system.

The Samoans were seen to be now all adherents of various Western faiths—Protestant, Roman Catholic, and Latter-day Saints. Traces of the older religion appear in ceremonial activities relating to elite groups such as the pouring of a libation in the kava-drinking ceremony and allusions in etiquette. But in the modern setting, Biblical and related references, and church activities, provide religious symbols and sanctions. When appropriate, the Samoan pastor or catechist, or a white church leader, may participate in secular ceremonial activities, and under some circumstances their voices carry great weight as being supernaturally oriented.

Samoan oratory, both in etiquette behavior and in relation to decision-making, rarely fails to include some rather generalized prayer form at its opening: "Thanks be to the Atua (God) for a safe assembly, " "Bless this occasion, " and so on. It is also likely to be sprinkled through with Biblical allusion, sometimes oblique to the point where a European, rarely so orally versed in the Bible as the Samoan, may fail to grasp the meaning. A Samoan letter, even when written by a reasonably well-educated Samoan, is similarly likely to start and end with religious salutations and to have Biblical references or exhortations scattered liberally though it. In connection with the self-government movements, Samoan spokesmen frequently expressed a sincere belief that "God will be able to tell us how to do the [governmental] tasks that we do not know how to do. " Certainly Samoan customs of gift-exchange, reciprocal hospitality, and the like have been fused by now inextricably with the Christian ethic of "brotherly love, " "charity, " and service, so that the Samoan mental picture of his own people and culture is that they are "the most Christian in the world. " A very influential and progressive chief, asked what solutions he had in view for the obviously fast increasing population of Samoans today in relation to quite limited good lands for plantation use, replied: "How do we know that God intends the Samoans to remain only in Samoa; perhaps he is preparing them as his special people, so that when the rest of the world is destroyed by atom warfare they may re-people it as Noah did after the flood. "

Mead and other modern observers have made a point that, with obsolescence of the old religious system, the sanctity of chiefs has tended to be replaced by the ceremonial of chieftainship. In terms of the older interpretation of chiefs as god-like and mediators with supernatural forces relating to spirits and ancestors, this tends to be true. Yet the "great royal personages" of the senior descent lines still evoke a measure of awe and even fear. Furthermore the churches have rested their lay leadership directly upon the elite hierarchy as represented among their adherents, so that religious sanctions of the new type support their authority.

Denominational differences are a source of rivalry and divisiveness today among the elite. In some situations they can put great strain upon community and kin cohesion, and a chief or orator who is an adherent of a "minority" faith may suffer some impairment to his prestige. Denominational groups struggle to get their adherents named to significant titles, as also to governmental and other positions of extra-Samoan leadership. But on essential secular matters religious ranks are likely to be closed. It is worth noting here that in the old religion there was a marked variability in terms of spirit forces which pertained to particular individuals, kin groups, and locality groups, and this may well be a factor in the modern Samoan tolerance of denominational differences within a religion-saturated setting of life. This tolerance is characteristic, indeed, of an attitude to personality widespread through Polynesia, and seen in other aspects of life in Samoa.

V. OPINION FORMATION AND DECISION-MAKING

1. The Texture of Samoan Interaction

In orally transmitted cultures such as that of Samoa, communication processes especially among elite persons may come to
have something of the character of an "art" or "game." In the
traditional setting, at least, virtually the whole gamut of situations
and problems which individuals may be called on to face have occurred more or less regularly, and solutions for them tend to be
institutionalized in the forms of patterned behavior. With the content of communication in the sense of the range of actions and expectations rather fixed, the techniques of communication themselves
have become a focus of interest.

Many observers have made this point directly or inferentially:
"Samoan leaders delight in talking"; "Samoans love discussion for
its own sake"; "What is enjoyed and sought is not the decision but
the prolonged drama of the fono proceedings". "A speaker is
applauded not for what he says but for his control of the nuances
of the speaking art." The analogy of a "game" particularly brings
out the fact that deliberation and negotiation have a recognized set
of rules and objectives—the "ideal" behavior; but interest moves
beyond the "basic strokes" which all must master to the purposeful
breaking of the "correct" order by those with virtuosity. Within
the defined bounds there exists in "real" behavior many kinds of
variability in the communication processes: the graceful performance of what is expected, the high pressure competition; the
exciting gambit; the trick play; the daring maneuver; the disguised
stroke; the dangerous edge beyond which essential rules are infringed. Tensions here may bring open breaks, so that the individual
may suffer ignominious failure or more or less serious penalties.
The communication "arts" provide an area of life in which the
Samoans move with such certainty that it is as "normative" to
deviate as to conform, and pleasure, excitement, and honor tend
to march with virtuosity in deviation.

The question inevitably arises as to how far the Samoan communication techniques prove efficient or inefficient in the face of
modern acculturation conditions and needs. All kinds of new problems have arisen which have required realistic decisions. Samoan
councils have been faced with new tasks and constitutional procedures
especially by government edict. Samoan leaders have had to negotiate with Europeans having very different communication techniques, e.g., "Roberts' rules of order," much more emphasis on
the decision-making objective, "democratic" representation, voting.
With increasing self-government they have become participants

along with Europeans in Western-type assemblies. How far, then, has it been possible to reconcile Samoan and Western communication behaviors?

An early administrative official, evidently exasperated in his first attempts to turn the Samoan Fono of Faipule or Advisory Assembly of Representatives into a modern parliamentary body, was led to write:

> This assembly serves to give the Samoans some
> field for the unlimited loquacity of which they
> are capable... A study of its meetings show
> that their deliberations are futile, that only reso-
> lutions in the most general terms are ever
> made, and that no practical matters are ever
> dealt with except on the rare occasions where
> the Administrator or other official has framed
> the resolution. A general distaste for the
> practical, and a lack of capacity for detail,
> prevent any Samoan assembly from being of
> actual direct benefit to the Administration.
> Meetings of the Fono are very wearisome after
> the first opening, on account of the vanity and
> futility of any discussions even on matters
> which the Samoans might be expected to under-
> stand. But the Faipules are there to talk and
> cannot be hurried.[1]

Clearly this official has no understanding of Samoan behavior and values in a deliberation process, yet a number of the points he made do have, behind the evaluative caricature, some validity as observations of Samoan communication at high elite and govern-mental levels for reasons to be seen.

2.   Individual and Group "Voices"

"Messages" leading to opinion formation may originate, in Samoa as elsewhere, from any point where a problem occurs. The matter may be gossiped about or otherwise talked out, opinions formed, and stands taken, at the level of the ordinary people if it is not a concern subject to elite notice and judgment.

---

[1] From an unpublished communication.

Local elite persons are likely to hear of problems under discussion. They will object if in their judgment any issue has an elite angle and is not brought to their attention. Inversely they will push the matter aside if they think it is not appropriate to their status.

An issue brought to the attention of an elite person may be such that he can render a personal decision outright. This, however, is very much the exception rather than the rule. It would be one of the usually few matters over which, by individual right, or by deliberately delegated authority, he already commands an absolute power (pule): say, disposal of a specific piece of land or of the products of certain trees, or directing a work party to undertake a given task. In the overwhelming number of instances the elite person would have to initiate a group deliberative process: this means, in Samoa, meetings of appropriate assemblies, usually of the fono or "council" type.

Reference of a problem to the appropriate group or groups assumes very great importance. As noted earlier a titleholder is essentially a responsible group representative. His "voice" is correspondingly a group voice. He must therefore correctly consult back to his adherent supporters as well as deal with his peers or superiors. Chapter II set out the formal and informal organizations or "collectivities" which might provide "voices" in a traditional deliberation process: the household, close kin, and community assemblies and the supravillage elite or matai assemblies of extended family, regional, and "all Samoa" character. Which deliberating group would be appropriate to handling a given problem is defined by tradition and custom: one involving the roles of untitled persons would, for example, be dealt with in household consultations or the interested community-level council. Concerns of the extended family units such as the naming of a major titleholder would call for joint deliberations by the various kin branches. Distinctive elite concerns, such as the naming of a spokesman from one council level to a higher council level would touch the sub-elite groupings lightly if at all.

3. The Significance of Group Responsibility

Whether or not, in a given problem situation, all adherents of a given titleholder are actually consulted, the weight of their support is nevertheless ideally always there as a generalized "voice, " back of his personal "voice. " In principle, adherents of an elite person share a collective responsibility, which implies in turn the right to be consulted and so to exercise at least an indirect

control over the titleholder. Samoan elite representation involves
one "voice" or vote per power bloc (i. e. , the adherent group),
not one to each individual person as such.

In the sections which follow, therefore, it must never be
forgotten that each elite member, in speaking publicly, has by
implication his group back of him. For his part the titleholder can
never afford to neglect the fact that the power to make or unmake
his authority lies with his adherents. He as an individual is bearing
the title and role with their consent, and if he fails to carry these
with dignity, honor, and satisfaction in his supporters' eyes he can
be rendered powerless, replaced, and even banished or otherwise
punished. At all levels the titleholder who loses the support of
his group is liable to repudiation, even though in practice this seems
to have very low incidence. Having this support he may engage in
conduct which the outside observer might judge as being "authoritarian, " "arbitrary, " even overbearing, and yet continue to receive
respect, veneration, and service.

The sensitivity of the elite person to the group he represents
tends to be a paramount factor in shaping his public positions. At
the village-council level this is not so significant as at higher
organizational levels. The interests of the community and its
constituent households and their close kin groups tend strongly to
coincide with those of the titleholders in the village council. In
wider consultations, however, the elite person is not only likely
to put the interest of his own community and immediate kin adherents first, but indeed has virtually a duty to do so. Only slowly,
and with constant likelihood of conflicts, are wider sensitivities
and loyalties gaining in balance—a problem of course not confined
to Samoa.

This factor operates not only in the higher echelons of Samoan
sociopolitical structure but also in relations with the governmental
superstructure. One of the writers has said elsewhere of the role
of the indigenous official in societies of this level of integration:

> [The] official, after all, is first and foremost a
> member of his own society, and personal, family,
> and community considerations are paramount.
> Where some government enactment runs counter
> to such interests it is likely to be quietly emasculated.
> If it gives opportunity for enhancing those interests,
> use may be made of it along [officially unauthorized]
> lines. [2]

_____

[2] Keesing, F. M. , The South Seas in the Modern World, p. 162.

The problems of political consolidation and effective self-government within such a society in the face of such limited and divisive
tendencies will be discussed in chapter IX.

The adherent group is here spoken of as if it were an entity.
But where higher or senior titles are involved, a great array of
adherent "voices" may have to be channeled in to make a single
"voice." The item under consideration may be passed up and
down, back and forth, through a number of echelons ranging from
the "grass root" non-elite views at a variety of household, close
kin, and community levels over Samoa, through village councils
and perhaps several levels of matai councils representative of
village, district, or great kin aggregations. Less formal consultations of many kinds may also take place depending on idiosyncratic and other variables. This is quite comparable with the
process in a government office or business where a memorandum
may not only have to be "cleared" across a number of established
desks, but also require informal conferences of line and staff
character.

The elite person is also sensitive to the opinions of those of
equal or higher authority. Emphasis has been laid to this point
upon consultation "downward" to the hierarchically lower adherent
group. The elite person, with the rare exception of the titleholders
in supreme authority, is also likely to have to consult "outward"
to peers or near peers, and "upward" on matters of serious importance to the titleholders of higher rank within the kin group or
geographic alignment. As a chief put it: "The respected traditional
habit of this country...is to refer matters to other posts of dignity."
Even where authority has definitely been delegated to the lower
ranking person or status position this may often be considered wise.
A lower ranking titleholder can hardly afford the risk of finding
himself aligned against a person of equal or higher authority with
whom he has interlocking relationships. In a matter of serious
ramifications he might want to consult a number of higher titleholders. Such "voices" might be brought into play directly or kept
behind the scenes. In the latter case their existence is likely to
be well known and taken into account in any deliberation process.

In the work of Samoan government officials, such as the
Pulenu'u (village mayor) or agricultural inspector, this dimension
can become particularly important. Such minor official positions
are likely to be held by persons of low rank, whether titleholders
or otherwise, whose effective authority is conditioned by the extent
to which they have the support of the more influential titleholders.
It would indeed be rare for, say, a village mayor, even under strong

government urging, to press his community beyond what his senior
titleholder kinsmen or the formulated elite opinion in the community
considered agreeable.

An elite assembly, it will be seen, tends to extend these same
principles in turn to its own deliberation processes. The diversified
"voices" brought together by the authorized participants may well
at first be markedly divergent.   A Samoan proverb is at times
applied to an assembly: "It is not a tunuma [tattooing-instrument
holder] in which all the instruments rest together, " i.e., people
are not all of one opinion, or "many men, many minds. " But step
by step a unified view is built up if at all possible, until finally it
is spelled out in the voice of one or more senior or authorized individuals who then speak as representatives of the assembly, backed
by the authority of the others.

A German governor, Dr. Schultz-Ewerth, who was a keen
student of Samoan custom, summarizes this process in speaking of
decision-making in a council:

> The decisions in this assembly are not carried by
> majority votes... The authority of one or more
> matais, who are called upon...as representatives,
> makes the decision... The influence of the one
> or more "deciding" matais is modified by the con-
> sulting vote (voices) of the others. Before the
> meeting (fono) private consultations (taupulenga)
> take place among the groups, in which the heads
> of different families exchange ideas, seeking to
> convince one another, and avoid disputes, so that
> the actual meeting appears to be the result of
> great preparations, and everyone knows before-
> hand more or less what will be said. Deep-lying
> differences of opinion were at one time settled by
> violence. However the German Government has
> undertaken to arbitrate in these cases, and by
> uninterrupted watchfulness over Samoan affairs
> to make for peace" ("The Most Important Principles
> of Samoan Family Law, " p. 45).

In the course of such consultations, many kinds of suasion
and "horse-trading" may occur in the attempt to get a consensus.
By concessions and modifications, the proponents of each viewpoint may try to win over dissidents, or a majority to gain the
support of a minority. Time may be required to take key points
back to the households and community groups, or to brother-

sister-linked kinsmen, the _feangainga_ (p. 51). On an appropriate matter advice may be sought from some technically specialized or well-informed source, such as today a pastor, medical practitioner, a part-Samoan leader, or a European government official. Cumulatively through such procedures, involving the equivalent of the political "smoke-filled room" and "lobby," something approaching unanimity is usually achieved. The formal _fono_, with its arguments and pronouncements, may therefore be almost a purely ceremonious affair. It forms a public demonstration of decisions already more or less arrived at.

Certain resemblances between such deliberative processes, and forms of elite communication in Western society are obvious. The following propositions might be postulated as appearing to have considerable common application:

1. Elite decisions tend to involve group responsibility rather than individual responsibility.

2. Elite decisions tend to be made only after problems have been brought into sharpest possible focus, usually in multiple consultations at a variety of hierarchical levels.

3. To be effective the views of an elite person, or a decision made by an elite group, must have marshaled behind it a weight of support from the adherent, the peer, and the superior groups concerned.

4. An understanding of elite decisions calls for analysis of all the "voices" involved, with their inherent rights and responsibilities.

In concluding this section, a distinction may be noted between a traditionally habituated society such as Samoa and the modern Western setting in the degree to which specific issues have to be institutionally assigned or delegated. This is not just a function of size or massiveness of organization, though this factor undoubtedly is influential. In Samoa, problems are easily referable to the responsible decision-makers. In the Western setting, by contrast, rapid change in the cultural milieu, the elaborate growth of new organizations, the lack of ability to forecast day-to-day issues, and similar well-known phenomena put a premium on formal mechanisms of problem anticipation and on formal allotment of responsibilities among organizations and individuals. A work chart on "assignment of responsibilities for decisions within line and staff organization" might seem to be as superfluous in the Samoan setting as a book on "how to win friends and influence people." Yet the need for precisely this type of elaboration and definition is beginning to arise, especially in connection with the development of new self-government organizations in both territories, as will be seen later, and involves difficult and troublesome adjustment.

A broad but significant illustration of the way traditional systems can dispense with formal distinctions and divisions of function is the lack of a stimulus among the Samoans to separate the legislative, executive, and judicial facets of decision-making. The same elite leader or council moves easily across the arc of deliberation in all these spheres. In the modern setting, the government authorities have been unable, despite efforts, to separate clearly the powers of a district representative as between legislative and executive authority, and find it difficult enough to keep him from those judicial spheres which have been assigned to judges, the more so as he freely exercises these facets of authority in his own Samoan spheres. Even in American Samoa, with the strong official emphasis on the American values involved in the separation of these responsibilities, progress is exceedingly slow in getting such a system understood and practiced. In elections of 1955, however, the American governor declared that no district executive official could be a candidate for legislative office; Samoan leaders holding such posts, and hitherto used to sitting in the legislature, were thus forced to make a choice. The problem specialist, sitting eight hours a day in his office, waiting for the social system to feed him technical business, is still a rare and mainly a very recent phenomenon in the Samoan setting.

4. The Weighting of Voices

In elite deliberation and decision-making the voice of each individual tends to carry weight according to his rank in the hierarchy and the power of the group he represents. Elite communication in general tends to be resistant to egalitarian principles except where peers and peer groups are involved. The situation in Samoa is comparable to the realistic facts of international diplomacy in which the prestige requirements of countries of vastly different size and power have to be met. The weighted voice is the other side of the coin of group representation: the voice that speaks for the more powerful group has the greatest weight.

In Samoan opinion formation and decision-making, the weight of the voice is likely to be more important than any other factor, including what is said. The Samoan tends to wait and listen for the deciding voice, the voice which by reason of its title, the group it represents, the range of opinion marshaled behind it, and its traditional role in Samoan affairs, is the voice of the leader. This is the point of a number of well-known Samoan proverbs and sayings of which the following are examples:

Ua feta'i le li'i: "The evening star leads others."
After the leading chief has spoken the others can
only follow.

Ua tu'u la le va'a tele: "The large canoe has
furled its sails." After the high chief's speech
has run its course and is "beached" or "at
anchor" it is of little use listening to lesser
"vessels." (But it can also have the meaning
that lesser "vessels" also have their right to
run their course, i.e., all should be heard.)

Ua ta le vila o le tama nei: "A competitive
song is being sung by a child." A high chief
will be listened to attentively for his expert
performance. But a lesser person will not be
heeded—his song is a childlike effort. (No
one should pretend to be what he is not.)

O le ngingili a nafa: "The sweet sound of the
hollow wooden gong." The experienced higher
chief can play the gong rhythms expertly, and
by comparison the lesser person will perform
like an amateur.

Faapū a tama ula: "Like the shell trumpet blown
by rowdy boys." A high chief's words carry like
the pu or shell trumpet of the authorized "herald"
announcing official news; but those of lesser
persons are poor.

The authority that marches with rank has been the subject
of many comments, all of which, if not seen in the context of the
group representation principle, can easily lead to misunderstanding.
A reader in "government" developed by a group of teachers for the
schools of American Samoa states quite baldly of Samoan decision-
making:

Every matai may give his opinion, but the highest
chief makes the decision to which all agree. [3]

---

[3] "Government" (mimeographed), by Brothers Herman and
Fred Henry, Dr. G. G. Brown, and Elisaia Iosefa.

Samoan informants, speaking in terms of normative behavior, state:

> It is the Samoan custom... once the high chiefs
> and orators have said this, though a person may
> think differently he will not speak out.

> The Samoans cannot go against the wishes of
> their highest chiefs.

On a political question a skeptical chief said:

> Others may disagree. But they are withholding
> opinions out of respect for high titleholders
> as is the Samoan custom.

A part-Samoan, speaking of the weight of the "royal" titles, said:

> Samoans do not easily oppose the views of the
> royal chiefs.　They are afraid of titles like
> that; as they progress it will be less so.

A younger educated Samoan, writing of the power of the highest chief in a village, says:

> [He] is the apex of all matters and affairs
> concerning the village.　His word is final.
> Nothing is official or legal without his
> knowledge and sanction.　His word used to
> be the life or death for criminals and
> offenders.　He can order a person, or a
> group of persons and even a whole family,
> to leave the village.　He has all power and
> many privileges, and he can do as he pleases.
> Out of caprice and mere show of rank and
> authority, he may hold up a meeting of the
> village council for several hours or even a
> whole day, and may order the councillors to
> disperse again until such a time as suits him. [4]

---

[4] From an unpublished MS. on "The Legal System of Samoa, " by Napoleon A. Tuiteleleapaga.

Particularly here in this last statement is the classic picture of the autocratic chief. To some extent the younger man writing this last quoted item appears to show a personal bias in the autocratic picture he draws of the principal village chief (he was living outside the village system), and there may be a "sour-grape" touch concerning the matai system which has some prevalence among de-Samoanized non-elite individuals; and he has probably also weighted his picture in terms of a stereotype of the "primitive" leader picked up from reading in the English language. Nevertheless, despite all that has been said to this point concerning the tempering of the power of the senior titleholder by responsibility and the balancing of authority, there is an element of fact in all the statements made that holds even in the "ideal" pattern.

Where there is no insecurity about the title, and the support of the adherent group is assured, the Samoan leader enjoys displaying his power, and is expected to do so. It is part of the demonstration of his superior title that he should show a certain amount of "God-like arrogance." An authoritarian mien and dignified but aggressive freedom of action is expected and approved in the really high titled person, and lesser people, titled or untitled, are inclined to take it meekly when the exalted one acts overbearingly. Only when he pushes matters beyond the limits of their patience and endurance is he likely to fall foul of his kinsmen and fellow chiefs. The writers, however, have observed plentiful tension-points in the relationship. In one village the high chief compelled entertainment of official visitors when the adherent group obviously was weary and rebellious after a hard day's labor. Persistently they offered passive resistance and the chief's anger sharpened till he seized a whip and lashed out at the young men and others, though not actually touching them. They gave way, but only sufficiently to save his face while preserving their own. In another village where the high chief was extremely rude in his remarks to his fellow matais they quietly withdrew, one by one, leaving him in lordly isolation. Certainly such cases as that cited, where a council is delayed just to demonstrate the power of the high chief, are liable to occur. But in so far as they arouse resentment and ill feeling they interfere with the appropriate respect and even awe which is the "ideal" of the Samoan relationship, and with the graceful patterns spoken of at the beginning of this chapter. It is important, however, to realize that such actions can enter into the real behavior of a "bad" matai.

Another factor here which can give room for an arbitrary margin of conduct is indeed inherent in the group responsibility principle—namely, that business in hand must of necessity be proc-

essed through one or more individual minds, and sometimes many.
The elite person can hardly escape putting his own idiosyncratic
mark on it, consciously or otherwise, as he performs his assigned
function as mediator. His own understandings and views must inevitably lodge to some extent in the "voice" that he passes on: a
phrasing, a vocal emphasis, a facial expression or other gesture.
He becomes a "gatekeeper" or critical intermediary, sifting and
coloring information.[5] As such a great temptation exists for the
elite person to impose idiosyncratic interpretations deliberately
upon "messages" in the interests of facilitating communication or
advancing other goals and values. That this happens in the Samoan
setting could be made the subject of many examples from Samoan
folklore and history as well as from field notes. Deliberate manipulation by orators, for example, of information to the advantage
of their chiefs and adherent groups approaches the character of
being a norm. The head of a technical department in American
Samoa shows the European's sense of this stress when he wrote in
his 1950 annual report:

> The persistent problem is to gain and hold the
> respect and cooperation of the influential Samoan
> Matais who control the actions of the people.[6]

The autocratic use and abuse of their powers is a temptation
which particularly faces higher elite leaders today. They are in a
position to continue to exercise and take advantage of their Samoan-
style authority while truncating their responsibilities and responsiveness to the traditional rights of their adherents. New forms of
power have become available in the modern setting—money, commerce, government authority, Christian sanctions, mass communication media—and because these tend to be free-floating and not tem-
pered by restraints and disciplines as they usually are in contemporary
Western society, they may be used to build up great personal power.
The picture of the autocratic chief has, perhaps surprisingly, more
chance of realization in such societies under conditions of modern
acculturation than in the closed cultural settings of precontact days.
The writers, if more space were available and the matter less
delicate, could give specific case histories here. It will have to be

---

[5] Chapter VIII has a fuller discussion of mediation, especially
in crosscultural contexts.

[6] Words are underlined by the present writers.

sufficient to say that only minor and partial tendencies show in this direction, and the number of higher titleholders who have cut themselves off sharply from Samoan-style obligations is exceedingly small. The Samoan social structure, including the title system, has tended to provide a considerably more stable force against such lines of sociopolitical change than that of most comparable small societies familiar to the writers in the Pacific and elsewhere. This matter will be discussed more fully in chapter VIII.

To this point the weight of voices has been discussed primarily in terms of the senior or highest titles. The principle is a consistent one, and the senior person in terms of prestige in any group— the senior woman in female affairs, the heir-apparent among untitled males, the eldest sibling over younger siblings, and so on— bears a weighted voice in decision-making.

Other variables, formal and informal in addition to rank or status position, also contribute to building up the strength of an opinion. The voice of age may carry weight, in terms of sheer experience; the voice of a specialist counts in technical matters, or again that of a woman over a man's where specifically female concerns are involved; the voice of the physically strong man, the beautiful girl, the dynamic personality, the educated individual, and so forth. Examples of this ever-present variability will be given in discussing personnel aspects of negotiation procedures.

5. The Equating of Opinion

How are multiple opinions, with different weighting, equated or consolidated into concerted opinions? What is the relation of the process to the Western concept of "voting," including "universal suffrage," "equal votes," and the "secret ballot"?

The peaceful integration of differing views is not an easy matter in Samoa, with its background traditions of violence and war. The language proliferates in terms and sayings which deal with disagreement and dissension, and the matter of reconciliation. For example:

> To oppose (faatu'i'ese, etc.); to disagree
> (faifesia, etc.); to reject (mele); to refuse
> saucily (fatala'ese); to laugh scornfully (masuasu);
> to use abusive language in a haughty manner
> (sisii); to use provoking words after being
> worsted (tauanau); to continue troublesome after
> the other party has given up and apologized
> (taufutifuti); to all talk together, causing

      confusion (tauiao); to be scolded on all sides
      (sona), metaphorically comparable to "laboring
      in a cross sea."

These are just a few of the many verbal discriminations which
Samoans make in relation to differences in views. Correspondingly,
the vocabulary of agreement shows recognized variants:

      To be unanimous (faatasi, to be together,
    to become one); to reconcile (sosoo, etc.); to
    make a concession in deference to another
    party (ai); to appease (faalotomalie, etc.);
    to strike hard bargains (tāungata); to be in
    two minds (fetoa'i, etc.).

Further examples are given in the linguistic annex.
    The idea of "voting" is familiar enough to Samoans in the
broad sense of equating opinion. It is expressed in the traditional
setting by assenting or dissenting voices, particularly in formal
proceedings of a council. This, however, is normally a public expression of opinion, without the elements of a "secret ballot."
"Equality" in voting shows most readily in consultations of peers or
near peers, hence where no strongly superior weighted voice is
present to serve as the locus of a single unified opinion. It tends
still to be almost inconceivable to most Samoans that the voice of
a powerful chief, traditionally with the right to speak for some large
district and relationship group with branches probably throughout
Samoa, should exercise a modern-style vote which would count for
no more than the voice of some young "nobody," perhaps an unmarried girl. The Western-style jury system, with its concept of
peers trying a peer, is still completely foreign and unacceptable.
When in 1931 a "Bill of Rights" was formulated for American Samoa,
this was the only section of the American Bill of Rights to be omitted.
In both territories an "assessor" system is used instead, with
Samoan associate judges or special "assessors," aiding the court in
making decisions. Coexistence of egalitarian political and judicial
rights with wide differences in economic and social power of individuals is, of course, a comparatively recent development throughout the Western world, with much unresolved tension; the Samoan
difficulty in this regard is therefore far from unique.
    Both American and New Zealand value systems weigh strongly
to the side of "democratic" representation. Egalitarian pressure
of New Zealand authorities upon the Samoan elite in the early days
of their control was undoubtedly an important factor in generating

the Mau movement (p. 26).   Both nations tend to make progress in
representative government an overt measure of Samoan competence
in modern political affairs.

The Samoan system of group responsibility combined with
hierarchical leadership as described earlier has left many observers
puzzled and with different judgments as to how far it is "democratic"
or "shows democratic tendencies." A modern Samoan word for
"democracy" is tutusa, the plural of "to be like, or equal," and
Samoans sometimes apply the term, even if perhaps somewhat
guardedly, to the system of matai representation as being a Samoan
form of "democracy."

In the modern setting of government the problem to Western
eyes becomes broadly one of how far the elite participant is present
in terms of his title and its privileges and honors, or as a genuine
representative of the group interest—that group in some cases being
more than just his traditional adherents but a district or even a
territory-wide group.   Here of course lies the rub.   If he were not
authorized to "represent" the people he would not hold the title.
If he is a bad representative he can in Samoan theory be replaced.
Even the "royal" chief, named to his title by way of great hierarchies of representative consultations, is subject to such rules.

The United Nations Mission of 1947 was clearly worried by
this problem.   In suggesting a place for the Fautua in the government as members of the Council of State it speaks of them as occupying these seats as "Representatives of the People" rather than
"royal" titleholders or "Royal Descendants" as such—and by implication removable should the people so will.   The district Faipule
of Western Samoa is even more overtly a "Representative." In the
former American Samoan Upper House, or House of Ali'i, which
was transformed in 1953 into an advisory council (p. 33), the
principle of representation has not been spelled out in this way in
the case of the twelve titles whose current incumbents are entitled
to sit; so that the implication comes somewhat nearer to, say, the
British House of Lords with emphasis on "privilege" rather than
"representation." The earlier and present forms of Lower House
in that territory, by contrast, stress the latter.   This analysis
suggests that Samoan elite participation in government is democratically
oriented to the extent that, in the given situation, overt stress is laid
on the "representative" rather than the traditional and ceremonious
status, and that the Samoan participants understand and accept this
theory.

"Voting" always tends to be a delicate procedural matter where
elite persons are concerned.   Crystallizing a decision from the
diversified and often competitive voices of a Samoan assembly, with

its usually wide gulfs in rank, is likely to call for ingenuity, discretion, restraint, coolheaded judgment, calculated risks, ability
to compromise, and other nuances of deliberation. Samoan language
is significantly rich in terms of such behavior variants, as will be
seen in the linguistic annex.

Voting, in the broad sense of giving the "franchise" or "universal suffrage" to Samoan adults at large has only very recently
been considered as a feasible possibility. It is significant that
the Samoan term palota, a "vote, " Samoanized from the English
word "ballot, " is one of the few modern political concepts for which
an indigenous Samoan term does not appear to have emerged, adapted
as necessary, into standardized usage. Discussion has centered
particularly on the issue as to whether representatives at the higher
levels might be elected at large "by popular vote" instead of by a
hierarchy of representatives on behalf of the mass base of adherent
groups. This, to many observers who want "democracy" in Samoa,
has been the missing element. While the election principle could
hardly involve at this time in Samoan history the naming of a "royal"
Fautua to his governmental post—Western Samoa is in the British
tradition—is it not reasonable, they ask, for membership in regular
legislative bodies and for some representative executive posts to be
subject to general suffrage?

Western-style "voting" has been introduced selectively into
modern governmental bodies in which Samoan leaders participate,
as in the Western Samoa Legislative Assembly, the Fono of Faipule
(Advisory Council of Representatives), and in both houses of the
legislature in American Samoa. Samoans have also long seen the
general franchise and secret ballot exercised in each territory:
in Western Samoa by the resident Europeans (i.e., mainly part-
Samoans) in electing five members to the Legislative Assembly,
and in American Samoa in providing representation for the small
resident group not living within the matai system (p. 33). Religious
denominational assemblies, too, including some attended abroad
by elite leaders, are settings in which Western-style voting is observed.

Something of a critical "tip-over" point in the acculturation
responses is currently occurring here in both territories, at least
in elite levels of "voice" consolidation under government auspices.
Coincident with the revisions, from 1948 on, of the structures and
powers of the central governmental bodies in Western Samoa under
stress of the self-government movement, Samoan leaders have
started voluntarily to experiment not only with "equal voting" but
also with the "secret ballot. " Samoan districts have in some instances tried out an election system in naming their Representatives

to the Fono of Faipules instead of using the Samoan method of talking
through to a unanimous name.   In this case, however, the majority-
minority decisions were limited to elite electors and not subject to
the general franchise.   A revealing glimpse is offered by the High
Commission in a Legislative Assembly debate of 1948 of the situation some two and a half months after the first series of district
"elections":

> Of the 41 Faipule...[to be] nominated [by
> Samoan Districts]...only 24 have been finally
> settled and the issue is still in doubt in [the
> others]... A Faipule is elected [in legal terms]
> by the majority of the matai in that district...
> [with] approval of the High Commissioner...
> In most-districts there are two or more villages,
> one bigger than the...others.   The result is
> that though there are agreements sometimes
> that another village shall have its turn, what
> happens often is that when the election arrives
> the larger village says, "No, we will elect
> the Faipule, " and the smaller villages are not
> represented... On the one side you have the
> people say "We have the majority of the matai...
> this is the law, we want the law, " on the other
> side Samoan custom says this, "That we have
> an agreement and arrangement, we should have
> our turn. "[7]

The initial introduction of the secret ballot in purely Samoan settings,
within this territory has also occurred in the Fono of Faipules.   Its
members, acting as peers in the official sense of being representatives
of their districts, have the responsibility for selecting the twelve

---

[7] Legislative Assembly Debates, Fifth Session 1948, p. 30.
Cases were discussed where the dominant village representatives
had refused "point blank" to meet even for discussion of the matter
with the minority in spite of official attempts at mediation.   Procedures have been ironed out in subsequent elections, or else districts have reverted quietly to the older methods of representation.

Samoan members of the Legislative Assembly. In 1950 of their
own volition they held a secret ballot for the first time to elect a
member to fill a vacancy. [8]

It is now possible to understand fully the responses of Samoan
leaders to those aspects of the Development Plan proposed by the
New Zealand government in 1953 which dealt with the constitution
of a new legislature (p. 30). It was hoped that the Samoan people
might be ready to accept a more equitable district representation
in terms of population densities, and also to move at least in more
politically advanced districts toward secret balloting and universal
suffrage. But it quickly became clear that the elite were adamant
against changes which would alter district alignments or carry the
vote beyond their own echelons. The delegates to the Constitutional
Convention of 1954 presented the New Zealand government with firm
views against any immediate changes in the system of district representation, for keeping both candidacy and voting within the matai
group, and for treating the secret ballot merely as a device for
settling disagreements.

A vivid expression of current elite opinion in Western Samoa
on the issue of matai voting versus the general suffrage occurs in
the record of a joint meeting in July 1955 of the Legislative Assembly and Fono of Faipule to consider the New Zealand government
reply to the recommendations of the Constitutional Convention.
The New Zealand statement had indicated a reluctant acceptance of
the principle of limiting the suffrage to matais "for the time being"
(p. 31).

> To'omata: I do not like to see that little
> phrase... I should sooner see that the matai
> system of voting should remain for all time.

> Fautua Tamasese (Chairman): We must
> bear in mind that New Zealand has to satisfy
> the United Nations with its reply...

---

[8] The winner of the ballot is reported to have received only
8 out of 41 votes, yet topped the list and so was named. A government official, while lauding the experiment, felt that the Samoans
had "a lot to learn" on voting procedures. For laudatory comment
on the action see Report of the United Nations Visiting Mission of
1950.

Tufuga: It looks to me that the New Zealand
Government has no desire whatsoever to maintain
the matai system or the matai method of voting...
I know that [it] will eventually try and introduce
universal suffrage to this country and it is up to
us to maintain that we stick by what has been
recommended by the Convention last year, because once we adopt universal suffrage we will
no longer be known as Samoans, we will be known
as Europeans... It is up to us to block all these
loop-holes and tell the New Zealand Government
that we would like our Government to be run as a
Samoan Government.

Fautua Tamasese: ·In New Zealand any adult
votes, so you can imagine why the Government is
always pressing the matter. That New Zealand
has this does not mean we have to follow its example.
We must remember that the universal franchise
was only introduced in the year 1880 and the women
were only allowed to take part in voting in 1919 or
1920. There are different forms in different countries,
and we have been used to our own form of voting.
We can have confidence that if we stick to our position
there will be nothing else except as the people
[sic!] decide. New Zealand's responsibility will
gradually be lessened as we manage our own
affairs. [9]

The chain of events summarized here lends support to a view
expressed in the report of the U.N. Visiting Mission of 1950, that:
"There is little prospect that the Samoans [of Western Samoa] will
agree to any widening of the franchise in the immediate future."
In American Samoa adoption of the franchise and the secret
ballot is proceeding more rapidly than in Western Samoa, though
still selectively. The territory is smaller; its hierarchical structure
by titles and regions is much more clearly defined and less complex; it is strongly under Americanization influences; and its leaders
would rather move politically toward the American norms under their

---

[9] Papers and Proceedings of Joint Meeting of the Legislative
Assembly and Fono of Faipule, and Meeting with Honourable the
Minister of Island Territories, Apia (mimeographed) pp. 8-13.

own volition, adapting them as they go to the Samoan setting, than
have them imposed arbitrarily by the Congress or other governing
bodies. The legislative houses have here long used an open ballot
system in the form of a show of hands. In 1952, as part of a reorganization outlined earlier (p. 33), use of the secret ballot was
agreed on. Adult suffrage was also made the basis for electing
members to the lower House of Representatives, though the new
Senate and the Council of Ali'i remain strongholds for Samoan methods
of representation. The experiment of holding such an election is
so interesting that a brief official report of the procedure may be
given:

> A committee of the Fono met for two weeks to
> set up a five-step election program and calendar.
> This called for an extensive as well as intensive
> educational program involving some 150 Samoan
> teachers to be followed by the registration of all
> those over 18 who wished to vote. Petitions were
> circulated that required at least 2% of the voting
> population of any candidate's county for political
> entrance. This was followed by publication of
> lists of registered voters and qualified candidates
> for each county... Time was then allotted for
> candidates to campaign which they did with a will.
> The local radio station and the weekly news-bulletins
> gave complete instructions... which aided greatly
> in disseminating the essential information that
> resulted in 4,861 people, or just over 65% of the
> eligible population, to register... General elections
> were held in all districts [over a period of one
> week, with] specially selected election teams to
> supervise the voting and make a careful public
> count of the results. [10]

The members elected to the Senate are all of _matai_ status.
So, too, are the top titleholders who constitute the advisory Council
of _Ali'i_, and on the executive side of government the district governors
and county chiefs (p. 33). The new lower House of Representatives,
however, opened out an opportunity for a major break in the Samoan

----

[10] From O le Fa'atonu, 40, 1 (Jan.-June, 1953). Two officials
from Western Samoa "observed" the election experiment.

pattern. Candidates of non-matai status emerged, and some received strong support. When votes were counted, seven of the
fifteen representatives elected from Samoan districts were not
holders of matai titles, so that with the two representatives of persons "not living under the matai system, " and one representative
of Swain's Island (p. 12), there were ten of eighteen members in
all not of matai status. Two members were women, one a representative of non-matai status electors, the other of Swain's Island.
In the second election which followed in 1954, out of the total membership of seventeen elected by Samoan counties, the number of
members of non-matai status dropped off to five, of whom one was
a woman. This could possibly mark a trend through which future
membership in the House of Representatives might become again
wholly a matter of electing persons of matai status. Meantime,
this lower house situation now offers one of the sharpest contrasts
between the political development of American Samoa and that of
Western Samoa—in the latter territory, representation from the
Samoan districts by non-matai or by women is still unthinkable.

    Where Samoans in either territory do "elect" representatives
in the modern sense to higher level offices, the modal expectation
is that (with the notable exception of the lower house in American
Samoa) those put in nomination will still be the appropriate senior
titleholders or else peers in rotation; so that much the same personnel
will be elected as would have been selected by traditional Samoan
methods. Even when breaks appear in the system, therefore, the
hierarchical representation principles are likely to prove very persistent. What will almost certainly be demonstrated is the fact,
too often obscured in emotionally charged discussions of "democracy" in Samoa, that the principles involved in the matai hierarchy and those involved in an elective system, universal franchise,
equal voting, and the secret ballot, can coexist just as economic
inequalities coexist with political democracy in most Western countries. The matai system may prove as capable of surviving universal suffrage as has the capitalist system.

    Under the new conditions, however, the way would be more
open for a group dissatisfied with its senior titleholder to replace
him for government representation purposes with a more competent
and better supported person, titled or otherwise, or for the titleholder to step aside if he wished to withdraw from practical political
tasks without loss of face. The only real stumbling block to wider
suffrage would be any arbitrary electorate alignment which does not
correspond to the traditional district and village groupings. This
would call for the much less familiar step of voting for representatives outside the range of customary representation, and indeed

could create extreme stresses wherever hierarchical principles of district and community elites were seriously infringed.

Samoan political leaders appear particularly anxious currently to conform to Western political techniques as a public indication of their preparedness for self-government. It may be expected, therefore, that in official settings open or secret voting will become rather rapidly established in essentially the same spheres as in Western parliamentary procedures (p. 152-55). In Samoan-style deliberations, however, the traditional methods of selecting representatives and otherwise equating opinions are likely to predominate for a long time, though with a few modern embellishments which creep in today in some situations such as asking for a show of hands rather than depending on speeches to reveal the various stands.

It may be expected, therefore, that long after equality in voting becomes accepted for territorial political purposes, the elite leadership pattern of traditional Samoa will hold strongly. Particularly is this apt to be so in the matter of nominations to higher positions subject to election. In Western Samoa, the non-elite Samoan is not very likely in the near future to have his voting choice widened beyond the elite personnel who would in the traditional order be eligible for the positions concerned. In American Samoa, however, this pattern is already loosening, as has been seen, in the case of personnel elected to the lower House of Representatives, and this could influence longer-term development among the younger generation in Western Samoa.

An additional element characteristic of the equating of opinion in a Samoan setting is that of a balance of power. Elite deliberation and decision-making tends to be marked by a balance of the power forces which have to be consolidated through political techniques to achieve unanimity. Power balancing in a symmetrical manner is a concept very deeply embedded in Samoan culture. There is a neat equilibrium of the powers and responsibilities of men and women, as also of the kinsmen in the male line and the female line; the chief is counterpoised by the orator; the weighted voice of the leading titleholder is balanced by the number of lesser voices of the consulting titleholders; in the old national polity there was the whole carefully balanced structure of the "royal" Samalietoa and Satupua lines, and of the Tumua and Pule orator groups (p. 23). This feeling for the need of pull and counterpull finds expression in many words of the language, and also in metaphor and proverb. Ua ifo i le ti a e a'e i le nonu, "the ti-palm and the nonu tree are the same height," i.e., be satisfied with the balance of affairs; se'ia silinga ifo maunga, se'ia silinga a'e vanu, "leveled will be the mountain, leveled too what is now the valley," i.e., imbalances will not persist. In fact

it may not be overstretching this element in Samoan life to note a
persistent love of the symmetrically balanced arrangment, emerging
in dancing, singing, and other arts, housing and house arrangements,
village layout, and many social alignments.

In every elite deliberation process there tends to be present
the potential of a balance of Samoan-style power. The "spice" of
Samoan politics is to maneuver the power blocks present into harmony and agreement for the purpose of achieving a decision or
action program. It was such maneuvering, including warfare,
royal marriages, gift giving, and other use of influence that in old
Samoa could achieve at times the concentration of all four "royal"
titles, two to each of the great "royal" power blocs, upon one person, thus achieving a ceremonial unity, or _Malo_ covering all Samoa. [11]

The balance of power elements at all levels in the Samoan
polity is regarded consciously by some thinking Samoan leaders as
a safeguard, and it probably has acted in this way, much as has the
separation of the three branches of government in the United States.
It keeps power from getting out of hand, or becoming too highly con-
centrated. It is one of the many factors that contribute to the often
remarked fact that "Samoans cannot be pushed around." If any elite
member gets too headstrong and aggressive, he will soon find himself up against an opposing power force. In village terms this means
primarily that the titleholders as a whole are usually capable of
acting as a check upon the leading chief, however godlike his prestige
and title.

Cases may also occur where the village council makes a decision which a vigorous section of the village does not approve. An
instance of this kind happened in 1950 in a prominent village on
Upolu. A stand taken by the village _fono_ ran counter to the wishes
of most of the women, or at least of their more vigorous leaders. [12]
The Women's Committee, after holding a meeting, marched down
in a body upon the assembled _fono_. Seeing them approaching the
latter hastily reversed itself. The household can be a setting for
similar happenings; even a child, feeling aggrieved, may move out
and attach himself or herself to another kin group.

---

[11] Except the three small islands of Manu'a in American
Samoa, which stood politically apart: see p. 23.

[12] _Fono_ members had been resisting a "progressive" titleholder in a matter of health improvement; the women's group, influenced particularly by this man's New Zealand—educated daughter,
took this vigorous step.

A traditional custom of great symbolic significance is still recognized and exercised in Samoan power—balancing and conciliation, a "ceremonial humbling" called ifonga. Perhaps having some counterpart in all elite behavior, it represents an open acknowledgment of apology or submission by one power unit to another, usually in the person of the titleholders concerned. It was often used in old days in the settlement of war and feuding. The public ceremony, involving prostration and passing over of property as a compensation equivalent, was required by the German governors on occasions to bring recalcitrant leaders into line.

One of the incidents of the Mau movement of Western Samoa during the 1920's involved an ifonga. A "royal" titleholder, the Tamasese of the time, had been banished to Savai'i by the New Zealand authorities for a legal infringement; the governor, on a visit to the area, was received with an ifonga by the whole community on Tamasese's behalf, but ignored it apparently through ignorance of its significance—it became one of the many sparks in the fires of the anti-government movement.

The balancing of power, however, always tends to involve tensions, so that the parties concerned are likely to seek to move toward greater unanimity. Especially where power situations produce, or have the potential of producing, an asymmetrical alignment, for example, a majority-minority stand, a conqueror-conquered relation, an upset of the reciprocity principle in give-and-take interaction, they are likely to be merely uneasy waystations in Samoan affairs. Problems of "unanimity" and of "opposition" therefore need to have special examination.

6. The Goal of Unanimity

Where a united stand is taken by an elite group it is often crucial to try to ascertain how far this represents genuine agreement or merely a public front of agreement. Government authorities throughout modern Samoan history, for example, have often been puzzled as to how to gauge the strength, genuineness, and potential permanence of apparently unanimous decisions by Samoan leaders, and how to estimate what undercover opposition might exist. Were they hearing a well-established opinion, or that of dominating leaders only? How firm or brittle was the agreement? How potentially powerful were any submerged contrary voices? These problems are still valid, and are significant for many other societies besides Samoa.

Elite negotiation is likely to be strongly oriented toward producing a public show of at least immediate unanimity. Obviously, in Samoa as elsewhere, there is much at stake, where elite persons enter into formal consultations, besides the problems at issue: the solidarity of their own groups, the issues of "peaceful coexistence, " the prestige of the negotiators. An appropriate Samoan saying is: ne'i te'a ma le fainga, "do not be far from the basket (when a group netting party is fishing), " i.e., in an important enterprise, be where opinion accumulates, as fish are driven by the nets into the giant basket at the head of the drive.

Elite opinion formation, therefore, is likely to involve every possible effort to delay or avoid a public position which aligns a majority against a minority. For this reason discussions and negotiations are likely to go on and on, in and out of formal meetings, until by suasion, compromise, or downright weariness, at least an outward appearance of unanimity is forthcoming, if only by a formal polite bowing to the prestige of the superior titleholder. Samoan custom is here buttressed by Christian principle; Samoans will often say that it is the brotherly duty of all to go as far as possible to come to agreement.[13] Not to do so in the intimate setting of the village and the kinship group may result in divisions and factions that tend to persist for generations, with corresponding loss of power and loss of pleasant associations for all the people concerned. Under old-time Samoan conditions, the impasse of a majority-minority situation might easily pass from verbal disagreement to open fighting and war.

Samoan culture significantly lacks here the precision of constitutional definition and political practice which Western systems have developed to establish proportionate relations between different opinion groups as a basis for acceptance of decisions. The Samoans recognized and used the concepts of "a majority" and "a minority." They carry, however, merely the general sense of "the greater number of contenders" (toatele), and "the smaller number of contenders" (toaitiiti). Precise extensions of this simple counting set, such as a "plurality, " a "quorum, " a "veto, " or legal definitions expressing a proportion (e.g., "a two-thirds majority"), appear to

---

[13] The writers have in their file the "doodle" of a literate Samoan high chief written at a meeting in which a "unanimous" opinion was being expressed to a government official. It reads: "Now is the time for all the good men to come to the aid of their party. It is the duty of the man to do a very good turn and if he can he will do so. "

have been nonexistent within the older semantic system, though Samoan equivalents have become established and recognized in modern times, at least for translating political documents from English. But they have effective meaning to Samoans still only to the extent that they operate in practice within the deliberation settings of government and mission.

A public show of unanimity tends to be valued proportionately to (1) the "integration" of the group concerned, and (2) the importance of the problem to that group. In Samoa it is most characteristic of the local village and its constituent groupings, bound together by close living and needs for co-operation. It is likely to be less pressed in the case of deliberations among the extended family branches or other supravillage groupings, which can rest on the more superficial and short-term unities of mutual convenience or self-interest, or of a balance of power.

Small intimate groups which have need to work and live together, as with the household and community units, cannot easily bear the stresses of open and continuous opposition. This aspect of decision-making has been widely reported by anthropologists as well as other observers. For example, an anthropologist with administrative experience in Melanesian island areas writes:

> When I was a District Officer in the Pacific Islands
> I used to get very annoyed because people would take
> a long time to decide anything. I then found that this
> was because they were not content with majority rule.
> They required unanimous consent to anything which
> concerned the village. So that if one person disagreed,
> that would mean the veto on the project. I still didn't
> fully understand until reading in anthropology made
> me realize that this was a consequence of the small
> size of the community. Everyone knew everyone
> else; furthermore nobody had anywhere else to go.
> An open quarrel would be a very serious thing,
> probably resulting in violence with all sorts of
> ramifications. So that it was highly important for
> the people to avoid any cause for quarrel, and any
> underlying hostility. [14]

[14] Belshaw, C.S., an anthropologist who has worked extensively in Melanesia and visiting at the University of British Columbia, in a talk given under the auspices of the Canadian Broadcasting Commission, 1954.

The reliability and permanence of expressed unanimity appears to lessen to the extent that the groups represented in elite negotiations do not share close common interests and associations; unanimity then tends to express less an agreement than a temporary balance of expedient forces. A high Samoan chief, advocating more effort at unanimity, said:

> We remember that our Samoan government in the past was unable to carry on in an orderly way because of different opinions, so that the country was in a constantly unsettled state.

The modern political history of Samoa could be interpreted usefully from this point of view as a struggle to extend the unanimity principle more effectively into wider spheres and on a longer-term basis, in the face of divisive forces seen as characteristic of supralocal organization. Far-seeing Samoan leaders, backed by governmental and mission agencies, have been trying to turn the Malo, in the older sense of an uneasy and largely ceremonious balance of the traditional alignments of great district and kin groups with their "royal" titleholders and the powerful Tumua and Pule orator groups (p. 23), into a stable and well-organized Samoan government. The leaders heading the recent self-government movement have been making strong efforts to draw and hold together a "unified Samoa." Christian ethic and nationalist aspirations have been arrayed to support peace and harmony.

The record shows considerable advances, as will be seen especially in chapter IX. But it has been noticeably easier for Samoan leaders to be unitedly "against" something than "for" something. Prestige stakes have often outweighed realistic agreement in producing a front of unanimity. "Concord" has not infrequently borne the marks of police enforcement and respect for the Western authority and power rather than voluntary abandonment of the Samoan methods of force. In the wider spheres of elite communication such unanimity as shows tends still to have the uncertain character of co-operation among balanced multiple power forces. Significantly, little tendency has shown in either the American or the New Zealand sections of Samoa for an institutionalized party system to arise, involving a majority-minority situation. Such a development is hardly to be expected until a much more secure sense of unity and of territory-wide integration has emerged. Yet the balanced principle seen as so widely operative in Samoan culture suggests it as a logical denouement for the future.

An attempt was made in 1951 by a small group of titleholders
in Western Samoa to found a modern style political party which they
called the "Samoan Democratic Party." This group, headed by a
very Westernized political leader, has had a membership in subsequent years of only about 100 of the approximately 3, 500 matai
titleholders in the territory. It has advocated forming a legislature
based on universal franchise, but with matais only as candidates;
it also seeks legislation to protect the dignity of Samoan customs.
Though the "Party" holds periodic meetings, it remains a minority
political organization rather than a parliamentary alignment.[15]

7. Opposition

In elite decisions an apparent unanimity may frequently cover
up submerged or covert opposition. A government official or other
person concerned with the representative character of Samoan
pronouncements must always be most careful as regards taking
them at their face value. The Samoan language has many terms
and sayings expressive of both public and covert opposition, as for
example, the grumbling and off-edge remarks of those who have
officially given way and agreed to an apparently "unanimous" group
decision (p. 120).
    At the personal level any individual, even a child, has a
recognized right of sorts to be non-co-operative and resistant to
authority. This is expressed notably in the term musu, "unwilling." This is perhaps a very essential form of freedom and privacy
in a group-oriented society, where co-operative pressures and the
absence of walls and therefore of physical seclusion might become
intolerable apart from some such safety valve. The person who is
musu is left to work it through or sulk it out alone. An entire group
may become un-co-operative in the same way. An elite titleholder
whose group ceases to respect and follow his leadership, or is
merely for the time being "mad" at him, can be rendered powerless
by such "passive resistance" techniques, which is one of the many
solid reasons why the elite leader is under compulsion to consult
with his group and get their consent and approval before rendering

---

[15] See Annual Reports under the category "Political Organizations." The dramatic objection of the "royal" chief Mata'afa,
at the Constitutional Convention of 1954, to his omission as one of
the proposed heads of state (p. 31) may foreshadow an organized
opposition group.

a decision, at least in any matter of general concern. A trader can find his store suddenly empty of customers if he arouses group hostilities.

Opposition can build up against an elite person to the extent that he may be ostracized, sent into banishment, or replaced. Grattan says of such opposition as it applies in the village fono setting:

> A matai who does not accept the otherwise unanimous opinion of the fono in regard to some decision may carry his view to the extent of refusing to accept the decision. He may be prevailed on to retract, but if he persists in his attitude, especially if that attitude covers a refusal to pay a fine of foodstuffs to the remainder of the matai [i.e., as compensation for the "wrong"] then he will probably be expelled from the fainganu'u [village social system] which means in effect that his social status and that of his family are no longer recognized. He is not allowed to attend meetings of the fono or to express his opinion on any matter that has come up for discussion; he is ostracized, and any assistance that he may offer in the maintenance or entertainment of village guests would be refused. He and his family cease to take part in village affairs until the breach is healed by the offering and the acceptance of his apology and usually the provision of a pig and other foodstuffs to mark his reentry into social life.
>
> The matai may be prepared to concede his fault, but public opinion may be such that for a time he must retire from social life. In such a case he will probably retire temporarily from the village, living with family connections elsewhere (op. cit., pp. 17-18).

The punishment of exile is put into effect only under the utmost provocation; yet the writers have notes on several cases where it has been called into play in recent years. All three modern governments—German, New Zealand, and American—have also used the custom as a political tool in dealing with "disaffected" or "recalcitrant" leaders.

The period immediately following a formal assembly is particularly likely to yield clues as to whether opposition exists. An
individual unwilling to set himself against a higher weighted view in
the public group may be under considerable tension to unburden
himself in private conversation. After a politically oriented meeting
attended by one of the writers, in which everyone ostensibly agreed
with pronouncements by the Samoan spokesmen, a younger chief
personally well-known to him deliberately sought him out, and not
only told of his opposition but pointed to other titleholders talking
around with private dissatisfaction. Faamali'upu means "to com-
plain after a matter is decided"; faatolo'ulu, to "find fault with a
decision"; faasautu, "to refuse to acknowledge authority"—these
are some of the many appropriate linguistic variants here. A
Samoan saying goes: "Although his nose is still swollen, he is
looking for trouble, " i. e. , a person, though his voice has been
overruled, is unsatisfied with the decision, and is trying to prove
that his position is right. Aamu has the strong meaning of "whis-
pering dissents with ridicule. " Fatu'ulu, "to store up grievances, "
has the further connotation of "thatching over old thatch. "

Where dissent is submerged for public purposes it does not
necessarily inhibit opposing groups or individuals from continuing
to influence the situation in terms of their contrary views. Such
persons or factions are likely to feel perfectly free to attempt to
"politic" their own opinion in every feasible way so as to lay the
groundwork for an ultimate reversal by the group of the decision
they dislike. In the same way throughout Samoan history, a conquered party, in acknowledging its submission to the pule (power)
of a temporarily stronger authority, will be expected to start making
plans of opposition and revival at the earliest possible time.

Where opposition is either culturally repressed or politically
suppressed small incidents are liable to trigger sudden, more or
less violent outbreaks. Samoan history has demonstrated repeatedly
that opposition to an official policy can start as a very personal and
local disgruntlement of an undercover nature, and before long emerge
as an organized Mau or "opinion" movement of some large segment
of the people. There seems little reason to believe that this was
entirely due to the alien nature of the government, or that new opposition movements against the administrations as now reorganized
are not a possibility at some time in the future. Such a movement
appears to be a characteristically Samoan form of opposition, the
other side of the coin of surface unanimity, and of the absence of
an organized, out-in-the-open opposition minority party. Indeed
it seems to be a more or less inevitable consequence of this absence
of an admitted opposition or minority party, observable in other

areas of like "unanimity" government. Where unanimity is the rule a great deal of frustration and undercover disaffection must exist; and where this accumulates to the point at which, for perhaps very different reasons, a great many of the power elements in the society become involved, a movement in opposition to the existing power structure is liable to emerge. The tip-over point in power balance at some periods will almost certainly be reached. The further course of such a movement depends, among other factors, on how far it is allowed open expression or is blocked by authoritarian techinques, as by official majorities on governmental bodies, by control of opinion media, or by forceful suppression.

Such movements serve as outlets for varied frustrations, only some of which are rational or even conscious, and which often differ widely in different segments of the population. They are likely to derive their unity primarily out of a negative "againstness"; any positive formulations they take on are liable to be very general indeed, as something to which all can give assent. Usually they have a mystical or symbolic rather than a practical or realistic character. No clear-cut definitions of aims and purposes is to be expected, since any such would be almost bound to cut across the elite and kin ambitions and motivations caught up in such a cause. The recent self-government movement itself, as will be seen later, bore many of these characteristics, and has been expressed on the Samoan side in the most general concepts. [16]

Dissension and opposition in elite groups can be most effectively brought into the open where participants are peers or near peers; marked heirarchical differences tend to inhibit them. Opposition by subordinates to opinions and decisions of important elite superiors tend to assume a private or even covert character. To give public expression to such opposition stands would involve showing

---

[16] The similarity between the modern political movements in Samoa and so-called "nativistic" movements on many other cultural frontiers may be noted. The Samoan "opinion" movements have had a large measure of cultural frustration of a general kind in their motivation, as well as more specifically political orientation. Such more naive movements as have occurred widely in Melanesia in the postwar period are well-named by a French anthropologist, Jean Guiart, "forerunners of nationalism." Anthropological literature on such movements is very extensive; see Keesing, F. M., Culture Change, an Analysis and Bibliography of Anthropological Sources to 1952.

disrespect and disloyalty to the powerful voices that have expressed
the "accepted" group position, and therefore by implication to the
group as a whole. Furthermore, resentment is likely to be aroused
in the leaders so attacked and their adherents, evoking sanctions
of various kinds against the open dissident, as shown in a previous
quotation (p. 40). So long, therefore, as the "unanimous" decision
"officially" stands, it is the only version likely to be heard freely.
In such settings rumor and intrigue rustle the underbrush.

Opposition may become so fundamental as to result in schis-
matic segmentation of hitherto integrated elite organizations. This
process has apparently been at work throughout Samoan history,
diversifying the structure and fostering local variability. It is one
aspect of the basic social process called by Bateson "schismogenesis."[17] Tendencies to factionalism, however, are particularly relevant to an understanding of the modern situation, as such
segmentation processes appear to have been accelerating. The
security values of alliance and the grim decisions and consolidations
of war which were characteristic of old Samoa are no longer part
of the scene where the white man's force keeps peace. Ethnological
analysis shows that a number of extended family units have been
breaking up, with former single titles being split among various
family branches, together with lands and honors; the main divisive
factor here seems to have been inability to agree on or to force a
decision relative to title succession. As an extreme instance, one
such title now has approximately a score of holders in different
localities. A number of cases have also occurred where there has
been a village division on vital issues, and because of pride and
strong family feeling the split has tended to persist for years or
permanently. For practical purposes the factions thus established
form separate villages, with correspondingly lessened political
and prestige importance, and also losses in pleasant social rapport
and cohesion. Religious denominationalism has in occasional instances resulted in whole community realignments of this kind.
On the other side of the picture there are discernible newer influences
making for greater cohesion in the Samoan society, as will be shown
especially in chapter IX.

In the Samoan setting the final instrumentality for producing
a decision among opposing parties was "the law of the club"—

---

[17] Bateson, G. "Culture Contact and Schismogenesis," Man,
25 (1935), pp. 178-83.

fighting. The incoming Europeans had to provide an alternative to war in the interests of law and order, judicial arbitration. In Western Samoa a special court (the Land and Titles Court) was set up to adjudicate cases dealing with two causes of dispute, land tenure and succession to titles, which involve intricacies of Samoan custom. In American Samoa these matters are handled by the high court along with other serious cases. A notable feature of the modern setting has been a frequent need for these courts to make a final decision among disputing claimants and family branches when an important title becomes vacant. In Western Samoa this has happened even with some appointments to the "royal" titles. Appeals to the court against an existing titleholder can also occur. In this sense the modern judicial system can serve as a divisive force as well as one making for unanimity in decision, and has contributed to segmentation processes.

8.   Some Further Implications of the Group

Responsibility Principle

A number of corollary propositions arise from the analysis in this chapter of the interplay of individual and group "voices." An obvious point is that elite persons, called on to formulate opinion, need time for proper consultation with the group or groups they represent. As an extension of an earlier discussion (p. 93) it may be said that elite persons are rarely in a position to make "spot" decisions in the fields of their responsibility.

This fact is surprisingly little realized by government officials and others in such areas. Too often they expect outright answers on new problems from an elite assembly during its session. They assume or imply that the representatives have the authority delegated to them on such specifics, or are in a position to exercise arbitrary authority. Lacking such results they tend to brand, as did the administrator cited at the beginning of the chapter, the proceedings of a Samoan assembly as "futile," "talking in generalities only," and so on. The Navy administration in American Samoa, however, was particularly successful in consultation with Samoan leaders in developing the type of over-all Fono schedule for business, in which projected legislation initiated either by Samoan groups or by the government could be discussed, ahead of final decision, at all levels. In the reorganized Legislative Assembly of Western Samoa the problem arose immediately of how long Samoan members should be given to frame their comments on motions after their introduction: officials wanted to allow one day only, but the Samoans asked for a longer period and in the end the decision was made to give at least seven days advance notice of motions. [18]

Where elite persons are forced, either by the pressure of circumstances or by external compulsion from higher authority, to render "spot" decisions, such decisions tend to have a purely tentative character until group reaction is forthcoming. The only circumstance in which such a forced decision is likely to "stick" is where no alternative is possible, for example, in some physical emergency such as a natural calamity. Where alternative solutions are available, any forced decision by an elite person is likely not only to be disputed, but to arouse automatic opposition in the adherent group because of the arbitrary circumstances involved; the decision has in it the seeds of its own destruction. Elite persons tend to make very effort to avoid being put into the position of taking personal stands. If forced to do so their "yes" or "no" answer is likely to be one of expediency rather than considered judgment. The history of Samoa is replete with examples of attempts to force decisions through elite leaders, and of the backlash of Samoan opinion. A strong word of disapproval, faafua'ava, means doing a thing without consulting the others concerned.

In a crisis calling for immediate or short-term decision the senior elite person available is correctly called on for definition of the situation; in turn he is likely to enlist both the "know how" of any specialist person available, and the more general opinion of any adherents present, as a basis for making his decision. The anthropological observer sees such unusual circumstances arising from time to time within the usually smooth stream of established habit. Negotiation by a longboat of a difficult reef passage in stormy weather will almost certainly find the chief giving directions with technical help from the experienced boatmen. A senior orator takes over smoothly, perhaps with aid from senior women, if an elite visitor comes into a community under emergency conditions where he could not send word ahead. A passenger bus may be ditched, and bystanders look to an elite person present to organize their efforts, under technical advice from the driver.

Any sudden removal of the responsible elite leader from an organized group situation is likely to break up the action pattern of his adherents, and in extreme instances may result in panic behavior. Should the correct elite person to whom a group looks for

---

[18] Legislative Assembly Debates, First Session 1948, pp. 8-28.

leadership be removed from active direction, the adherent personnel
is likely to lose its momentum, and in crisis situations to lapse into
disorder or panic. This happened, according to oral history and
folklore, in old-time battles when death of a leader caused a force
to break up and even to surrender. In 1929, in a clash at Apia
between parading "Mau" movement supporters and the constabulary,
the shooting of the highest chief present, the Tamasese of the time,
brought about a complete scattering of the demonstrators, who for
the most part in the case of men fled to the hills. "Banishment"
of a leader from his community or district has been a familiar pattern both in old Samoa and during later government regimes to
break up organized activity.[19]

In elite communication, correlation tends to be high between
the seriousness of a problem and the hierarchical level at which
final decision-making is handled. A Samoan proverb, using the
analogy of trapping fish, contrasts small quickly built traps with
big traps which call for the construction efforts of a whole community: trifles should be settled by the parties concerned without
making a fuss, but a major problem has to be handled with a big
trap. Consideration of an issue in a formal meeting of top elite
persons is indicative of its high, usually group-wide importance:
a breach of custom or law which threatens the interaction equilibrium
of the community or between communities, the marriage of high-
born persons, governmental problems of concern to the High Commissioner or Governor. It would be a useful measuring device,
in the all too little understood methodology of analyzing the value
systems of a culture, to use the lodgment of decision-making in
elite hierarchies as one significant index of the degree that given
values might be counted "basic" or "focal."

Subordinates are not good negotiators in matters above their
station, especially in view of the great sensitivity to elite factors.
An individual rarely makes decisions that pertain to elite levels
above his own station if at all avoidable, and if circumstances should
demand it or ambition motivate it he is likely to experience corresponding insecurity. Mead, in her analysis of the role of the individual in Samoan culture (1928b), stresses the strong tendency for

---

[19] The effectiveness of banishment by government edict,
however, has depended on whether it is recognized by Samoan
opinion; the group concerned has, in perhaps most cases, placed
the leadership correspondingly upon actual or symbolic substitutes—
in the case of the "Mau" movement in Western Samoa the senior
women—and the group entity has not been shattered.

a person to keep level-with persons of the same status, but never to emerge to notice as an individual pressing beyond the rest.

Inversely, it would demean higher elite persons, and shame their adherents, for them to take action on matters appropriate to decisions by those lower in the hierarchy. When one of the "royal" chiefs gave a radio talk promoting some improvements in taro culture there was a strong Samoa-wide reaction, a resentment that he was lowering his dignity by talking of such matters, and also that he was "not an expert" in this agricultural field and didn't "know anything about taro growing!"

This is one example of the many misunderstandings and conflicts which have occurred throughout modern Samoan governmental history through the reference of a problem to a wrong level; as by asking high chiefs to take action in matters of sanitation or baby care, or rank and file persons, because of their ability, to handle elite roles. It provides a rather sharp contrast with the Western milieu where an elite person tends to be expected to know and have an expert opinion about everything.

Still another facet of such relationships is also true: an elite individual has his security threatened if matters pertaining to his status are referred to his subordinates or to his rivals in power. A Samoan titleholder, and also his adherent group whose prestige is vested in his position, is always watchful of this. Again the orator is the specialist in keeping the tensions here from fastening on specific issues. As would be expected, outside government officials unfamiliar with the nuances of Samoan custom have been prone to mistakes here, and Samoan memories are long when important titleholders have been involved.

A subordinate consistently uncongenial to or publicly running counter to a higher elite person is likely to "lose his job" or to be bypassed and lose influence. Only a powerful personality backed by general public opinion or by great locality strength is likely to risk this situation. In connection with the self-government movement of 1947 in Western Samoa a top-level orator in one of the key villages and districts stood out consistently against the views of the highest level leaders in his extended kin group. In order that the petition sent to the United Nations might be unanimous, a substitute was named to put a signature in his place.

Elite persons are in a particularly vulnerable position in relation to their subordinate aids and supporters. In Samoa, this is especially so in the case of the chief in relation to his talking chief, who is the expert in ceremonial as well as many technical

matters. In modern communication across language barriers the
parties concerned are notably at the mercy of their interpreters.
The writers years ago in Samoa were present when a high government official was deliberately fooled in a serious land transaction,
and the people of the district were also purposely misled by the
skillful manipulation of the facts by the linguistic intermediaries,
all in the interests of certain chiefs present from outside the district. Other cases could be cited but the naming of personalities
involved would be invidious and the cases somewhat pointless if not
spelled out in detail.

A competent leader knows his vulnerability in regard to specialist subordinates and is likely to prolong interaction so as to
probe the alleged facts involved. He is also sensitive to the need
for checking and testing the integrity of subordinates in a position
to manipulate the facts on which decision-making rests. One reason for the desire of many Samoan leaders for more thorough teaching of the English language is to reduce the dependence of the
leaders on the services of interpreters in cross-cultural operations
(pp. 212-14).

To the extent that elite statuses and roles are "achieved"
rather than "ascribed," i.e., subject to elective and competitive
factors, communication behavior is likely to involve increased
responsiveness to group opinion. There also tends to be a higher
incidence of personal tensions and stresses, a selection of types
of individuals who can bear the brunt of such tensions and stresses,
and a greater turnover of personnel. In Samoa, as seen in chapter
III, succession to titles involves such achieved status emphasis,
and it bites deeper in the case of the higher elite titles where rivalry is generated among aspirants and their supporting kin and district factions. This is in contrast to numbers of other Oceanic
societies where ascriptive factors of seniority and primogeniture
give more secure expectations, and patterns of responsibility and
strain take on different perspective.

At the same time, the Samoan elite operate within a very
well defined status and role structure which cushions strain and
competition. Such factors would not appear by and large to be
present with such intensity as, say, in the top managerial elites of
Western industrial corporations. Rather, the Samoan higher elite
might have its parallel more in modern governmental structure
with its combination of mobility and civil service tenure.

9. Problems of Measuring Opinion

A general implication which shows clearly in the discussion to this point is the great difficulty of gauging Samoan public opinion in the sense of mass opinion: what is on view is likely to be always the formal opinion as processed through elite formulation mechanisms. Particularly difficult, and in some respects perhaps impossible, is the application of communication measurement techniques established in research on Western societies.

It is rarely possible in a hierarchical society such as Samoa to get a public expression of individual opinion or minority opinion on any issue that has been "processed" through the elite leadership system; and any secret polling would be resented. Elite subjects must be dealt with through elite channels. Thus, of Samoans who have testified before the various government investigatory bodies on political affairs in each territory, only a handful have expressed points of view that differed from the standard patterns as voiced by the leaders, and these in virtually every case were individuals who have lived outside of Samoa, and who were markedly deviant in Samoan terms. In relation to the self-government petition to the United Nations sent by the leaders of Western Samoa in 1947, the only strong opposition by any group came from one whole district, Falealili. Throughout Samoan history this particular district has had a traditional right and duty to voice opposition where it deemed appropriate. In the old Samoan polity it was a Tumua area with special "opposition" rights—the district is known ceremoniously as "the conscience of the 'Malietoa'"; so that this was part of an expected pattern.

Outsiders who are used to a ready formulation of individual judgment find particularly disconcerting the wall of inhibition here. It is a rare, socially deviant individual even among the elite who would be prepared to express his personal opinion outside the proper communication channels on any issue that has been or is due to be "processed," through the group leadership system. For a non-elite person to yield a considered personal judgment in this way to an outsider would be virtually unthinkable. In such a milieu an opinion poller can obviously have thin pickings only, and random sampling response techniques on any public question would be ruled out. Should a subject of elite concern be raised it would be passed off in some polite way or the interrogator referred to the appropriate titled person.

An investigator needing information must obviously go to the persons who not only command it but also have the right to impart it, i.e., a purposive and controlled rather than a random type of sampling. In the case of elite matters, this would be to the appropriate chief or orator at the highest level of authorized communication. This is one of the main techniques of the ethnologist in handling his informant samples: going to elite leaders on elite topics, to specialists on their own expert data, to women, and even to children on appropriate concerns.

VI. CONSULTATION AND DELIBERATION PROCEDURES

1. Organized Deliberation

The focus of this chapter will be upon the procedures of a formal assembly or _fono_. To what extent in such an orally trans-mitted tradition are consultation practices standardized and orderly? How is business conducted? Who participates actively? What characteristic tensions arise and how are they resolved? How far are the proceedings public or subject to "security"? How are decisions formulated and the record kept, especially when writing techniques have not been available in the traditional setting? How far are Samoan procedures congruent to, or compatible with, those introduced by Europeans?

A formal deliberation involving elite persons calls for an orderly conduct of business. In a traditional-style assembly it is particularly the task of recognized or assigned orators to conduct a meeting in correct fashion. In one dealing with modern govern-ment business it would be the village mayor, county chief, or other responsible official. Such an elite assembly brings into play the full range of negotiation arts.

2. The Order of Business

Oral equivalents of a written agenda exist. A formal meeting will almost always have the range and order of business announced and agreed on beforehand. "The discussion of the day," the "subject of the meeting," or equivalent definition of topics, will frequently include the term faia "to be acted on, to be done." One of the synonyms for a consultation process is faamafolafola, "to spread out" as one spreads out the fingers. A Samoan proverb applied to the orderly conduct of discussion likens it to a bunch of bananas which are picked as they ripen in succession from the top down-wards, and some of which will need to be thrown away as damaged by birds or flying foxes, i.e., irrelevant. Another proverb equates keeping to the business in hand with steering a straight course in a canoe.

This is not to imply that the Samoan approach is necessarily direct and "business-like." Within the ostensible frame of reference, other (and perhaps more real and vital) topics may lurk. The agenda of the day may, so to speak, serve as a front, and be so understood by everyone. A Samoan is hardly likely to take at face value the first expressed interest of an outsider, but will probe his ideas in the expectation that his real "agenda" is still being held back. A

Samoan may ask in due course some polite and devious equivalent
of: "Behind all this talk, what is your real business?"

Because of the Samoan sense of an orderly conduct of business,
it is easy for Samoan elite members to pass over into a Western-
style consultation in which a written agenda defines the subject
matter. In dealing with Europeans, however, lack of clarity as to
content often results in talking at cross-purposes. Clear preliminary
understanding of any proposed agenda therefore becomes particularly
crucial where ethnic lines have to be crossed.

Elements of "protocol" and ceremony such as were discussed
in a previous chapter are essential precedents of the formal order
of business. All must be seated. A kava drinking ceremony is
essential, and nowadays a Christian prayer may be added. The
names of all those present may be acknowledged in a welcoming
speech. If visitors are involved the "Who's Who" (fa'alupenga) of
hosts and visitors will also be included for ceremonious identification. Characteristically there are long silences as participants feel
each other out and enjoy the sense of solidarity that assembling together promotes. Trivia may be exchanged (talanoa, "to chat inconsequentially") and food served. When the orator or official in
charge deems the time appropriate, or a signal comes to him from
the senior chief, the formal deliberation starts.

A set opening statement by one or more parties to a consultation is recognized as appropriate, usually giving an exposé of
the business in hand. One of several terms for an opening speech,
faalangatā, can also be used for giving the first blow to commence
a match with clubs (one of the traditional contests of skill at which
the elite were particularly trained and expert). Another, suamua,
has a literal meaning of digging up or tossing up first. Certain
orators gain a reputation for being especially skilled practitioners
of the art of making an opening speech.

In small face-to-face groups procedures do not call for the
elaborate ordering of business characteristic of larger "parliamentary" type assemblies. Samoan leaders have become familiar
with Western-style formulae used in offices and meetings, and
equivalents have now been established in the Samoan language,
e.g., "a motion," "plenary session," "in committee," "adjourn-
ment." Such finesse in negotiation concepts and procedures, however, does not show in the traditional conduct of business. The
niceties of negotiation, as will be seen, lie rather in the play of
oratory, status factors, personal variants, timing, and other factors more appropriate to the context of an oral record. It is a
question, however, how far comparable small elite groups engaging
in Western-style negotiation pay much more attention than Samoans

do to formal business procedures at least in private meetings and committees.

The closing of a major elite assembly tends to be especially marked by honorific and ceremonial behavior. When the last significant business has been dealt with, that is, the views of the senior or authorized spokesman have been expressed on every item, participants will normally want to follow with honorific and laudatory statements, and then the presiding officer will conclude with a formal closing speech of ceremonious character. An ethnologist has a sense of a break here in which participants signalize, usually with reluctance, the disintegration of the particular micro-society or cultural subsystem which has been built up in the course of deliberation.

3. Participation

As seen earlier, participation in an elite assembly has two major facets: (1) the right to speak; (2) the right to be present in a spectator-supporter category.

Based on their field notes the writers would judge that the number of speakers, or at least major speakers, in a typical formal deliberation process is usually from four to six. This may well approximate an ideal number for elite decision-making. A lesser number could well tend to make action too private or conspiratorial, and leave some of the variables without explicit examination; a larger number makes communication increasingly formal and oratorical, and may induce over-much audience effect and diversity of content.

The size of the house structure and the number of its honorific posts used as back rests serve as constant controlling devices in this respect. The voices of speakers can carry easily across the house floor and the beehive-like roof structure appears to be acoustically good. It was noted how each higher level of fono drops out enough of the participants, in active and spectator roles, to keep this face-to-face character of the deliberating group within an approximately constant range in number.

In larger groups developed through the needs of modern government, as for instance the 41 members of the Fono of Faipule, the number of speaking participants is still likely to be that of the typical traditional style fono. In four full days of discussion in a 1951 session of the American Samoa House of Representatives, which had 54 members at the time, only four chiefs spoke frequently or to any length. Seven others raised their voices briefly on occasions, one other gave a final peroration, the remaining 42 simply voted, i.e., were silent participants. Much the same was true of the Samoan representatives in the early sessions of the Legislative Assembly of Western Samoa, where procedures generally are in modern style. In sessions held from 1948 to 1951 the number of active participants among the twelve Samoan members rarely exceeded four to six in any one session, covering several days. In later sessions, however, this pattern became sharply changed as Samoan representatives gained knowledge of Western parliamentary procedure (pp. 152-55).

A reminder needs hardly to be given here that the nonspeaking supporters present at elite meetings will already have had their say on the questions under discussion in lower echelon meetings, just as will those not entitled to be present at all.

At higher elite levels the active or speaking participants are likely to approximate to a "peer group," even while occupying relative hierarchical statuses one to another. This would be less true of the village fono and smaller kin assemblies where any high ranking titleholders in the group will sit along with the lowest ranking titleholders of the locality, though even here all are present in their common capacity as household or kin representatives. It becomes increasingly true as representatives assemble in higher level councils. Here the small number of speakers are likely, subject to the differentiation between chiefs and orators, to be of closely coordinate rank.

In modern councils, especially under government auspices, this traditional pattern has tended to become somewhat diversified. Here the business is likely to include consideration of technical questions requiring expertness in European-oriented matters. At such points the traditionally senior spokesmen may deliberately make way, or "yield the floor" to lesser ranking persons who have acquired a specialist or mediator role. The writers have a list of some ten considerably Europeanized Samoan and part-Samoan titleholders in Western Samoa, ranging from fairly low to fairly high rank, who frequently speak or otherwise take the lead in this modernized context even in meetings at which the top "royal" titleholders are present. One such lower ranking individual, competent and trusted, was named by his fellows to serve for a period as presiding officer of the Samoan advisory council, the Fono of Faipule. Such exceptions further illustrate the readiness of Samoans to vary an ideal pattern for functional purposes.

In elite communication there is a marked tendency for all persons with a right to speak on a topic to do so, even though the materials may be repetitive and in agreement with the general view-point, or of another viewpoint already stated; this gives overt rec-ognition to their group, and exercises their rights and responsibilities. This may be thought of as fundamentally a diplomatic procedure, rather than a parliamentary or business meeting procedure. To European observers the reiteration involved may appear to be in-efficient as well as perhaps boring. "Samoans," they will say, "bring up the same business over and over." Its significance is all too rarely understood.

The highest elite person or persons are likely to speak at the points in a discussion where their statements, with their priority weighting, will have maximum effect. Such a senior elite person may choose to speak early, especially if he has strong convictions, wants to give guidance to the discussion, or knows that prior in-formal consultations have made clear a unanimous stand. More usually he will let others carry the active roles and then make his own pronouncements directly or through his orator at or near the end of the discussion. The presiding senior orator, at a district meeting attended by the writers, allowed everyone else to speak first, then started his closing speech as follows:

> Opportunity has been given for the chiefs and
> orators to state an opinion, so individuals have
> expressed their thoughts freely. And now I
> shall summarize the various views...

Such a procedure appears to be especially favored when a problem has not been resolved, and the senior person wants to obtain a full sense of the varied viewpoints and assess their im-plications problem-wise and status-wise before taking a strong step and committing himself and his group. Doubtless in important matters he will have worked out a relevant strategy with the re-sponsible director of the deliberation if not presiding himself, so that he will not be asked to participate other than at the time he chooses.

How far persons of lower status should speak publicly in the presence of superior elite persons, especially if expressing opposi-tion views, appears always to be a high-tension, or ambivalent, area in a formal elite discussion process. This point was stressed in the last chapter in connection with the differential weighting of voices. A part-Samoan leader said:

> The Samoans have formalities. No one is to
> express himself freely at meetings. They have
> their high chiefs and orators, and although a
> lesser chief's opinion might differ on the sub-
> ject at issue, he usually will not dare to express
> it in their presence.

Samoans of lesser rank have a marked tendency to await cues as to
the views of the highest chief or chiefs present. Until these are
forthcoming they are likely to talk, if at all, noncommittally and
tactfully. On the other hand, strong motivation exists for a lesser
person to show his mettle by taking an independent stand or exercising initiative—he has an eye for his constituents, and for demonstrating special competence which might lead him to be considered
for a higher title.

The risks which this entails are illustrated by the series of
proverbs cited earlier (p. 99) in which the superior chief is pictured as the expert, the lower one a kind of presuming amateur.
The presiding senior orator, in a district meeting at which one of
the writers was present, put everyone neatly in their places by
remarking of the opinions expressed on one current political issue:

> Just as with a successful catch in fishing, when
> there are some big fish and some small fish, you
> can keep the big one and throw out the little ones,
> so as regards the different views expressed here
> you can take your pick...

Another saying, often used as a kind of prefacing apology by a lower
ranking person differing with, or presuming to speak in the presence
of, a higher titleholder is ua faaifo le na'aloa i lona taomanga mutia:
"The pigeon catching net has been placed on the grass which is
pressed down." Pigeon netting being a sport of chiefs, the chief
has put down his pigeon pole (his own opinion) and the grass no
longer stands upright, i. e., lesser views cannot stand straight up
like normal grass would because they have been depressed by the
heavy weight of the senior chief's words. Vivilu is "to be forward";
it also has the sense of "beginning to understand and talk as a child."
Even so, the very existence of, and variation in, such metaphorical
sayings indicates the expectation that lesser persons will talk up
even with new or opposing ideas, and not just be "rubber stamp"
conformists to superior elite opinion. Positive encouragement is
provided in another phrase, o le laulalo a Asiata, "the intercession
of Asiata, " referring to an incident where a chief of that name gave

advice to "King" Fonoti in a song, and was given special honors
and rights as a result, i. e., good fearless advice will be accepted
even by a king and will be rewarded. The individual who tries himself out in this way, however, does well to be adroit in the graces
of respect, deference, and other honorific niceties.

4. Time Dimensions

Elite deliberation is likely to move slowly and be exceedingly
time-consuming as compared to everyday communication behavior.
As with the characteristic diplomacy of modern states, participation
in important meetings cannot be set to an anticipated timetable.

Elite persons may have to assemble from distant communities
involving indefinite travel arrangments; they can easily free themselves of day to day responsibilities in their own communities;
their physical wants during meetings are looked after by relatives
or by hosts other than relatives; they come ready to savor the sociopolitical game to its fullest. Quick or "spot" decisions, as discussed in the last chapter, are contrary to the responsibility principle. In connection with the self-determination movements of
modern times, elite groupings have stayed at the assembly centers
at times for weeks and even months. Samoan decison-making at
elite levels is likely indeed to move as slowly as the problem situation will bear, with full devotion meantime to the arts and pleasures
of negotiation.

Samoan oratory relating to timing of decisions can exasperate
the uninitiated outsider. "We listen," an orator may say, "and the
longer you stay the larger the understanding we have. If you stay
many days, perhaps you will receive a communication from us."
Or again, "We are not rushed or hurried in giving you our views..."
To express even a quick convergence of views over a simple problem might, in neglecting the respect for "negotiation for its own
sake," cast a reflection upon the prestige and dignity of those involved.

Non-elite persons today, often women or untitled men, may
express impatience or even profess contempt for the "endless
talk" and ceremony involved in elite gatherings and proceedings.
Indeed there is a discernible tendency for the actual practical affairs
to slip into hands freed from too much of the ritualistic: thus the
talking chief in the past took over more and more the practical affairs
of the chief, and today the women, as being less elaborately concerned in ceremonial are taking over a great deal of the practical
running of affairs in many villages, and in family matters, as when
the faletua actually runs the store which her husband "owns."

Devices to expedite procedures of elite communication, especially of important _fono_ gatherings, have been developing noticeably, keyed to modern clock and calendar values. Partly this indicates the increasing spur of necessity in the shape of new problems. But partly, too, they reflect acculturative influences from Western-style assemblies, including boards and committees, in which an increasing number of Samoans are participating along with Europeans and part-Samoans.

In the Western Samoa Legislative Assembly inaugurated in 1948, modern parliamentary procedures have been followed under the chairmanship of the New Zealand High Commissioner. Samoan members, new to these techniques in most cases, expressed to the writers their amazement over the speed with which it becomes possible to transact business. Speaking in the inaugural session the High Commissioner said:

> I know that in Samoan custom many words of
> politeness are used which are essential in the
> proper oratory as practiced by the Samoan people,
> and also that it is customary for all members of
> a meeting to speak on a subject even though they
> may be repeating in different words what has
> already been said. Now... I... wish to point
> out that if we were to carry on our business on
> those lines we would take a tremendously long
> time to get any business done. I am asking you
> now in this Assembly... to come as quickly to
> the point as possible with a minimum of intro-
> duction. All that is necessary is for you to
> address the chair and then go straight on with
> what you have to say.

He asks them to avoid repetition of the same view, simply showing opinion as it comes to a vote.[1]

In a later session the matter was under discussion of how the reports of the Assembly could best be shared with the people. It was suggested that the district _Faipule_ should each have a copy, and also be assigned the responsibility of making them known to their constituents. High chief Tofa made this revealing comment on the Samoan procedure that would be involved:

---

[1] Legislative Assembly Debates, First Session, 1948, p. 23.

> The Samoan custom is that when there is a
> gathering of chiefs and orators the chief whose
> [home] they are in must provide food for the gath-
> ering. And if the faipule are going to try to
> explain to the people the proceedings of the
> Assembly meetings it will take perhaps a week
> and for that whole week he would provide food
> for the gathering to uphold the dignity according
> to Samoan custom. Perhaps it may go well for
> the first time...but in the long run I am sure he
> will not be able to provide food for the people
> [and that he would therefore bypass the respon-
> sibility].

It was proposed instead to broadcast Assembly proceedings. [2]
Speaking to the first session of the Assembly in 1949 the European
Secretary of Samoan Affairs had occasion to remark out of his long
experience: "the length of a fono in this country is quite unpre-
dictable."[3] Nevertheless, time sequences in the Samoan style fono
have their characteristic patterns. A meeting that goes on too
long for comfort occasions the saying "the mat is hot," which refers
to the cross-legged posture on the floor sitting-mat: the Samoan
attention-span, as well as posture repose, has its limits. The
term faaaale, by contrast means "to conduct affairs expeditiously."
  Elite deliberation tends to be staccato and chronologically
segmented, with relatively short direct interaction periods, and
breaks for intragroup or individual review, planning, and relaxation
of tension. Both unduly foreshortened and unduly prolonged interaction make for inefficiency.
  Participation by the authors in very numerous consultations
with Samoan elite groups, especially in village settings, suggests
that the modal time for effective communication sequences lies
somewhere about one and a half to two hours. Briefer time periods
are likely to truncate a proper exchange of views in terms of the
number of persons likely to want, or be authorized, to speak, or
to satisfy the amenities of good talk. Beyond that the discussion
is likely to die out or become trivial, or excuses be found for participants to leave.
  Urgency and focus as interpreted by the parties concerned
appear to be more important in elite decision taking than simplicity

---

[2] Legislative Assembly Debates, 2nd session, 1948 p. 95.
[3] Ibid., 1948, 2nd session, p. 139.

or complexity of problem: definition of priorities therefore becomes of great significance in "agenda" making for elite communication, and only limited correlation exists between seriousness of
problem and length of time needed to reach decision. In the face
of an imperative need, therefore, an agreed timetable or listing
of priorities will readily be established, and decisions formulated—even though they are likely to be held as amorphous and
malleable as circumstances permit, leaving room for manipulation.
Anyone wishing to gain a quick decision does well to bring the situation into the focus of a crisis.

5. Public Versus Private Deliberation

To what degree deliberation should best be public or private
is probably always a tension area in elite communication. In Samoa
as elsewhere privacy gives greater room for statements and negotiation without being committed. On the other side of the coin,
public proceedings are an exercise in responsibility to adherent
group opinion. Secrecy, about which a number of terms in the
Samoan language center, tends to arouse suspicion and distrust.
But it probably does so on the whole much less in Samoa, with its
oral mobility and extensive talking out of problems, than in the
Western milieu of "classified" documentation and closed doors.
Physical privacy in the sense of being out of sight is very
difficult to achieve in Samoa with its open houses and personalized
relations. A traditional saying, "Laloifi was here," recalls as
newsworthy the fact that a chief was able to practice club fighting
in a "secret place" away from his village. "Security" in such an
oral culture is rather a matter of who is within earshot. Every
Samoan is taught from childhood to be prepared to respect, unless
otherwise authorized, the privacy of an elite assembly by being
out of the range of voices, as also by creating no noise within range
of the meeting.
In Samoa the problem of privacy tends to be determined for
each separate meeting rather than on the basis of general directives
or legal definitions as in Western-style assemblies. At any point,
spectator audiences of lower or untitled persons can be waved out
of the meeting place if previously permitted to be present. On
really important occasions the problem is resolved by having no
one casually within earshot, as for example in higher Samoan-style
fonos or the hearings of the official Land and Titles Court.
The equivalent of "security classification" may attach to important topics of elite concern, with severe sanctions against breaches.
Certain categories of "classified information" are traditionally

recognized, and even today public discussion of them brings down strong disapproval or active penalties. Kin groups guard privately, for example, their genealogies and lore relating to land rights and chiefly titles, and even in the privacy of the modern court reveal them cautiously in the face of intergroup disputes. One of the leading chiefs in Western Samoa came in for severe criticism recently for quoting mythological material in talks over the local radio, this taken from an ethnographic source. The term sa— "reserved, " "sacred"—is a main verbal mark of such classification. Discussion in camera perhaps comes more easily to a Samoan elite person than it does to many Western legislators.

Elite decision-making tends to involve a measure of individual anonymity for the participants, i.e., an institutionalization of responsibility rather than personal acts. Decisions are made "by the fono, " by "the ali'i and faipule, " etc., rather than by the individual titleholders involved as such. This is important in communities where close ties of kin and friendship make it peculiarly hard to say "no." Acting institutionally, behind this measure of personal anonymity, the Samoan elite are able to adopt action and ethical positions, mete out fines and penalties, and make decisions that it would be most difficult for them to reach where their individual responsibility was involved. Where the decision is formulated through the voice of the highest chief, he is buttressed by his institutional backing from the larger group and so freed from what might otherwise be unbearable personal onus or pressure.

Where formal decisions are required to be made in public, they are likely to have been formulated in minutiae through private conversations, "committee" work, and other informal procedures beforehand, so that the public act tends to be symbolic and appropriate to public relations. It will be recalled that Dr. Schultz-Ewerth noted of the fono in his day that it "gave the appearance of great preparation, " that it was the result of much preliminary private consultation and negotiation outside of the formal fono session. The proposition would be especially true to the extent that the status factors involved tend to inhibit open negotiation, or the issues to be dealt with involve delicacy or the potential of dissension. In such cases the symbolism of final public demonstrations of agreement becomes particularly significant.

6. Oratory

The art of speaking well is probably more emphasized and influential in elite communication within an orally transmitted culture than in one where records are kept in writing. To Samoans the ability to give an outstanding speech is one of the most valued accomplishments. The vocabulary relative to characteristics of oratory is profuse.

To exhort skillfully is apoapo, which can also mean to poise the spear; faaleileia is to speak inspiringly, or with the voice of a god. O upu matuia, quoted earlier, signifies "words with points like a sharp fish spear," that is, penetrating words which may arouse emotions advantageously or otherwise, e. g., creating friends, arousing hope, hurting feelings, creating enmity. By contrast, o upu matatutupa, "words with blunt points," are flabby, covering up, or merely talking to hide inefficiency. One speaker may evoke the saying O le upenga valavala, "a net with a wide mesh," i. e., he has brains like a sieve, a great talker but no action; another will evoke o le upenga putuputu, ". . . with a close mesh," i. e., a person of wisdom who pays attention to detail. To prepare a speech is faamoe—which can also mean "to put to sleep."

Stress has been laid upon the importance of honorifics, and correct usage here is of the utmost importance in elite communication. "To speak hastily without honorifics," "to speak without showing respect," is inexcusable unless justified by emergency. A speaker addresses himself first to "the Dignity of the fono." The good speaker will "talk respectfully," "compliment," "express admiration," and otherwise take full and leisurely account of the niceties of manners. Should a speaker have to differ with a superior he has available appropriately apologetic sayings, e. g., faifesea, vaeane, "with due apologies." Dictionary-wise it appears significant, however, that a proportionately larger number of synonyms relate to showing "disrespect" and other deviant behavior than to correspondingly correct behavior. Possibly this is a very widely distributed metalinguistic tendency—to take notice of the deviant may be as universal as for the eye to follow movement.

A modern Samoan speech is likely to contain Biblical references, often obscure or allegorical passages which show virtuosity in command of the scriptures and also put the weight of religious sanction upon what is being said. A Western speaker who can display such knowledge gains kudos in Samoan eyes. A former administrator, going to a rather tense political meeting, specifically armed himself with an obscure Biblical reference which sent Samoan leaders in haste to their own copies. Presumably the use of religious reference had its counterpart in former times in relation to traditional religious materials. Some of the older mythology and folklore materials may still be put to use in oratory.

Samoans, as do so many comparable peoples whose life represents an orderly round of affairs, like the spice of a joke or laugh

in a speech; there are a number of terms for "joking," "laughing."
These range in meaning from good-humored jesting which is likened
to "the tacking of a vessel," to jeering, mocking, and ridicule.   To
call a person vangivangi has the jocular implication that he is a great
liar and jester.   A visitor does well to be cautious, however, until
he knows very well the local conventions in matters of joking, as
also other borderlands of good taste such as telling "humorous"
stories, and skating the edges of obscenity and profanity.

A speaker who is hesitant may be prompted (taulangilangi,
etc.); or he may deliberately nono, or "stop to await prompting,"
so as to secure an effect.   To cut off or interrupt a speech has the
metaphorical equivalents of "turning the head of a canoe," "damming
the course of running water," or "twisting a rope."   Faaselevei is
"to interrupt a speaker."   Faasi' ungutu is "talking to a person while
looking away from him."   Tano is "to leave a speech unanswered
and introduce another subject."   Faasalaē is "addressing one person and meaning it for another."   Sapo is "catching up a word and
answering it."   Faamālofie is "talking indistinctly or childishly."
Sasi is "making a slip of the tongue" (also being delirious).   Tavale
is "speaking without thought" ("to cut wood without measuring it").
Talavale is "to tell a sob story."   Nānunga is "to talk nonsense."
Faalolo'i, "to desire earnestly," conveys the metaphor of "being
dark and lowering."   Samoan-style gesture is important, and must
be understood to get the full import of a speech, e. g., faamafulifuli,
"to sway from side to side in contempt or anger"; fulufululele, "to
place the hands on the loins or hips when arguing forcefully, or
quarrelling."

A few further examples may be given here to show Samoan
discernment of behavior variants in communication (the translations
are mainly from standard Samoan vocabularies):

> Complimentary: sensible; clearheaded; clever;
> proud-bearing; good-voiced; mild; zealous;
> grateful; courageous (a standing rock which cannot
> be moved); earnest; truthful; modest; persevering;
> persuasive; wholehearted.

> Uncomplimentary: rapid-talking (like a chattering
> bird); wordy; loud-talking; shallow-grained; ignorant-
> looking; timid; boasting; shaming by reciting faults;
> menacing; using bad language; difficult; scolding;
> abusive; misleading; lying; evading; making excuses;
> obstinate; deceiving; insinuating; exaggerating;
> presumptuous; stigmatizing; acting as a foolish

person; boorish; easily persuaded; confused;
childish; halfhearted; making a great show of
a little; doleful; rude; haughty or contemptuous;
overbearing; irritable; ungrateful (the term also
means empty-handed, and left-handed); sullen;
surly; sulky; mischievous; swollen with pride;
cowardly (also the name of a gelatinous fish);
promising but not performing; inconsiderate;
careless; grumbling; quarrelsome; puffed up
with pride (carried away by the wind); a great
talker who disregards truth.

Reopening a topic once a decision has been made occurs, but
it is frowned on unless fully justified. "The ufu fish is sleeping,
and the paipai crab is at rest, " goes a saying used as a reproof,
i. e. , the meeting is finished and no more need be said. Faatuāma'o
is "to tell a message after the time for it is past. " In the same
way, talking out of turn or saying something unwisely may be reproved with: "Do not make a noise above the ngana (a shy fish
easily disturbed), " i. e. , the "fish" of deliberation are shy and too
much careless noise will frighten them away. A speaker straying
away from the point or being devious will be chided: "Why not keep
your va'a (canoe) to a straight course?" or "A crooked niu (coconut
palm) is easily climbed. "

Samoan oratorical practices have tended to carry over into
Western-style meetings. In this, however, a critical shift seems
to be currently under way in the case of more educated and higher
elite leaders. The "value of time" is becoming known to them, and
also a sense of keeping honorifics separate from practical business.
Verbatim records of government bodies show an increasing facility
among Samoan spokesmen to speak in the rather brusque Western
manner, and to participate in informal give-and-take discussion.
The writers have heard a top Samoan representative, speaking in
a government setting with an audience of senior titleholders as
spectator-supporters, giving most carefully a Samoan-style speech,
but breaking in parenthetically here and there in English to give
brief pointed comments on what he really means to convey. The
problem of equating a Samoan address with an English translation
might be illustrated in closing this section with an item reported in
O le Fa'atonu, the government newspaper of American Samoa. The
Samoan text reads, with parallel literal translation, though without
analysis of the social groupings referred to honorifically:

Ua tonu ma filifilia nei,	Completed correct and decided
i le finagalo pa'ia o le	by the (chiefs') will sacred
Aofia Aoao o lo tatou	of the Assembly Supreme of our
Manu'a Tele, i le Ulu ma	Manu'a Great, by the Ten and
susunga i Ali'i, i le nofo	their highnesses the Chiefs,
i To'oto'o ma lo tataou	by the seat by To'oto'o (supporters)
atunu'u, o le a faia so	and our villages, the obtaining
tatou va'a.	for us a ship.

The English text of the decison reads "The Supreme Council of
Great Manu'a has solemnly decided to acquire a vessel for our
people."

7. Negotiation

Elite interaction tends to be cautious and devious rather than
frank and frontal. A number of students of Samoan custom have
said that this aspect of deliberation and negotiation has been elaborated into a major art or exercise in virtuosity. At times it
might well appear that decisions are reached with reluctance, the
interaction experience being the focal point of interest as an exercise
of prestige and skill and a source of enjoyment.

"No one," says a part-Samoan, "is to express his opinion
freely at the meetings." A chief states: "It is the Samoan custom
to go around, not to come straight forward and say what you think."
To "go around about in speaking" is denoted by the word taani'o;
to "proceed with caution," by paopaomuli, i.e., "the end of the
canoe." Mālele means "to say something in a public speech in
order to satisfy the public or fellow members of a fono without
having any intentions of carrying it out." "To ponder," fuafua, has
the significant parallel meaning of "to take aim with a spear," but
the "spear" may be deliberately aimed so as not to hit the target
directly. Faafisi, "to entangle" as by a vine, also implies to manipulate a person's words so as to "wrest a meaning" from them for
one's own purposes. As pointed out already, an opinion is likely
to be couched in devious mythological, historical, or Biblical
allusion, or in other terms that "hedge" against finding oneself
later in a position in opposition to that of a top elite person or the
majority stand. There must be room left for retraction without
loss of dignity. Maintaining room to maneuver, when done by a
number of participants, makes the whole interaction process a
cautious and devious exercise.

"Truth" and "fact" may be somewhat tentative concepts in
elite communication at least in the sense that a position or opinion

may be revealed step by step, or approached deviously, in the
interests of negotiation and in the light of the status factors involved.
This seems true even in Western "political" or "diplomatic" behavior, where the individual is trained from childhood to respect
truth and to "sign on the dotted line" with the sense of an oath backed
by realistic penalties.

Again words abound: alo, "to conceal"; aviti, "to give a false
report"; faasese, "to mislead (to bring the head of a canoe to the
wind so as to leave the sails flapping)"; faatangā, "to pretend";
lave, "to be intricate"; ni'o, "to say something and then try to deny
the meaning attached to it." In Samoan deliberation it often appears
to be part of the "game" to locate specific fact beneath the surface
of speech. A proverb runs o fetalainga e malū a e ivia, "words that
are gentle but bony," referring to a species of fish which looks
fleshy and tempting but is really full of bones; such words may be
mild, soft, diplomatic, but on further examination are full of hidden
points and meaning.

It has become a stock item in the training of anthropologists
and other comparable workers going into non-Western cultural
settings to warn them not to accept an affirmative or negative stand
at face value. Should relations be friendly, the first desire is likely
to be to please a person of prestige; inversely an individual without
in-group rapport is fair game to be deceived, tricked, or otherwise
handled according to expediency. This is another elementary matter
which can vitiate the work of communication researchers going into
such areas with questionnaires, no matter how expertly constructed
(p. 129). The same factors, however, are operative where Samoan
discussants have no close in-group affiliation.

The exposure of real views and intentions, under such circumstances, becomes something like a strip-tease; a major part of the
interest is in taking off the garments one by one. It would indeed be
blatant and rude to "come in naked" with the proposition that concerns the meeting. This aspect of elite communication is disconcerting to most Americans and New Zealanders, except as they may
be schooled in the diplomatic arts; the communication modes of both
these peoples are oriented toward directness and "truth."

Elite negotiation tends to be brittle and sensitive to divisive
factors, the latter particularly critical where communication among
the elite persons concerned is oriented toward goals of consolidation
or equilibrium. Here the Samoan vocabulary, sampled in a previous
section (p. 103) and in the linguistic annex (subhead 5), speaks for
itself. Words dealing with contending, raising the voice, dissenting,
refusing, importuning, threatening, quarreling, manifesting anger,
provoking, inciting, abusing, being discontented, scolding, showing

disrespect, standing firm, and the like, are numerous, with many synonyms and nuances. Taïngā, "pained with words, " also can have the connotation of being "speared in a mortal part. " Also significant are terms which indicate courtesy or politeness along with dissent, e. g., faamolemole, "to make smooth" (a word which occurs constantly in Samoan talk as a kind of "excuse me, " spoken genuinely but sometimes with tongue in cheek).

Other words were cited expressing the sensitivities of agreement, reconciliation, and compromise. The equating of opinion, including the question of "voting, " has been dealt with earlier. An interesting metaphoric term is liualo, "to be favorable, " with the sense of persons turning the abdomen to one another; it also has its opposite, fetuatuana'i, "to disagree, " with the sense of sitting with backs to one another. A senior leader may say to an arguing or quarreling group: ia matua i le o-o, "let it finish with an o-o shout. " The o-o comes at the conclusion of certain songs to indicate the end, so that the exhortation has the implication of "great as is the music of your speech, let us settle it amicably rather than by violence. "

While Samoan elite persons are prone to engage in high-tension behavior in consultations among themselves, they are unlikely to show overt dissension before a European unless they know him well. Samoan leaders, however, are not loath to criticize openly, attack, or otherwise engage in divisive behavior in relation to government officials, or part-Samoans and other European-status residents, especially those whom they consider to be on an equal or lower status level.

Elite persons, even when manifesting extremes of hostility to one another, are likely to continue to participate in interaction situations because of the group and class responsibilities involved. "Taking a walk" from a formal consultation would be likely to have the same serious connotation of a deliberate public break between the groups concerned, and not just individuals, as it does in international diplomacy. Elite individuals who have battled it out bitterly today may face each other with apparent amicability tomorrow. The government official and Samoan leader who have been at loggerheads in the official council room during the day meet with no outward show of hard feelings at an evening social occasion. Tension, in other words, tends to become diffused and depersonalized in elite interaction. Two individuals who may be known as great personal friends may have to disagree firmly in terms of group opinion. Conversely two individuals who are mutually persona non grata may engage in outwardly amicable relationships on behalf of their groups.

Even so, personal qualities and relationships inevitably do affect such role playing.

8. Personal Factors

Elite communication tends to be a highly personalized process. Personal (idiosyncratic) variables tend to affect strongly an elite negotiation process, even when in formal terms interaction is between representatives of institutionalized groups. Decision-making is likely to be facilitated or retarded according to the extent to which the participants are congruent in characteristics and interests.

Increasingly in recent years personality and interest differences among Samoans have sharpened. Samoan culture fosters sensitivity to personality differences, yet these are rather secondary to role differences—the importance of carrying through one's status obligations with dignity and correctness. This balance of interest to the role side rather than the idiosyncratic personality side is supported statistically by analysis of terms in the language.

Today, however, experiences outside of Samoan culture have reinforced personality differences in many important cases. Two influential chiefs, one in each territory, were observed by the writers having great difficulty in their relationships in fono gatherings because of their individual "un-Samoanness"; it led them into undiplomatic abruptness and impatience with Samoan procedure, "rudeness" in their chiefly roles in the interests of "getting things done," "getting ahead"; and ambivalence and insecurity in relation both to Samoan and to European goals. These qualities promoted in the more typically Samoan individuals around them attitudes of being "musu" or unco-operative and sulky. Cases of this kind are likely to increase.

Observable in the Samoan setting, these clashes of personality and interest are much more to the fore in the crosscultural contacts among elites—where Samoans are dealing with part-Samoans or with Europeans. Non-Samoan individuals in the administration who by temperament, training, or experience have become congruent with Samoan personalities are of inestimable value to harmonious relations and the smooth working of governmental machinery. Too often in both territories such unique individuals have not been held in the service of Samoa over long periods. Indeed their compatibility with Samoans has tended to make them suspect with their administrative superiors. Yet there have been some notable exceptions. Personality clashes and frictions have contributed heavily to problems of administration.

Strong correlation is likely to show between the ease of decision-making and the extent to which the negotiating persons and their institutional contexts are coequal and compatible.

The fono at all levels tends to bring together people of roughly equivalent rank and status - it is in the nature of an assembly of peers; at the village level, despite what has been said about the dominance of leading titleholders, all present are there in their capacity as village matais. At district level they will be people of district prestige status, and so on. This is a major factor in the operational strength of fono organization.

The sharing of common interests—also language and other symbolic media of communication—facilitates decision-making. Decision-making is easiest in the kin-community setting, and becomes more difficult in the widespread district level, and at the territorial level. It is very much harder where the European-Samoan situation is involved.

In the various councils involving Europeans or co-operation with Europeans, as in the governor's advisory council in American Samoa for example, the essential proceedings are in English. This linguistic situation, and the problems involved more generally with mediation needs, will be dealt with in chapter VIII. Where a translation process is required it more than doubles the time involved in any decision-making.

9. Decisions

The problem of how decisions are formulated, made known, and kept on the record in a predominantly oral medium is a particularly challenging one. Here writing serves one of its major functions in a literate tradition, notably in relation to long-term preservation and verification.

Terms relating to decisions convey various shades of meaning. The term most used for "a decision," at least in modern legal documents, is i'unga, from i'u, "finish, to end, to fulfill"; other terms have such significance as "to give authority," "to promise," "to unfold," "to produce a representative view," "to spread abroad," "to cause to appear," "to have brought concord," "to provide the answer," "to bring desires together," "to receive by the ear," "to command," "to be the firm testimony," "to narrate," "to proclaim" (see linguistic annex).

The final pronouncement of elite decisions is correctly made by or in the name of the senior elite person or persons involved.

To report the words or the decision of a whole group in the words of one person is indicated by the verb molitasi. The decision of a fono is typically announced in the words of the highest chief, either directly or through the senior orator. The decision has his prestige without of course at the same time involving him in personal responsibility. In the words of a talking chief in a speech in 1947: "The people do not recognize any [decision] unless the ruling chief of their group pronounces it." Correspondingly, in government màtters, the Samoans would expect any significant decision to bear the authorization of the senior official responsible: in important elite matters usually that of the head of the government.

At the point of elite decision-making, attention is likely to be focused upon minimum problem units of great specificity. The issues involved must be clearly defined and understood by all parties concerned. Marked effort is likely to be directed in preliminary discussion toward bringing these out sharply, so that hidden factors which may cause misunderstanding or ambiguity can be avoided as far as possible. Certain experienced chiefs and orators are recognized as particularly expert at such problem analysis. It would be an impression, however, that the lack of a written medium in Samoan assemblies makes this much less sure, and indeed much less consciously emphasized, than in comparable Western-style discussion where a record can be taken and meticulously analyzed in relation to building up an adequate text for a decision.

Elite decisions tend to be verbalized in sparse or minimal statements of explicit semantic character. Specific wording is all-important. Such statements must have a shared interpretation among all the parties so as to minimize the possibility of future disagreement or dispute as to their import. Ambiguity or long-windedness at least in the essential content would be particularly detrimental to the record in an orally carried tradition. That decisions can sometimes be poorly formulated is indicated by such words as avevalea and ta'uvalea, having the meaning of being "badly reported."

In the Samoan setting an important opinion or decision is frequently given memorability and affective or symbolic weighting by being thrown into a brief word picture, metaphor, or analogy, or else by attaching to it some well-recognized traditional or Biblical precedent or allusion. This, together with the fact that it was promulgated in the words of some senior leader, reinforces its memorable character. The Samoans are well aware of the power of words and slogans.

Such explicit verbalization becomes particularly necessary, yet is particularly difficult, when two or more different linguistic

media are involved. The problem here is to get statements which
match in exact translation. Serious enough where any metalinguistic contexts show marked contrasts, it is undoubtedly rendered
even more troublesome when one or more of the media involved is
carried in an oral tradition so that precise written texts cannot be
carefully equated and placed on the record. The position has been
eased somewhat in modern Samoa, at least in official matters, by
the use of the written Samoan language, and by progressive stand-
ardization of Samoan terms or Samoanized English terms to cover
the technicalities of political and legal proceedings, e.g., "proc-
lamations, " "laws, " "ordinances, " "rules, " "regulations."

Elite decisions are likely to be limited to the principles or
generalities of the problem in hand, leaving the details of definition
and implementation to specialists and other interested parties.
Samoan elite assemblies connected with the self-government movement in Western Samoa, for example, were conspicuously unwilling
or unable, even after weeks of meetings and after repeated official
requests, to formulate specifics on any proposed organization for
a new government; all statements forthcoming were of great generality, though strongly set in the direction of the self-government
objectives. It would on the whole be outside the action and prestige
spheres of elite persons to work out the specifics of a problem,
even in the rare situations where they have the ability and training
to do so. Only if the lower level specialists and other interested
parties fail to agree on the detailed implications of a decision would
these be brought to the elite level concerned. The accusations of
"vagueness" and "talking in generalities" sometimes brought against
Samoan fonos is also frequently leveled against Western diplomatic
procedures and decisions.

Public promulgation of an elite decision tends to be a formal
and ceremonious act. A decision at the community level may be
formally promulgated by an orator assigned to make the announcement; he may summon public attention by blowing a pu or shell
trumpet. In a higher level meeting, young men ("runners") may
carry the decision as quickly as possible to all localities where
there are interested parties.

Any important decision is likely to become a subject of ani-
mated conversation for some time. A relevant Samoan saying is
ua taimalie o ve'a, "a piece of good fortune for the woodhen"; just
as unusual morsels may turn up at times to add to the diet of this
bird, so a chief's speech may provide "something which arouses
thought and discussion among the many—the chief has handed out
special pieces of mental food. " The words will be searched for
the "bones" in the soft flesh as in the sense of the proverb quoted

earlier. In due course the pronouncement may be cited in speeches
as a precedent or justification for future action: the orator of today will often recall significant words of important leaders from
generations back.

10. The Record

Preservation of a record in an orally transmitted culture is
likely to be the prime responsibility of communication specialists.
Even so it necessarily has an evanescence and precariousness not
present when it is put in writing; it can also be subjected to manipulation by interested parties. In Samoa the task of keeping elite
records lies primarily with the orators. As in many comparable
societies, such experts in communication are skilled in verbal recall and reproduction. Recently, after a major political meeting
with government authorities in a rather isolated district where the
senior chief made an important pronouncement, a delegation of
five top chiefs and orators made a special journey to the government
center to clarify a possible misunderstanding of one phrase in the
statement.
       Under such conditions, it must also be recognized that a
purely oral record is more vulnerable to manipulation by interested
parties than a written archive. The ethnologist in Samoa, following
up historical and sociopolitical data having status and prestige
significance, is likely to find variants in the record from village to
village or kin group to kin group. Official court proceedings are
plagued by inconsistencies in claims made by different family branches
regarding historic rights in land and succession to titles. In any
case, what will be remembered is likely to be the unusual or exceptional—just as in folklore it is so often the variant in the cultural
norm which excites the interest and points the moral: the rightful
heir displaced by the usurper, the supernatural intervention, the
sexual deviation, and so forth. The general record, of course,
tends to recede in importance quickly, and so to be forgotten or at
most stored in the archives of aged memories.
       Samoan leaders, increasingly becoming aware of the value
of a written record through governmental, mission, and commercial
settings, show a discernible tendency to put important matters in
writing. The keeping of verbatim proceedings of modern legislative
bodies is perhaps the most influential factor here, as top elite persons become sensitive to the importance of an accurate record.
In American Samoa the keeping of district, county, and village
records has become a standard part of governmental activities.

11. Modern Parliamentary Procedures

The emphasis in the preceding discussion has been upon
Samoan procedures. To round out the contemporary picture it
must be recognized that Samoan political leaders have been undergoing a quite amazing acculturative shift toward acceptance of
Western parliamentary procedures. This started somewhat earlier
in the legislative bodies of American Samoa, where the handling of
business came by the 1940's to approximate to American forms.
But its most spectacular development has been among Samoan members of the Legislative Assembly of Western Samoa from about
1950 on.

Up to this time participation by Samoan members in the latter
Assembly, which was formed in 1948, and in a Legislative Council
which preceded it (with four Samoan members), tended to be limited
to a few "spokesmen" in the Samoan fashion. Not the least of the
stumbling blocks appeared to be the sheer unfamiliarity of all but the
few most Westernized leaders with the honorifics and procedures
of parliamentary behavior, e.g., addressing the chair, moving and
seconding motions, the order of debate, the arts of politeness and
of criticism. Problems of translation between English and Samoan
gave added complexities. The early debate records of the Assembly
are therefore dominated by the "voices" of the High Commissioner
as president, explaining procedures as well as the business, the
six official members who are executive heads of key departments,
and the more vocal of the five European elected members. Samoan
opinion was presented mainly by one of the two Fautua, Tamasese,
and by some three of the 12 Samoan members. Decisions were
unanimous on virtually every item of business, even where differences
of opinion appeared in the discussion.

By contrast, the later debates show great virtuosity on the
part of Samoan members in handling even intricacies of procedure.
Parliamentary slips are rare, though they still occur. All Samoans
are participating at a number of points, and speeches are longer
and more fluent. Samoan intervention is notably vigorous when
matters touch directly the Samoan community concerns—roads,
education, health, radio. Budget debates also show very active
Samoan participation, with a strong slant toward economies at points
of lesser direct interest to the Samoan community, e.g., official
housing and transport. The High Commissioner and the official members take more of a guiding and expositionary role, rather than one
of direct decision-making, and there is a strong effort to get the
Samoan majority to crystallize decisions. This is facilitated by

the great amount of preliminary work done in the Executive Council
and the legislative committees. The trends referred to here can
be demonstrated in some measure by presenting summaries of
participation in sample Legislative Council debates over the years
from 1948 to 1955:

October-November 1948: In 140 pages of debate
the major speaking role was carried by the High
Commissioner as president; the six official members together spoke 126 times; the three European
members present spoke 121, 54, and 14 times
respectively; the two Fautua spoke 17 and 3 times
respectively; and of 11 Samoan Members present
only 8 took active part, speaking respectively 38, 33,
29, 9, 2, 2, 2, and 1 times. Of the three Samoan
members dominating participation, two are markedly
Westernized and of part-European ancestry. Official
members, while generally confining their remarks
to expositions and explanations of activities in their
fields of responsibility, frequently took direct steps,
along with the High Commissioner, to secure
affirmative votes on the business in hand.

June 1949: In 140 pages of debate the major speaking
role was again carried by the High Commissioner as
president; the six official members together spoke
120 times; three European members present spoke
115, 16, and 13 times respectively; one of the two
Fautua spoke 14 times and the other did not speak;
and ten Samoan members spoke the following number
of times: 67, 47, 38, 14, 9, 8, 8, 6, 6, 2. The same
three Samoans dominated participation as in the
1948 debate. With a moderate number of exceptions Samoan interventions were very brief and
five Samoan members did little other than propose
or second motions.

August 1954: In 230 pages of debate the High
Commissioner confined his remarks mainly to
procedural matters; the six official members
together spoke 111 times; four European members spoke 58, 32, 11, and 5 times respectively;
the two Fautua spoke 8 times and once respectively;
and twelve Samoan members spoke the following

number of times: 31, 12, 10, 9, 7, 7, 7,
6, 6, 5, 5, 3. The last group, however,
involved in general much longer interventions.

March 1955: In 260 pages of debate the six
official members together spoke 277 times;
four European members spoke 78, 34, 21,
and 10 times respectively; the two Fautua
spoke 18 times and once respectively; and
twelve Samoan members spoke the following
number of times: 56, 32, 21, 13, 11, 9, 8,
7, 6, 6, 3, 1. [4]

In the debates of 1948 several divisions occurred, in which,
on some point of marked concern to the administration, an official
minority lined up en bloc against the nonofficial members. Subsequently this formal technique of recording individual votes lapsed,
and even when differences emerged in debate the passing of motions
showed an outward unanimity. In 1954, a heated issue arose as to
whether the government should purchase a barge for transporting
Samoan-produced bananas and other goods, and so possibly under-
cutting transport by private commercial interests. A formal division
was called for, resulting in an alignment of 9 Samoan votes and
4 official votes for the proposal and 4 European votes, 4 Samoan
votes, and 1 official vote against it. [5] In this and subsequent sessions into 1955 a number of divisions were called for, in which
members voted in amazingly varied combinations. In May 1954,
for example, on a labor bill item, the "Ayes" comprised the Fautua
Tamasese, 4 European members, 6 Samoan members, and one
official member; the "Noes" comprised the Fautua Malietoa, one
European member, 5 Samoan members, and 3 official members.
In March 1955, on a customs schedule item, the "Ayes" comprised
the Fautua Tamasese, 3 European members, and 9 Samoan mem-

---

[4] These statistical analyses are tabulated from the verbatim
debates of the sessions cited. Western parliamentary expressions
are so catching, it would seem, that they carry Samoan oratory at
times beyond local realities, as where a member from an outer
area may say: "On behalf of the taxpayers of my district..." This
glosses over the fact that since the mid-1920's Samoans have not
paid taxes, their financial contributions to government having been
collected indirectly as through export and import duties.

[5] Legislature Assembly Debates, First Session 1954, p. 48.

bers; the "Noes, " the Fautua Maletoa, 1 European member, 2 Samoan members, and 4 official members. This emphasis on individual responsibility is undoubtedly an important forward step in Samoan political competence.

The parliamentary experience being gained by Western Samoan leaders in this body is in turn being carried over selectively into Samoan political assemblies. The Fono of Faipule has had a number of meetings jointly with the Legislative Assembly in connection with self-government planning, and its members thus come to participate in Western procedures. As noted at an earlier point, the higher elite are becoming increasingly adept at shifting back and forth as appropriate between the Samoan-style political behaviors and Western-style political behaviors. In September 1955 the New Zealand government made an opportunity for a delegation of Western Samoa politicos to visit and observe the New Zealand Parliament in session. The Samoans reportedly were privately rather shocked at the informal and earthy nature of some of the parliamentary proceedings they saw as compared with their own.

VII. THE ELITE AND MASS COMMUNICATION TECHNIQUES

1. The Impact of Mass Media

To this point the focus has been upon Samoan elite communication as demonstrating a traditional and oral system still func-
tioning today. Modern factors have been brought into the picture,
but mainly as an unspotlighted background or deliberate contrast.
Here it is appropriate to change the angle and depth. The focus
in this and the next two chapters is on the elite in the "cross-cultural" or "acculturative" setting, involving new communication
processes and the new contacts, problems, and goals of contemporary Samoa.

The past thirty years, and particularly the post—World War
II period, have witnessed a spectacular development of modern
communication techniques. While these involve so-called mass
media—the written word, motion pictures, radio—it will be seen
that vital roles in their manipulation are played by the traditional
elite. Even when operations of the new media are in the hands of
government or other agencies external to the Samoan indigenous
setting, they tend to fall strongly under the influence of the Samoan
leaders, and to be geared to the goals and purposes which they
will be seen as espousing (chapter IX). In many respects they have
become an extension of the traditional setting of communication
viewed above; but in others they have in them a marked potential
for change.

The materials in this chapter lend themselves only selectively
to formulation of general propositions relating to elite communication behavior. They do, however, bear upon a statement, made by
a group of communication specialists in formulating the research
program from which this study took its start, to the effect that:
"Foreigners can reach the ear of the masses of some countries
only by addressing those who control the mass media" (p. 1).
The broad and rather obvious proposition to which this chapter
addresses itself might be spelled out as follows: the impact of
modern mass media tends to be strongly influenced by, and in
some respects is controlled by, the elite and particularly by those
elite persons who command the linguistic and other skills of mediation.

In a traditionally oral culture, literacy becomes perhaps the
most profound of all acculturation influences. But its long-term
effectiveness depends on the quantity and nature of text materials
which become accessible. The impact of the written word in Samoa
has had two facets: one, literacy and the accessibility of reading

materials in the Samoan language; the other, literacy and accessibility of materials in the English language.

2.   The Written Vernacular

The early concentration of mission effort upon making the Samoans literate in their own language was referred to previously (p. 6). Samoan adults and young people are in a very limited sense almost universally literate in the Samoan language. They write their names, read government notices, and may send or receive written correspondence or follow passages of the Bible and other religious works. Even with very low-level teaching, the basic idea of written symbols in a completely phonetic system where spelling exactitudes are not expected or standardized seems to be fairly easily acquired. Such written materials as are in circulation in Samoa are likely to be used till they fall to pieces.

Despite this literacy there has been very little written material in the aggregate in the Samoan language accessible to the mass base of the population. Mission press texts, government notices, and other materials, when they come into the village, tend to lodge in the wooden chests in which valuable goods of the elite person are stored. Children's texts prepared for government and mission school use, perhaps the most extensive part of the more permanent literature by now, are kept in school lockups outside of classroom hours. This is understandable to a point, as exposed paper materials rapidly deteriorate in the topics through dampness and insects; until specially treated papers suited to the tropics, such as are currently the subject of experiments, [1] are available and used, the life expectancy of reading materials is likely to remain brief.

The Bible and derivate religious literature have been from the first the mainstay of Samoan reading. One of the mission presses put out around 1900 a Samoan translation of Lamb's Tales from Shakespeare, and this has provided models for many Samoan plays produced for church fund-raising and ceremonial entertainment.

-----

[1] The South Pacific Commission has recently included consideration of this problem in its research program on behalf of territorial administrations in the area.

The Navy administration in American Samoa issued for many years an official "newspaper," O le Fa'atonu (literally "the-causing-to-be-correct"), with parallel Samoan and English text materials. [2] The New Zealand administration in Western Samoa has issued fairly numerous official documents in printed or mimeographed form, including a printed monthly official journal in Samoan, O le Savali (the "emissary"). These government publications have been mainly instrumental in standardizing Samoan language adaptations to political and other modern terminology beyond what Biblical translation by the missions had established earlier.

A commercial newspaper has been published, with some break periods, in Apia since the German period, and has included special articles in Samoan, or additional translations of English articles, together with notices and advertisements of interest to Samoans. This is especially so in the case of the current weekly newspaper, Samoa Bulletin (with the Samoan subtitle Tusitala Samoa), developed in Western Samoa since the war. The Bulletin had in 1954 a circulation of approximately 1,400 copies, of which several hundred were bought by the government at a reduced rate and distributed free to Samoan officials and other key Samoans throughout the territory. Many of the "letters to the editor" are from Samoan readers. In the postwar period, too, the New Zealand authorities have been getting written and printed in that Dominion an excellent Samoan School Journal for use in the Western Samoa schools. Three of the mission bodies are also issuing periodicals in Samoan, with mainly religious themes. The current trend is toward an expansion and diversification of such popular materials at the news level for both adults and children. But, in the words of an educator, "Very little in the way of sound, attractive, well-produced secular literature is available for present general distribution or sale."

A problem of literacy in hitherto oral vernaculars, often serious in such areas, has been that of standardizing an orthography (writing system). Samoa has been fortunate in that, as with other Polynesian speech, its phonemic system has less units than are current in English. With certain adaptations established by the early mission bodies they can be reproduced within the scope of

---

[2] Recently this has become a quarterly, and a weekly called Failauga Samoa ("Samoa News") added (circulation about 3,000).

standard type or print. Where standard hand types were being used,
however, as in the government and mission presses, the proliferation of vowels in Samoa has been running them short of type. [3]
The problem of standardizing the spelling of Samoan words, too,
has still not been fully solved. Government and mission translators, as well as the individual Samoan writing more informally,
are likely to transcribe words according to the reactions of the
moment to their sounds, rather than in fixed orthographic patterns.
This confusion, however, is getting ironed out as frequency of
public usage in writing gives them increasingly an imprimatur of
standard recognition.

In American Samoa, the naval authorities acceded in the
1930's to a proposal by the Samoan legislature to permit Samoan
supervision of text materials on Samoan custom used in the school
system. [4] This stricture developed from fears that children would
be presented with versions of things Samoan which could be incorrect, infringing the Samoan proprieties or undermining authority.
It applies to materials both in Samoan and in English such as were
being experimented with at the time by the school authorities to
offset a previous overemphasis in the curriculum on English language materials and non-Samoan contents (p. 248). This is the
most overt instance known to the writers of elite control over reading
sources. But the great bulk of text materials so far written in Samoa
have been prepared whether directly or through assistance to European authors, by elite, or elite-oriented, persons. A quotation
given earlier (pp. 143-44) from the American Samoa newspaper shows
how carefully the Samoan elite ceremonious niceties are taken into
account. The impression of the writers is that all authors of Samoan

---

[3] Reported in the Legislative Assembly Debates, Second Session 1948, p. 92.
    [4] Section 582 of the Code of American Samoa; it reads in part:
"Matters relative to Samoan custom, culture and traditions shall
not be taught in the schools...unless the materials to be taught has
been approved by a majority of the District Governors upon advice
of the High Chiefs and High Talking Chiefs or approved by the
Governor, and furthermore, no article, book, or other publication
shall be printed or presented to a publisher or editor for publication
by any student or person connected with the Department of Education relative to Samoan Custom relative to [these matters unless so
approved in writing]. "

text materials, in knowing the Samoan language, lean over backwards to avoid infringing elite sensitivities, in view of hostile reactions which such infringements could evoke on the part of leading Samoans.

Sessions of the Legislative Assembly of Western Samoa include discussions indicative of the interest of Samoan elite representatives in having more printed source materials made available to their people, especially in the Samoan language. In 1948 the Secretary of Samoan Affairs reported that 2,000 copies of the Government journal (O le Savali) were being distributed free to Samoan officials and leaders throughout the territory, and that it was expected when a paper shortage could be overcome that the issue would be increased to about 4,000. The pressure of space was serious, as Samoans were using it increasingly for paid advertisements relative to community and church activities. The following are extracts showing some of the Samoan opinions expressed:

> Hon. Fautua Tamasese: This newspaper, the "Savali," was for the purpose of publishing... political matters of the government... I ask that in the future the "Savali" should contain resolutions or debates in this Assembly... it would be very very useful for the people of Samoa to learn what is going on here in the management of the government of their country.
> Hon. Tuala (points out that over a period there had been great dissatisfaction of Samoans regarding the public debt of Samoa to New Zealand:) ...the reason of the great dissatisfaction of the Samoans of the time. They did not know how this debt was incurred... When the estimates were printed in the Samoan language in the "Savali" the dissatisfaction of the great part of the people was then allayed... I really think that the debates and reports of the present Assembly should have the first preference to any other matter that should come up for advertisement in the "Savali."
> Hon. Secretary of Native Affairs: The matter of printing subscription lists, opening of cricket matches, etc. ...was started by my predecessor for the purpose of giving a service to the people. The number of such insertions has reached a total

which was not contemplated... but it is now too
late to stop it without giving offence...
Hon. Asiata: I suggest that the circulation of
the "Savali" be increased... the very large villages
only get two or three copies. It appears that
most of the offences against the law are due to
the fact that the offenders have not read the
"Savali."
Hon. Lavea: ... in big villages where there are
about one hundred chiefs and orators they receive
only about 10 "Savali"... one "Savali" has to go
around about ten readers which is not very good.
I am sure that if the people were fully informed
of the things going on in Apia there would be very
few offenders of the law, and very little criticism.
Hon. Tamasese: I think you will agree with me
that the most vigorous enemy of Samoa is ignorance
because they have no understanding of what is going
on in the management and administration of the
Government. [5]

It will be seen from the above that in top elite opinion better mass
information about the affairs of government is believed to be preventive of dissatisfaction and criticism of the current leadership,
and that offenses against the law are caused by ignorance of regulations and of government purposes. It will be noted, too, that it
is assumed that the readers of the "ten" copies of the Savali in a
big village will still be the "hundred" matais—there is no mention
of persons of non-matai status. Elite matters are for the elite,
and it is the responsibility still of the matai that his family know
the law through him and hear of government affairs through him.

It is hardly to be expected that the small Samoan population
can support any really extensive vernacular literature, as is hap-
pening in some village-living zones with a broad demographic and
linguistic base. Furthermore, for the more technical literature,
it would appear to be quite inefficient as well as uneconomical to
translate texts from English into Samoan, e.g., as with more complex mathematical and other specialized operations. A people
having a localized vernacular can advance effectively beyond a very
limited point in communication experience only by mastering some
wider linguistic medium; in this case, English.

[5] Legislative Assembly Debates, Second Session 1948, pp. 89-
99. As of January 1955 the Savali distribution was approximately
2, 500.

3.   Written Sources in English

Bilingualism is increasingly becoming the objective for such
a population as that of Samoa, with its own deep-rooted customary
setting where the vernacular is essential, yet with needs for the
confident control of a language medium that gives access to the
knowledge of the larger world.   The much greater emphasis on
English language teaching in American Samoan schools combines
with more intensive contacts with English-speaking traditions to
put the Samoans of that territory well ahead, on the whole, of
those in Western Samoa in relation to such bilingualism.

In American Samoa, literacy in English is very widely spread
in the limited sense that all Samoans who were of school age in
the last quarter century have had at least some elementary reading
and writing in English through compulsory government school attendance.   Western Samoa has introduced English much more recently and at higher grades only, so that there is no approach to
a mass base of literacy in English.   In both territories it is written
and spoken most widely around the ports.   Good control of English
is in both territories still the accomplishment of a few, mostly
persons of higher elite status and their families.   Putting it in
another way, bilingual competence has become in itself both a
mark of, and a means to, higher eliteness.   It will be seen that
mediation at more sophisticated levels across the language barrier
is mostly carried on by a limited number of mediators, of whom
part-Samoans are the most numerous and facile group, and who
are treated as persons of special eliteness (p. 206).

With this background, the availability and use of English
text materials becomes of selective importance only.   Their
content tends in fact to reach the Samoan mass audience either
through the better English speakers among the Samoan group, or
else indirectly through mediators translating the ideas to Samoan
elite persons who then may pass them on in the Samoan medium.
The hazards involved in these steps will be discussed in a section
on "interpretation" (pp. 212-14).   The generalization might be made
that elite persons can on the whole exercise the role of censors as
to what ideas from all but very general and elementary written
texts reach the mass audience—a situation typical in such village-
living groups.

A British visitor to Western Samoa has recently taken the
territory to task for its lack of commercial book outlets, and com-
pares it most unfavorably to the larger central Pacific territory

of Fiji, which has a number of bookstores. [6] A survey of local
stores showed them as carrying a small range of somewhat ephemeral
fiction and a few reference works such as dictionaries and "ready
reckoners." The English sections of the local commercial newspaper, the Samoa Bulletin, are widely available through government
distribution (p. 158) and otherwise. The government also prints an
official Gazette in English several times a year, and distributes a
daily mimeographed "Press News" summarizing outside events. In
American Samoa the government now issues a mimeographed daily
news bulletin, with a printing in 1955 of 500, of which 200 go to
schools, and the new quarterly O le Fa'atonu in English and Samoan
with a printing of 2,500. Other periodicals come by post to very
narrow Samoan audiences, e.g., the Pacific Islands Monthly, a
small Australian journal of the islands; the Quarterly Bulletin of
the South Pacific Commission; and New Zealand and American publications. Samoans readily pass around picture magazines and mail-
order catalogs when these fall into their hands. Adults may also look
at English textbooks which the children study in school.

The possibility of stimulating English reading by peoples such
as the Samoans through the development of libraries has been considerably discussed, with emphasis on problems of carrying library
materials to the village. [7] In American Samoa during the 1930's a
special "library fale (house)" was built under official impetus to
house books donated from Hawaii and the United States mainland.
These were later incorporated with the library of the high school of
American Samoa. The books have had prestige value but limited
use, and certainly borrowing habits have not significantly reached the
village level. In Western Samoa a very small European library has
operated at times, and its books are used by a few town-living elite
Samoans. Mission centers have sometimes carried a few English
books. The central education department has also done what it can

---

[6] Pacific Islands Monthly, January 1954, p. 48.

[7] This has been a world-wide concern of UNESCO. It has
also been given prominence in the social development program of
the South Pacific Commission for the two Samoas and other territories in the area. The latter maintains a South Pacific Literature
Bureau in Sydney, Australia, to help locate and prepare suitable
texts, and also carries news of reading materials suited to island
use in its Quarterly Bulletin.

to circulate a considerable quantity of books purchased with funds from the New Zealand—controlled Reparations Estates (p. 243) to villages through the schools and teachers and has set up libraries in some of the larger schools. But though the service is reported to be popular it has as of 1953 no special organization or staffing to give it continuity. A Commission on District and Village Government, in a report of 1950 (p. 29), advocated establishing an itinerant library system to reach local communities; it also pointed out that if one Samoan reads a book "the information in it will spread much further by word of mouth."

Reading tastes of Samoans do not appear to show much patterning as yet, though some "pulps" and pocket-size works were seen usually in European-style village homes along with sometimes an older tropics-ravaged book which a family was cherishing perhaps as a gift from a European visitor. (A high chief confided to the writers that he had sent for and read Forever Amber, and was disgusted by its "unpleasant," "dirty" contents.) The desk and shelves of one well-educated high chief living in town and one village orator of high rank were seen, however, to be quite well stocked with journals and books. Some of the Samoan medical practitioners were subscribers to overseas medical journals. These are rare straws in a wind that is going to blow more strongly. The Commission on District and Village Government, referred to above, and consisting significantly of leading Samoans with one European only as chairman, stated:

> The main need [as regards reading] is to make the knowledge contained in books available to the people of the villages [as happens in New Zealand]... Otherwise, many of the leaders in district and village affairs will not be able to serve their people to the fullest extent of their ability... We have met a number of people [in a village-to-village survey] who are anxious to pursue their studies, on subjects such as agriculture or cooperative organization, by means of books. [8]

---

[8] Final Report, 1950, pp. 70-71.

A Samoan leader named to the Legislative Assembly from an outer district gave the writers the difficult assignment of sending him "books on government and economics which can help me." The written word on world affairs and technical subjects has in it for the elite person a new potentiality both for exercising power and for giving service.

Use of the written word has on the whole moved slowly as a medium of mass communication to date, except in very limited spheres. General reading in either Samoan or English has not become a wide habit. Selective mediation from written sources, especially by elite persons, and subject to the hazards of interpretation, is the rule. The situation here shows the more starkly in that the much later coming media of motion pictures and radio have already well outstripped the written word in mass appeal to Samoan audiences.

4. Visual Media

Visual presentations can obviously be of great influence in cross-cultural situations where verbal and written intercommunication systems are imperfectly integrated, as in Samoa. The question, however, as to what is actually perceived with discrimination, and what interpretive responses are invoked in one cultural tradition by visual images relating to another, is not well understood. Clearly there is ample room apart from the original selection of materials to be presented, for mediator manipulation of the impact that such visual materials have upon cross-cultural audiences.

Practically all Samoans now see commercial motion pictures periodically. In addition to Western-style theaters at the ports, with regular programs on most nights, indoor or outdoor "bush" theaters have sprung up at main rural centers with periodic presentations, and even the showing of itinerant movies from a truck in the villages. Nearly always there is a "packed house." The enterprises are privately owned, mostly by part-Samoan businessmen, though for many years the Navy allowed Samoans in American Samoa to attend the free movies which were part of the recreational program for naval personnel. The filming of several full-length movies in Samoan settings has added to this sophistication, e.g., Flaherty's early Moana of the South Seas; Gary Cooper in the recent color film Return to Paradise.

A quarter century ago motion pictures were limited to presentations at the port centers only. But actors such as Tamamiki (Tom Mix) and Araloiti (Harold Lloyd) were Samoan "heroes," their names known even in the isolated villages. One of the writers' observations of the time is summarized in the following statement:

> The influence of motion-pictures upon Samoan
> youth cannot be overestimated. In Apia alone
> something like 1,000 Samoans attend the [two]
> theaters weekly, many more than once; the free
> Navy movies are also very popular at Pango Pango.
> From observation [it was] found the great majority
> of "fans" to be aged from about 16 to 25. Their
> special passsion is for "wild west" pictures, with
> horses, guns, and fighting...and in Apia no
> performance [was seen] without one of these
> accompanying the more sophisticated films shown
> for the benefit of the [non-Samoan] community.
> According to the manager of one theater the
> Samoan audiences are learning English rapidly
> through the medium of the sub-titles [they
> were silents] and gaining an increasing "compre-
> hension" of what the stories are about (Modern
> Samoa, p. 441).

The statement about learning English was perhaps unduly enthusiastic,
the more so as then and for some years longer a "narrator" stood
at the side of the screen and interpreted in Samoan what was said
and done as the film proceeded. Nevertheless, in the modern theater,
with English "talkie" sound tracks, it is no longer considered
necessary to have any formal interpretation.

      To the older "wild westerns" and slapstick comedies, still
popular, have been added mystery thrillers and gangster themes as
a favorite Samoan diet. The "serial" also continues to have a vogue.
On the whole the films sent by the commercial distributors to both
Samoan territories, as to so many comparable parts of the world,
are low grade and often many years old. The impact of films on the
mind of the villager might be suggested by listing the titles shown in
six village theaters in outer districts of Western Samoa for the four
week ends of August 19 to September 16, 1955:

> Films: Hellfire; Violent Hour; Lovely to Look At;
> Suspense; California Conquest; Tycoon; Springtime
> in the Sierras; Captain Blood, Fugitive; Combat
> Squad; South Side 1-1000; Walls Came Tumbling
> Down; Voodoo Tiger; Rio Grande; Sinbad the Sailor;
> Honey Chile; Sport of Kings; Yukon Manhunt.
> Serials: The Iron Claw; Daredevils of the West.

The low quality of many films, or their unsuitability for
Samoan audiences, has been a matter of running criticism by officials
and others, and has provoked discussions in the Legislative Assembly
of Western Samoa.   The local distributors have consistently made
representations to the metropolitan agencies for better class films,
but they apparently cannot break the overseas distribution chain.
Some films, after preview, have been considered unsuitable for
local audiences. [9]   The High Commissioner, speaking in the Legislative Assembly, said of the situation: "The general quality of films
[received] is very low—we get a very large quantity of poor films."
But the legislators expressed confidence that the local theater management was doing the best that could be done, and considered that government censorship would not improve the situation. [10]

An increasing use has been made by the administrations in
both territories of educational films, film strips, and slides.   The
lead in this has been taken by the medical departments.   The mobile
medical units have used such visual aids regularly in the villages on
their periodic visits as part of their work in preventive and educational
medicine.   They have also been used effectively by the educational
departments, and for Western Samoa such materials have been sup-
plied by the New Zealand Department of Education National Film
Library.   Their popularity and effectiveness in the health programs
indicates that they could with profit be used much more extensively
on all educational fronts if more of the right types of materials were
available. [11]

The writers, talking to a circle of chiefs in an isolated village
in Western Samoa, were confronted by the question as to why Americans appeared so violent and lawless in the movies, yet were so
orderly and friendly when seen in American Samoa.   This provoked
an interesting discussion in which the point became understood that,

---

[9] Western Samoa had for a time a Citizens' Board to review
films, but this lapsed, and at present the commercial management
meets the censorship problem in the light of its knowledge of local
opinion.

[10] Legislative Assembly Debates, Second Session 1948,
pp. 88, 138ff.

[11] The South Pacific Commission is working on this problem
as part of an extensive visual aid program; see a report on visual
aids in both Samoas as part of a larger survey by Moore, A. L.
Visual Aids in Education in the South Pacific.   South Pacific Commission Technical Paper 4, (1950), Noumea, New Caledonia; also
the Commission's Quarterly Bulletin.

as with Samoan audiences listening to folklore, American audiences were interested in a "story," often an escape theme or one in which exceptional rather than everyday events were depicted. This illustrates how peoples such as the Samoans can be puzzled as to how to interpret what they see and hear from another cultural medium by way of films, unless trouble is taken to distinguish between the documentary theme and the storytelling theme. Films of American life are nearly all of this latter class, but New Zealand, with almost no film industry, is almost never shown to Samoan audiences other than in perhaps rather idealized documentaries which put on a government tourist bureau show—a factor perhaps significant for "image" building as discussed in the next chapter.

Elite influences on this communication medium, as implied in the discussion above, operate on the whole indirectly. The more Westernized titleholders are noticeably frequent movie-goers, and are likely to be most "movie literate" at least among the mature adults. Though they cannot exert much say on the types of movies coming to Samoa they can and do speak out on the quality of films shown. Undoubtedly they are called on by their adherent groups for a lot of interpretation relating to particular films, their themes, and their actors. With Europeans, they consider the modern film of gangsterism and violence a seriously disorganizing influence on youth, and largely responsible for delinquency and periodic "crime waves" around Apia. In such an oral culture, with limited outside contacts, any film which emerges to special Samoan notice is likely to be the subject of prolonged discussion and dissection, much as is the speech of an elite leader. This popular modern medium, however, is on the whole the least subject to elite control.

5. Radio

Radio appears to fit with great facility into an oral milieu where persons are accustomed to speaking and listening rather than to reading and writing. As a mass medium it is a more recent phenomenon in Samoa, but in its total acculturative impact perhaps surpasses already that of the motion picture.

A government "wireless" and cable station, and private radio sets, have existed at the town center in each territory for many years, and "radio telephone" stations are also located at key administrative centers in outer districts. Wide use of radio, however, is a postwar phenomenon. Both governments now maintain small broadcasting stations with local programs as major instruments of policy and education as well as entertainment.

The Western Samoa administration established its broadcasting station in 1948, and as gifts of the New Zealand government
installed in practically every village a battery-driven radio receiving
set. These sets were so fixed that only the local station could be
received. They were placed usually in the house of the leading chief
and were serviced by government technicians, all costs being met
by the administration. The governor and other high officials were
in this way able to talk directly to the villagers, who for the rest
were presented with brief news summaries and with entertainment
programs in both English and Samoan. A broadcasting committee
was established as one of the five standing committees of the Legislative Assembly. (In 1954 it was merged into a committee jointly
with education.)

Radio listening became at first enormously popular, and
added notably to the current oral coin of daily village affairs. It
also tended to extend Samoan wakefulness and the consumption of
lamp fuel. Soon, however, the enterprise began to falter. As host,
the leading chief was more or less bound to offer hospitality to
listeners and the nightly groups became a drain on his resources.
In some communities the chiefs used the radios as exclusive personal possessions. Families did not like their children out late,
and perhaps being noisy as their listening patience lapsed. The
sets, affected by the tropical climate, proved expensive to service
(the cost in 1949 alone totaled about $11,500). The writers, on
going into villages, found the sets often out of order. In 1947 the
United Nations Mission criticized restriction of reception to the
local station as an arbitrary matter. The audience in many villages
fell off.

Partly to overcome these difficulties and partly as a prelude
to experiments with the use of the village radios in education, many
of the village radios were transferred to the village schoolhouses
and put in charge of the schoolteachers, or else additional government radios were installed in the schools. Many of the elite were
by then buying their own private short-wave radio sets, which could
listen in to "any part of the world. " By 1949 it was reported in the
Legislative Assembly that in some villages three out of every ten
matais had their own sets, and they were installed in all the village
schools; in some villages there were six or more sets. [12]

---

[12] Legislative Assembly Debates, First Session 1949,
p. 139.

In 1950-51 a comprehensive radio survey was conducted by
a party of officials and Samoan leaders throughout all villages. In
addition to considering problems of set maintenance and desirable
program content, this party demonstrated and took orders for a
compact and inexpensive British receiver-type developed for tropical
conditions (the Berec "saucepan" set). The findings of the survey
may be summarized as follows :

1. Trouble as regards village sets was confirmed
very widely. Maintenance and use had deteriorated.
The system of having one in the school, and/or one
in the chief's house was unsatisfactory. The radios
ran out of batteries, other than at the schools, and
the local stores also tended to run out. When the
novelty wore off it was too much trouble to go down
to the school or radio fale (house) to listen, or the
chief gave up encouraging group listening. Even the
teacher was "lazy" about operating the set many
evenings. Everyone did not want to listen to the
same programs.

2. Enquiries as to whether the Samoans were
willing now to assume the cost of the maintenance
of the village radios showed Samoans as very unwilling to do so, the characteristic reply being:
"If they are a gift why should we pay on them?"
Yet the attitude to the administration showed
significant change since the self-government
modifications. In village after village the elite
leaders said something to this effect: "It is our
malo [government]. If our malo says we pay on
the village radios for maintenance we pay. It
is our malo."

3. An eager demand showed for the new type
of set, so that there will be many homes with
radios. The cost of maintenance should be only
about $5 a year, easily managed by a village family.
Orders for the new sets were running high—already
65 from that village, 35 from this one.

4. Reactions to programs revealed the following
general trends:
    a. Broadcasts of the verbatim proceedings
of the Samoan legislature, begun in 1949 as a

result of a decision of the legislature "to educate
the Samoan people in the matter of their country's
politics," were tremendously popular and influential.

b.   There were requests in most villages for
more "world affairs," "explained so Samoans can
understand them."

c.   There were strong requests in most villages
for more territorial political information, especially
for talks by people holding government posts explaining their work.

d.   Musical programs, both local and those from
Honolulu, were very popular.

e.   Samoan children's programs, apart from
the school programs, were popular.

f.   The women's programs were unfavorably received almost everywhere. "Why should we listen
to a woman we do not know, telling us to do this and
that to our babies, children, or food? We have the
nurse of our own village, the teacher, or pastor to
tell us. How do these strangers know what is suitable
for our village?" This comment was typical.

Improvements in the system followed this radio survey,
though many of the difficulties are deep-set in the cultural context
and will persist into the future. The opposition of the elite to the
women's programs indicated in the last item, for example, seems
to have a larger significance. Partly it appears to reflect the conservative face in relation to women's expanding roles, but it is also
a demonstration that Samoans still prefer to look to their known
local officials and "experts" for practical guidance. They want individuals they know personally and trust to help them to make adaptations to their own local conditions, not advice via mass media.
"The government agricultural officer can tell the Pulenu'u and he
will tell us." This dependence on known individuals for technical
information rather than on the unknown broadcaster seems typical
of the highly personalized Samoan village setting, and probably of
the village viewpoint in much of the world. The radio or other mass
media is looked to essentially for news or general information on
local and world affairs, and for entertainment.

As of 1954, official statistics showed a total of 1,205 privately owned radio receiving sets in Western Samoa, together with
192 government-issued sets, of which 127 were in village schools.
Private purchasers can obtain "saucepan" sets at cost from the

government, and owners pay a small tax on each set. The government broadcasting service does all repair work, bringing the necessary maintenance supplies into the territory, and charging the
costs to the owner or, in the case of government sets, to the appropriate account. Almost every session of the Legislative Assembly
involves lively discussion of radio problems: high maintenance costs
are questioned; complaints are voiced when repair services are
slow; transport of sets from outer districts to the central repair
shop offers serious problems; certain districts with poor daytime
reception because of mountainous terrain want better service; the
content of programs is criticized. The following extracts from a
1955 debate in the Legislative Assembly reveal some highlights of
the current situation:

>   Superintendent of Radio: Approximately 600 sets
>   come annually to the Radio Station for repair
>   and maintenance... [and others are handled
>   by an itinerant technician]. All these costs
>   are charged to private owners or to the
>   Education and Secretariat departments.
>
>   Hon. To'omata: I have seen teachers coming
>   in almost every week with sets for repairs...
>   I noticed in one instance that... it was
>   about two weeks before [one teacher] returned
>   with the set. [This involves costs of passage,
>   freight, and school time.]
>
>   Hon. Director of Education: We are very perturbed
>   when a teacher is away for several days...
>   We have tried to send sets, but they get
>   damaged by rain and seawater, and are almost
>   useless on their return... We are trying
>   to get sets collected and several brought by
>   one teacher, and also trying to devise a sea-
>   proof container for transport...
>
>   Superintendent of Radio: We are having a lot of
>   trouble not only with moisture and seawater,
>   but also with misuse... It appears that it
>   might have been a bad policy to have made
>   these receivers fixed on 2 AP [the local
>   station because I think that approximately
>   80 percent of the [government] receivers
>   that come in for repairs have been tampered

with and they have apparently been put on to
cover the more normal broadcasting band...

Hon. Fonoti: The problem of looking after sets
has been discussed many times in the past...
[and there has been] the assurance that school
sets are not used except for school broadcasting. Now it seems they have other uses.
I ask for strict rules so they will not be used
at other times.

Hon. To'omata: For the benefit of those listeners
[in outer districts] it is suggested that the musical
program during the Samoan session should be
considerably reduced by allowing more time to
be given to world news and happenings in
different parts of the world, that is, foreign
news. As we all know, on Mondays, Tuesdays
and Saturdays we have a two hour program in
Samoan. Most of the time...we find that so
many musical programs are included that when
it comes to the foreign news the announcer will
only read news items for about 9 minutes, and
in some instances only 5 minutes. [Three
quarters of the Samoan population] do not understand one word of English and therefore do not
want to listen to English songs... [I suggest
that programs be organized] so that at least
25 minutes is set aside for foreign [and local]
news... I have seen it myself that most of
[the people] switch off the radio when music
and brass bands are on the air. They only
switch on the radio again when Samoan news,
local news and foreign news is announced.

Director of Broadcasting: The amount and quality
of the news and other materials besides entertainment has very greatly increased. A great
deal of work is involved to provide original
material as against...records. Taking it
down from overseas, typing, simplifying,
and translating...all takes a very great deal
of time. Where this is done in other countries
there are larger staffs of specialists to handle
it and also library and other facilities, rather

than one person only to handle the bulk of
translation. [13]

The statement of the last Samoan speaker on the content of
programs gives a somewhat unbalanced picture. The Samoan entertainment program includes not only Western music but also presentations of music and drama by Samoan groups. Special plays
are now being written by Samoans for broadcasting. But the major
impact is undoubtedly of the non-Samoan materials. A Samoan
who had tuned into the Apia station on the weekend of September 16,
1955, would have heard, apart from the Saturday evening two-hour
program in Samoan, the following:

Friday
6:30   Mary Feeney Sings
6:45   The Music of Irving Berlin
7:30   Comedy and Contrast
8:30   Down Memory Lane with Bing Crosby
8:45   Waltz Time in Vienna
9:00   A Man and His Music. . . Edward German

Saturday
6:30   H. M. Royal Marine Band
7:30   Where Science and Faith Meet. . . B. B. C. Talk

Sunday
6:30   Keyboard Kings
6:45   Patti Page Sings
7:00   Soft Lights and Sweet Music
7:15   Peer Gynt Suite No. 1

The desire for more information about outside world happenings
as revealed in the sources cited above, was also a "must" in all of
the personal contacts of the writers with the Samoan villagers. The
experience of the local broadcasting authorities, confirmed by that
of the writers, however, has been:

   1. That the interest, while genuine, has so
little informational ground support that explanations

---

[13] Legislative Assembly Debates, First Session 1955, pp. 86-
95; see also First Session 1953, pp. 47-48, 119-21; First Session
1954, pp. 48-49, 62-77.

have to be brief, and in Samoan terms. Every
world news item has to be set into an informational
background, an editorial essay, on the geography,
history, people, etc. involved.

2. Explanatory backgrounds have to be in terms
meaningful to people who have never moved out of
sight of a coconut palm. They have to be brief,
simple, yet with an element of drama, fashioned
for people whose life experiences are almost entirely
in terms of intimate human relationships.

A current events report for radio broadcasting purposes, worked
out perhaps monthly, with background materials to meet the above
requirements, could obviously be a great service, not only to Samoa,
but to the village-living non-Western world more generally. As it
is, the hard-worked radio staff, with only a meager bookshelf and
reference file, does its best to meet these conditions more or less
impromptu.

Western Samoa has won recognition, in the radio field, for
its special experiments in using the village school sets as a major
educational device. The work of a central broadcasting staff of
European and Samoan teachers has helped in overcoming a main
roadblock to advancing competence in schooling: a shortage of well-
trained village level teachers. Model lessons broadcast to the schools
have been very effective in demonstrating good teaching methods to
the Samoan teacher. Each grade throughout the government school
system has had an hour each week of broadcast lessons, of which
one-half hour is in Samoan, and one-half hour in the English language, the latter mainly instruction in its correct use. As of 1955
it was officially estimated that the programs were reaching 14,000
children in government schools and some 7,000 in mission schools.
The class teacher is expected to be an active participant in this
teaching, and has carefully written instructions well ahead of time as
to what will be covered in each lesson. The story is told of one of
the early broadcasts in which the Samoan teacher-commentator,
somewhat of a humorist, began his lesson this way:

Good morning, boys and girls. Yesterday
your teacher told you that you were to have a
lesson this morning on fish, and he told you
each to bring along a small fish. Now, look
at the fish that your teacher told you to bring.

> Or, if he forgot to tell you to bring a fish, well,
> look at the fish he has drawn on the blackboard.
> If he forgot to tell you to bring a fish, and if he
> has not drawn a fish on the blackboard, well, just
> look at the lazy face of your teacher. [14]

The writers heard samples of these radio-school lessons, dropping in unannounced at various schools both close to and distant from the Apia center. In all cases the attention and interest of children seemed very good, and the intelligent participation of the class teacher excellent. Paced as they were, however, to the mediocre pupils of the isolated districts, who form the great majority of the listeners, the broadcasts must have been excruciatingly boring to brighter pupils, and to those who already had some working knowledge of the English language as being in more accessible centers or stimulated households. This seems to be a fundamental, probably ineradicable, element in mass media teaching. There is none of the flexibility to individual pupil, individual class, individual district, that a good teacher supplies. Therefore such teaching is probably being used to the limit which is profitable or even tolerable. Nevertheless such radio-school classwork is conditioning a whole generation of young Samoans to active radio listening.

Getting information by radio is by now becoming as habitual to adults and children alike in the Western Samoan villages as is the reading of the morning paper and listening to broadcast news in the United States. Crowds are also likely to be on hand in the evenings at the government broadcasting station, comprising out-of-town visitors as well as townspeople, especially when well-known Samoan troupes are singing or presenting plays. A Samoan leader, speaking in the Legislative Assembly, stressed the unifying influence of radio:

> Since the installation of...broadcasting sets in
> the villages, the Samoans are more or less getting
> together...and understand each other. In my

---

[14] Quoted in "The Village School," a paper presented by the Western Samoa Delegation to the First South Pacific Conference (the advisory body of the South Pacific Commission comprising representatives of the island population) in Suva, Fiji, 1950.

village on Sunday nights all the people of
different religions like the L.M.S., Catholics,
Methodists, assemble together in the same
fale [house] and listen to whatever service is
conducted. That, I think, in itself makes these
broadcastings worthwhile. It is bringing the
people together.

From the viewpoint of the New Zealand authorities the political as well as educational significance of this whole radio experiment is obvious. The High Commissioner, in a Legislative
Assembly debate, emphasized its special value in helping the people
in the outer districts "to be with us in what we are doing." In 1954,
for example, the whole proceedings of the Constitutional Convention
were broadcast, with the idea of bringing the village listener directly
into touch with highest level political deliberations. Besides political

matters spokesmen can present agricultural, health, and other
technical information directly to the radio audience.
    How do the elite enter into this radio picture, and how far
are they able to use it to influence opinion? An early feature of the
program became regular broadcasts by the two "royal" chiefs in
their roles as Fautua (High Advisers). Their broadcasts, combining
Samoan with modern ideas, have personalized and symbolized the
new Samoan political leadership functions that go with recent "self-
government" experiments. They represent, as a Samoan put
it, the "dignity" of Samoa "coming into the village." Though criticisms
have been generated about some of their broadcast materials being
inappropriate and demeaning to persons of such status, their presentations have been on the whole an educative influence both on the
people and on the leaders themselves.
    On a broader base, the Samoan representatives in the Legis-
lative Assembly and the Samoan Fono of Faipule (Advisory Council
of Representatives) have been sensitive to radio activities. The
broadcasting of Legislative Assembly proceedings has, as indicated,
been popular as well as influential. The ordinary Samoan can hear,
through this and related individual talks, the elite views at the top
of the representative hierarchy, and not just at the bottom through
the traditional family and community consultation. The process
acts two ways: in reinforcing the elite views in mass opinion, but
also in making elite persons more guarded against infringing that
opinion. Some remarks by different speakers, taken from radio

debates in Legislative Council proceedings will show how leading
Samoans feel that radio is intimately related to national pride, unity,
and development.

> Owing to the lack of news and entertainment
> in the villages, it is common knowledge that
> the people of Samoa have great pleasure in
> criticizing anything and everything.
>
> Instead of listening to false rumours they will
> [now] get the truth from our broadcasts direct
> to them.
>
> One.and all are very content to listen in every
> night to the entertainment, information and
> education that is derived from these receiving
> sets.
>
> We have the best broadcasting system in the
> Pacific.
>
> This broadcasting service of ours...has now
> become part of the life of Samoa...part of our
> progress and our growth toward unity and
> nationhood of Samoa.
>
> In Samoa we are taking the lead in these matters
> in the Pacific. [Regarding the eagerness for
> more private sets] Samoa is not satisfied and
> is always reaching for something better, which
> I think is a very good thing. [15]

The Samoan elite, as seen above, also have opportunities
to exercise influence in radio matters at the village level. The
eagerness of local leaders for larger contacts brings to mind a major hoax played by an untitled youth in 1930 on the fono of his village.
Coming from Apia, he built a fake radio and when other men of the
'aumanga went to work he adjourned to the set and made pronouncements on larger affairs that made him something of a village oracle;
his "news" broadcasts, however, led him into falsities, and when

---

[15] Legislative Assembly Debates, Second Session 1948,
p. 108; Fifth Session 1948, p. 30; First Session 1949, pp. 102, 104-
5, 140.

found out he was summarily banished from his community.   The
village titleholder of today, besides having most access to the broadcasts, is likely to rely on radio materials increasingly for his news
and views, and in turn transmit them to his adherents, according
to his own interpretations.   This perhaps is the most potent zone of
elite supervisòn and control in this new medium.

In American Samoa, it was not until 1952 that the government
installed a local broadcasting station.   Until then private radio listeners, mainly part-Samoan and some of the more educated Samoans,
had listening choices which included the Honolulu and U.S. Armed
Services broadcasts as well as the Western Samoa station.   But the
people at the village level had not become radio-minded.

The new station is directed by the education department
under its adult information and education program.   It has been
broadcasting five evenings weekly in Samoan and English, with programs of news, instruction, and entertainment.   Training has been
given to a small group in radio communications; but no move has
been made to provide free sets or servicing.   An earlier attempt
by the education department to use the school broadcasts of Western
Samoa had failed, not least of all because of differences in English
speaking accent.   A daily (broadcasting program) called "The School
of the Air" is beamed to the local village schools.   Without doubt these
new developments in American Samoa will bring radio into the forefront as a communication medium.

6. Other Media

Both territories have government-maintained telephone services operating in and around the port areas.   The Apia service had
in 1953 a total of 328 units but nearly all are to government or European outlets; only a few elite Samoan homes, nearly all with official
connections, have direct access to the telephone, and there is only
one public call station.   The Pago Pago service in American Samoa
has about one-third this number of units.   Government postal services in both territories include sub-postoffices in the outer districts,
carrying light but increasing mail to and from Samoan correspondents

In the modern setting, Samoans in both territories have made
free use of an entirely new instrument for expressing representative
opinion: the written petition.   Though petitions have so far been
limited primarily to documents signed by titleholders on behalf of
their groups, they have in the Samoan setting an important relation
to mass opinion.   In Western Samoa such petitions have gone even
beyond the New Zealand authorities to the United Nations.   In American

Samoa they have been sent on to Washington, D. C. , including the
desk of the President. Petitioning has also been established as a
procedure by which adherents of a matai title may make known
their views to the court on matters of succession and of fitness of
an incumbent.

It would require specific study of any given petition process
to ascertain how far the opinions and signatures represented carry
the weight of solid unanimous opinion and proper authority. The
Samoan setting has lent itself at times to ready manipulation and
misrepresentation. This can be illustrated from the Journal of
the American Samoa legislature in connection with a conflict of
opinion in 1951 as to the worth of a dismissed attorney-general;
it reports that even numbers of important chiefs signed "blank sheets
of petition collectors, " that petitions in English were signed by
Samoans unable to read English, that many signatures were forged
without awareness of the persons concerned, and that in one case
the names of twelve minor children were written in on a list pur-
porting to be names of representative titleholders. [16] In verbatim
committee proceedings, in which witnesses were giving reasons
for having signed the petition, the following exchange occurred,
well illustrative of the play of Samoan customary factors involved:

> Q. (To a local chief) Is there any Samoan
> law according to the ostracising of a person
> refusing to sign a petition as this one?
>
> A.   There is no law...but it is customary to
> the Samoan people to punish by ostracising,
> with food, fine mats, when they do not carry
> out the will of the leaders...

------

[16] Legislature of American Samoa, Fono Journal, Special
Session August 1951, Report on Committee Hearings, pp. 1-50.
Certain leaders indicated that they understood the petition forms
they signed were to ask that the official concerned be reinstated,
but the actual document showed them as making accusations against
the governor. The incident led to considerable conflict, and to
ostracism of several titleholders and their families.

Q. So that is the reason why you signed the
petition because of your political position and
respect for the other chiefs who signed it?

A. Yes.

Q. Your "yes"... would automatically let
other members of your family sign... according
to the Samoan custom?

A. That is right; when the matai agrees to
something the members of the family do the same,
whether they like it or not.

Q. What were your reasons for [signing]?

A. I had no reason whatsoever but signed
only because of my respect for the other chiefs
according to the Samoan custom.

It can be expected that in the Samoan setting the written petition
technique will continue as an appropriate and important way of putting
on record a group view and that it will increasingly be used by widely
based groups as well as through titleholder representation.

In many ways the most significant of all media of communication continues to be the traditional pattern of an itinerant journey
and holding of assemblies in the districts and villages. United
Nations Visiting Missions, government visitors from the metropolitan countries, senior administration personnel, and also top
mission personnel, all employ profitably this face-to-face type of
contact. The coming of a distinguished visitor is as ever a high
point in the round of life. His business, if properly transacted with
the appropriate combination of the ceremonial and practical, has a
shock force which no indirect medium can have. The Commission
on District and Village Government put this into perspective as
follows:

Broadcasting and the distribution of books
are two of the means by which knowledge
can be made available to the people. But
there is another means more important
than either. That is personal contact...
Of course, our proposal is not new. The
Government has a long tradition of official
malaga [journey]... With the increased
participation of the people in their own

> government, they are more necessary than
> ever... What is needed at the present time
> is thorough discussion with district repre-
> sentatives of important issues. [17]

The visitor's supplementary stock of friendly news and gossip
will also be easily welcomed, and can be made an opportunity to use
the type of informal and oblique influence to which the Samoans respond so sensitively. He will, of course, be in the hands of the
elite, as indicated in the quotation; but the village families will
quickly have everything out in the open.

7. Wider Implications

The more general implications of this picture of mass communication among such village-living peoples as the Samoans, of
whom there are many millions throughout the world, are obvious
enough. They are wide open to receive information; but the accessible materials are inadequate and often of unsuitable form.
Acute need exists for suitable written texts in English and
other widely used language media on paper processed for preservation under local conditions; for aid in the establishment of village
library facilities; for circuits of well-prepared visual materials;
for radio program scripts suited to the needs of isolated villagers.
These problems are fortunately coming increasingly under the
attention of the national authorities, and are also concerns of the
South Pacific Commission and other international agencies.

---

[17] Final Report of the Committee (1950), p. 71.

VIII. ELITES AND CROSS-CULTURAL COMMUNICATION: IMAGES AND MEDIATORS

1. Factors Influencing Cross-cultural Interaction

The focus of this and the following chapter will be upon elite communication behavior in its cross-cultural, or "international," aspects. How, it may be asked, is such behavior conditioned by the images which Samoan leaders have of themselves and of the part-Samoan and white groups with whom they have contact, and in turn by the images which these latter have of the Samoans? What goals are the respective elites promoting, and how far are they congruent or different, even opposed? What sensitivities, stresses, anxieties, affect the communication milieu? Who are the effective mediators? To what extent in each territory are communication techniques adequate for national or total group consolidation?

As seen already at various points the "encoding and decoding" of messages between Samoan and non-Samoan elite groups is particularly open to "noise" in the sense of breaks and interferences in communication. At the same time an increasing milieu of common understanding and interest has been fostered in recent years among Samoans, part-Samoans, resident Europeans, and other active participants in the local situation. Moreover, in each of these groups, various kinds of mediators have been emerging whose roles, especially at elite levels, have become critically important.

To localize and record the images which such groups have built up of one another, and their relation to self-images, calls for an exercise in generalization approximating to those represented in "national character" studies. For Samoa an extensive amount of written material exists, but this mainly delineates how Westerners perceive Samoans and evaluate Samoan behavior; for the corresponding Samoan views of non-Samoans the student can depend to some extent on legislative proceedings and other sources, but in the main must lean on field work data. In building up the picture here, the method will frequently be to give what appear to the writers to be representative statements of elite persons.

2. The Samoan "World View"

Elite communication across cultural boundaries tends to be strongly subject to the biases of "ethnocentrism." Even granting what has been said above about the very recent radio listening, the world view of the great majority of middle-aged and older Samoans is still primarily that of a villager with vague perceptions and perspectives on external conditions, and inevitably measuring what he hears and sees in his own terms. Younger Samoans nearer their school geography lessons would even yet tend to put Samoa centrally and largely on a mental map of the world. Among the elite, who are likely to do more traveling and otherwise have the widest contacts, only a rather small sophisticated minority have real knowledge of the world outside Samoa and to some extent its immediate island neighbors.

A marked ambivalence shows here which may influence communication behavior. On the whole the Samoans show no humility in thinking of themselves and their roles in relation to other peoples in and outside Samoa. They have something of a reputation, in the general perspectives of Pacific island peoples of being "proud," "independent," "self-centered," even "conceited." At the same time, their sense that the European has superior instruments of power, and dominates their affairs, bites deep. Samoan spokesmen will speak of Samoa as "a small and weak country," needing protection and help from more powerful peoples. The implications of these attitudes will be discussed below as they relate to self-government and other goals.

Europeans, from their side, while themselves subject often in marked degree to ethnocentric tendencies, have rarely been reticent about stigmatizing the limited nature of Samoan horizons. Too often it is assumed that even a top elite leader must be ignorant of wider affairs; this, indeed, is one of the bulwark arguments by the European for continued outside control in the face of the self-government movement.

Modern communication media bring to the more literate Samoan a selective awareness of secular history and contemporary affairs. In 1930, for example, the Mau movement leaders used the slogan "Samoa for the Samoans" and other political techniques which were derived from Asian self-government movements. In 1947 the banners paraded before the United Nations Mission spelled out such quotations as "Good government is no substitute for self-government," and spokesmen talked of "dictatorship," a "New Deal," and the "Atlantic Charter." Several educated Samoan leaders, as of 1951, were aware in general terms of communism as an expanding world force, while feeling that it could gain no foothold in their own society.

Under the older League of Nations system, from 1920 to 1945, Western Samoans appeared to have vague notions only of what their relation to the League and its mandate system implied. The United Nations Trusteeship system, however, is much better understood, not least of all because their communication can be in some respects direct as in the right to "petition" and in periodic face-to-face consultations with visiting U.N. Missions. Samoan leaders are beginning to meet, too, technical workers from the U.N. Special Agencies. The United Nations becomes in Samoan respect oratory the "father of the world," the "privilege and dignity of the world."

Increasing regional knowledge of the Pacific area is also a marked feature of the contemporary communication setting. Samoans had mythological and historical links with Tonga, Fiji, and some nearby groups before the coming of Europeans. Subsequently they have been travelers in minor degree within the Polynesian and Melanesian island zones. Some mutual settlement and intermarriage has occurred. Representative football and cricket teams meet in competition. Notable has been the role of Samoan men and women as mission teachers and nurses along the mission fringe of Melanesia, sometimes in the van of pacification; Samoans contribute money, too, to the Melanesian missions. A sense of the need to Christianize the world's "heathen" has been a strong part of their century-old Christian faith. Recently, Samoans have felt pride in successes of several Samoan boxers and wrestlers abroad. Families with members overseas, as in Hawaii or New Zealand, are likely to keep in touch and so get news of outside places and events.

Since 1948, Samoan relations with other Pacific islands have been accelerated through establishment by the six governments with territories in the area of the South Pacific Commission as a consultative and advisory body on mutual economic and social problems. Samoan elite leaders from each territory, including the two Fautua, have attended and taken an important role in meetings of its advisory body representative of the resident populations, the "South Pacific Conference."[1]

In assessing the implications of this great expansion of Samoan horizons, it is clear that the newer "world view" is reinforcing among the Samoans the consciousness of their own "national" identity and ethnic uniqueness. Higher elite leaders are also in the van of a slowly growing trend toward feeling some common identity with other Polynesian and Pacific island peoples, and even a sense of participation in the world community. As a top leader put it: "This

---

[1] See Reports of South Pacific Conferences, obtainable from the South Pacific Commission headquarters in Noumea, New Caledonia.

country will run altogether with the world, and will adhere to any
laws made by the United Nations for the safety of the world."

Samoan images of European and other specific peoples are
likely to be clear only to the extent that these have had living representatives in Samoa. For each known group, too, there tend to be
limited stereotypes based on observed characteristics and roles.
The writers, traveling through remote Samoan villages in 1930,
found the people often hard put to identify them: not fitting, as then
rare scientific visitors, into the standard categories of official,
trader, or orthodox missionary, they were rumored variously to be
missionaries of a new faith or a Hollywood screen star and wife
traveling incognito.

3.   Samoans and "Foreigners"

Samoans have from the time of early contacts called white
men papalangi, often translated as "strangers from the sky." The
term historically tends to convey the eliteness, even superiority,
that was noted earlier as affecting communication with Europeans.
The Samoan speaker will frequently contrast the faaSamoa, or "way
of Samoa" with the faapapalangi or the "foreign way." The general
set of relationships is perhaps caught up in the following frank statement made to the writers by an educated orator with whom they had
special rapport: "It is hard for the Europeans and Samoans to work
together. The views of the Europeans are far more advanced, and
our people are not in a position to be able to keep up. They will
say 'yes' in an argument out of gladness to get out of it, to have the
matter over with instead of prolonging any discusssion."

Effective communication by elites across cultural boundaries
is likely to be facilitated to the extent that the interacting cultural
systems are "compatible" or "congruent." Starting from this most
general viewpoint, Samoan and non-Samoan behavior have involved
from the first some footholds of mutual perception and comprehension
which can bridge the differences between their cultural, societal
and personality characteristics (p. 8). Not least interesting are
congruences that act in a kind of inverse manner. The Samoan way
of life, or at least an idealized image of it, as with the South Sea
tradition more generally, represents to many Europeans a kind of
life in which the types of behavior which bring them tension and anxiety at home—economic pressures, sex prohibitions, the demands
of clock and calendar—are supposedly absent: the "escape-dream"
picturing the Samoans as "happy-go-lucky" dwellers in an easy
"elysium" has had currency in fact since the days of the early white

voyagers. Correspondingly, the Samoan may see the white man as
commanding secrets of power and bountiful resources, and sitting
in fonos of world prestige, which represent levels of authority and
respect beyond those of his own culture. John Williams, the first
white missionary, quotes a Samoan chief as saying, even at his first
arrival:

> I look...at the wisdom of these worshippers
> of Jehovah, and see how superior they are...
> Their ships...can traverse the tempest-
> driven ocean for months with perfect safety...
> Their axes are so hard and sharp... Now I
> conclude that the God who has given to His
> white worshippers these valuable things must
> be wiser than our gods... We all want these
> articles, and my proposition is, that the God
> who gave them should be our God.

The zones of overlap and congruence between Samoan and
Western cultures are constantly expanding through acculturative influences. This is primarily a matter of Samoans selectively learning
elements from whites. But the non-Samoan also gains a working
knowledge of Samoan culture to the extent that he has continuing contacts e.g., etiquette, foods, a scattered vocabulary of useful words.
A tendency therefore exists, though manifested in different degrees
among individuals and groups, for the older stereotypes of the papalangi to give way to increasingly realistic images.

Samoans have had their major contacts with officials and
others from the United States and New Zealand, and before that
from Germany and Great Britain. They may also meet French Roman
Catholic personnel, though these are now few as compared with later
coming English-speaking mission workers. A few individuals from
a considerable number of other Western nationalities have also settled in Samoa, and may have part-Samoan descendants. Some have
also recently come on United Nations Missions. Chinese were formerly numerous in Western Samoa as a plantation labor force, but
nearly all were returned home by the 1930's, and only a few elderly
men and several respected trading families remain; again there are
many part-Samoan descendants. A few Japanese and Indians have
rounded out the Samoan picture of Asian peoples. Samoans also meet
a variety of other Pacific islanders, Melanesian and Polynesian.
Those who have traveled abroad get this range of contacts correspondingly widened.

The images or stereotypes which peoples gain of one another
in cross-cultural contacts as relating to "national character" and
"modal personality" play a vital role in elite communication as representing expectations of behavior and motivation. Communication
tends to be facilitated or retarded according to how far these images
or stereotypes are congruent or otherwise. Elite persons are likely
to conform to the expected roles in order to be understood most effectively.

It would be possible to delineate more or less distinctive
Samoan images and stereotypes for all such groups to the extent
they have emerged significantly. Peretania (Great Britain), for
example, represents an image of historic British benignity and dominance, standing back of New Zealand and still powerful in neighboring South Pacific territories; the symbols of royalty play an important
part here, but the rest of the picture tends to be vague. Some sentiment has been manifested among elite persons to have Peretania
take Samoa under its protection as with neighboring Tonga, but it
is hardly a political force. The German image is mostly vague and
likely to be associated with authoritarian compulsions; but some of
the part-Samoans of German ancestry keep alive the German tradition. The Chinese image is perhaps mostly of a friendly, hard-
working, and generous person, but of low status and "heathen" background. The determining units in the current situation of elite relations are those concerned with the New Zealanders and Americans.
Before these are examined, however, a further general dimension
of interaction needs to be analyzed somewhat more, namely, the
factor of assumed white superiority.

4. Historic White "Superiority"

Elite communication is particularly sensitive where discriminations exist based on concepts of relative superiority and inferiority. This problem, world-wide in scale, is manifested in Samoa to
the extent that the top posts and the ultimate controls of government
continue to be held by whites, implying Samoan subordination and incompetence, and that the social and economic milieu are pervaded
by assumptions and behaviors with these implications.

The images which Europeans still generally possess of themselves and their roles have been the familiar ones of the frontier:
the enlightened developer, the civilized succorer, the knowledgeable
guider, and so forth. The local European resident is likely to recite
readily a series of stereotyped images of a Samoan as "childlike, "
"incompetent, " "gullible, " and otherwise needing, and accepting
gratefully, European leadership. These typical frontier attitudes,

however, make many white newcomers such as those in administration and mission work exceedingly uncomfortable. Both the Americans and the New Zealanders, with strong egalitarian values at home, tend to be under strain and unable to comport themselves well, in the face of the hierarchical aspects of what is increasingly labeled "discrimination." Furthermore, they soon become aware of increasing Samoan tension in the face of such historic relations.

From the Samoan side, as already indicated, a marked ambivalence has shown here. On the one hand such a people has shown from the first days of contact strong respect elements vis-a-vis the European. But on the other, the images of self-worth have not been unduly impaired. Samoan culture allows for attitudes of persistent humility and subordination in the face of an imbalance of relationships. Furthermore, the older aura of respect—even approaching awe in the case of the higher elite persons—has tended to wear thin with greater familiarity and with knowledge of the larger trends of world relations in which assignment of automatic superiority to white peoples has become obsolescent. The Samoan image of themselves here goes back in part to a coloring and idealization of the proud "Golden Age" of the nineteenth century "independent" kingship and the older Samoa back of it; partly it is constructed from the newer focus of a growing desire to be independent at all costs of the white man's dominance, and increasing realization of the latter's powerlessness short of armed force to maintain such dominance.

Both the Samoan elite leader and the European of status, whatever the contemporary communication context, are likely to find overtones of tension along these lines intruding to color interaction. Unless the rare informality of rapport exists, the Samoan will either assume the conventional pose of respect if he so gauges the status of the European, or else he will assert his own superiority in ways which the European is likely to call "arrogant, " "overbearing, " etc. The American or New Zealander may well try to talk as an equal, or as a friend, and find to his puzzlement or exasperation, or chagrin, that a formal and hierarchical behavior is forthcoming. If he assumes the pose of superiority, he gets conformity in the form of deference; but another in the sequence of incidents is consummated which, talked about by Samoans, feeds the currents of sensitivity. The extent to which such factors operate consciously or nonconsciously in any given situation would have to be weighed in terms of the specific interaction case.

Verbal expressions of the Samoan attitudes here are not hard for the field worker to come by. A vivid case in point was an out-

burst by a senior Samoan employee with almost a lifetime of service
in one of the government departments, as part of his explanation of
the modern self-government movements:

> The white people look down on us. Samoan
> employees are paid lower salaries for the
> same work. This is not fair. All this [self-
> government] activity is because of the different
> races of people. Being brown, we don't want
> the white authority upon us. We want to be
> free. This is the real thing. Self-government
> for us is a racial difference. If we have the
> run of self-government it means that we will
> expel the whites. The Samoans look to white
> people as their boss and they don't like that.
> Things cannot be continued as they are now, so
> there must be a change.

A white mission leader said:

> I think there is more than appears on the
> surface. There is not only a desire for self-
> government, but it is the dislike of the white
> man, and this because of the way the white man
> has treated these people. For instance, the
> dentist charges a Samoan 30 shillings cash
> for filling a tooth, but charges a white man
> 10 shillings and sixpence, perhaps on credit
> terms, for the same job... The Samoans
> know these facts and they resent this.

The derivative effects in present-day Samoa of the great
accumulation of social tension here indicated are multiple. On the
Samoan side, as will be seen, they feed strongly the dynamic of
the "self-government" or nationalist movements, of the moves to
get status "equality" with Europeans in many spheres, and support
for education and other benefits which appear to give access to
modern-style "power." More extremely, these tensions have shown
in desires by some to cut off further European entry to Samoa other
than those who marry Samoans; even, at the height of the self-government movement in 1947, to expel resident Europeans and part-
Samoans of European status who will not accept assimilation into
the Samoan milieu; to monopolize trade; to "go back to the old ways";

to root out "subversive" Western influences such as the increased
powers of women and untitled men as over against matai authority.
Though thinking leaders recognize that "protection" by larger external power is needed for the security of a small people they want
it as far as possible "without strings."

5. Samoans and New Zealanders

The images which the Samoan elite have of New Zealanders
are inevitably varied and complex in view of experiences over more
than four decades of administrative and other associations. Currently
there are strong respect elements among both Samoan and part-Samoan
leaders for the integrity of the New Zealand administration, its disinterested devotion to the welfare of the people and territory, diligence,
and willingness to meet the aspirations of self-government. Confidence is often expressed with every show of sincerity, that "New
Zealand is the proper country to protect us, as she has the understanding and knowledge of the people of Samoa, and is familiar to
us"; "New Zealand and the United Nations will give us help and wise
guidance in managing the affairs of Samoa."
This is on the whole a great change from widely prevailing
sentiments over much of the New Zealand regime in Western Samoa,
colored as it was by extensive nonco-operation and opposition. It
reflects the wisdom and restraint of the handful of key officials who
have been engineering the shift toward greater self-government, and
the willingness and ability of the few key top elite leaders of both
Samoans and part-Samoans to co-operate in these efforts. Previously
New Zealanders had borne the brunt over the years of almost every
conceivable criticism which Samoan ingenuity could conjure up:
often being damned as much for doing as for not doing. Few administrations in the history of colonial affairs can have been accused
openly of so much, or made the scapegoat on so many points of
tension.[2] Furthermore, Samoan spokesmen have not been hesitant
to point out that New Zealand is, in international terms, a proportionately "small and weak" country just as Samoa is.

---

[2] The critical literature, including statements of witnesses
before government investigating bodies, opposition newspapers,
petitions, books and pamphlets, reached a special crescendo in the
period 1927 to 1936: see especially Keesing, Modern Samoa, and
Stanner, The South Seas in Transition, for references.

Space does not permit detailed examination of the factors at work except as they come out here and there in the study: New Zealand policies, the impact of specific personalities and events, and pervading all, the desire of the Samoans to throw off alien control and pressure, no matter how "enlightened" and "disinterested. " But note may be taken of the important interplay between the New Zealand and Samoan character structures in the image building and communication processes.

The pervasive group values and modal personality of New Zealanders not only are markedly different from those of Samoans, but in some respects appear to represent extreme opposites. The Samoan, taking his own self-image as the standard, is likely to react negatively, or to misunderstand, such New Zealand traits as egalitarianism, frugality, playing down of display and ostentation, puritan sex standards, straighforward directness and sincerity, strong sense of duty and punctuality, and heavy stress on self-responsibility, internalized guilt-sanction, and repressive (self-regulating) controls in child and adult behavior. To the extent that a Samoan comes to admire and emulate these traits he must inevitably become insecure and critical concerning Samoan behavior.

The New Zealander correspondingly tends to be critical of the image which Samoan traits convey to him, e. g. , the stress on hierarchy, the flair for dramatic display, ceremoniousness, and circumlocution, the emphasis on group-responsibility, with externalized shame-sanction, and suppressive (group-regulating) controls. Especially in the early days of the New Zealand regime, strong efforts were made to reduce the privilege aspects of titleholders, stop "wasteful" property exchanges, reduce "unnecessary" travel and meetings, step up the pace of work, encourage saving, correct sex "deviations, " reward individual initiative as in schools, village baby care, and sanitation. Inevitably such well-intentioned pressures provided overt grievances to which deeper tensions became attached, i. e. , they became the more superficial "causes" of antigovernment movements.

The contrasts drawn here help to explain the remark of a part-Samoan leader, speaking of the popularity of a deceased New Zealand prime minister in Samoa : "It speaks well for him, as Samoans are not inclined to like New Zealanders at any time. " New Zealanders, for their part, are likely to be guardedly critical of Samoan character. The factors involved at times produce dramatic contrasts. The writers have on record numbers of public ceremonies, for example, with the parts played by New Zealand officials clipped to an irreducible minimum, underplayed with close-lipped precision and sharp, restrained motions; the corresponding parts played by Samoan elite, with elaborations of status exhibition, leisurely oratory, superb staging and gestures, full play of emotional content and artistic expression and lavish hospitality and displays of gifts; the slow, dignified, rollingly fluid, and graceful gestures of the Samoans in speech and in action setting off the angular, quiet, often nervously tense behavior of the New Zealanders. The contrasts tend to be sharpest in relation to the lesser New Zealand personnel: the top officials, as a result of diplomatic or comparable training and experience, cope better with this cross-cultural situation. Certainly this "alienness" of the seconded officials from New Zealand is a factor in the strong desire among Western Samoan leaders to replace them as fast as possible with local-born persons.

It can be understood why, except for the still few Samoans and part-Samoans who have been strongly influenced by New Zealand contacts, and the very few New Zealanders who have established local rapport, relations between the local elites and New Zealanders do not tend to have great closeness or warmth. Attitudes from the Samoan side tend to be ambivalent, between a grudging admiration and a tolerant dislike verging at times towards pity. "They seem to get so little fun out of life!" was a remark heard repeatedly in local circles. On the other side of the relationship the New Zealander also shows some ambivalence. A helpful factor is that he displays on the whole less racial prejudice than is customary in such territories. He is also more genuinely and disinterestedly devoted to local welfare than is usual in a colonial area, and is genuinely egalitarian in attitudes. There is, however, enough carry-over of older slants to make most New Zealanders avoid easy comradely behavior with Samoans, both in and out of government, and keep a considerable social distance. "Fraternization" is not only officially discouraged but tends to bear the stigma of "going native." It is overtly symbolic that the New Zealand administration has never permitted any Samoan government employee or even schoolboy to wear trousers: a Samoan waistcloth and bare feet or leather sandals are required; to date the Legislative Assembly has made no move to change this situation, the Samoan style having developed increasing symbolic meaning in relation to "nationalism" and cultural conservation.

6. Samoans and Americans

The images which Samoans have of white Americans are conditioned by the highly selective character of contacts with United States citizens. A small number of American residents, mainly establishing themselves prior to 1900 in both territorial zones, apparently demonstrated the character traits popularly counted "Ameri-

can, " e. g., go-getting in business, prudent, egalitarian. These
characteristics tend to persist where they have left part-Samoan
families. Beyond these few, contacts have been mainly with United
States Navy personnel with transient shipboard personnel, and with
the short-lived but large influx of Marines and other military forces
in both territories during World War II. In American Samoa, civilian
government personnel have been represented in any number only from
1951 on.

The Navy relationships which dominated the American Samoa
scene for a half century have set the main patterns of communication
behavior. Naval officer and enlisted rankings and attitudes regarding
rank fitted with great congruence into Samoan elite and non-elite
rankings and attitudes. The elite in both groups did not "fraternize"
with rank and file people within or across the cultural boundaries.
Outside of the officer personnel, relations of enlisted men with
Samoans were as far as possible restricted, but so far as they occurred they tended to be on an intimate, casual level. As Samoans
were trained to specialized work within the Navy establishment they
were for the most part treated by American fellow workers as "junior" colleagues, at least in more recent years. One of the writers
commented on this relationship as it was demonstrated by a naval
medical officer in discussing the medical cases of the day over cig-
arettes and coffee with his Samoan medical practitioners, along
with other colleagues. The medical officer said, rather gruffly,
"Good God, they're human, aren't they! And they're probably smarter
than I am to have gotten where they are with the amount of schooling
they've been given!"

Senior Navy officers in the ceremonious proceedings of naval
affairs carefully fitted the chiefs in with their own hierarchy, paying
meticulous attention to protocol. Drills and parades provided a form
of public display as dear to Samoan as to Navy hearts. The main discriminations about which much was heard was the exclusiveness of
the officers' club and the restriction of liquor to naval personnel.
However, the bans applied to all local civilians including whites and
part-Samoans, not specifically to Samoans as such. No attempt was
made to restrict Samoans employed by the administration to Samoan-
style dress as in Western Samoa. The "Fita Fita" or local Samoan
Navy guard had a distinctive, Samoan-style uniform, of which they
were proud, but other Samoans wore regulation service uniforms or
else could elect Western-style civilian clothing appropriate to their
jobs.

Unquestionably there were incidents of private discrimination
and prejudice, but on the whole there was less obvious and externalized "social distance." Samoans for the most part were employed

in unskilled or semiskilled jobs, but those who achieved status moved fairly comfortably in the American circles to which they had access. In the closing period of the Naval administration, more American civilians were brought in and developed still further the "colleague" relationship with their Samoan fellow workers as part of the task of training personnel so far as possible to replace white mainlanders. Numbers of these white civilians were from Hawaii or California, and used to working with fellow Americans of different racial backgrounds.

The wartime contacts with United States armed forces units would make a special study in themselves. Gray armadas landed massive materiel and many hundreds of men in both territories. Bases were built; roads cut; needs for workers brought the activities of whole villages out of their traditional round; money circulated freely; military supplies stimulated new wants and tastes, at least in the immediate perspectives; in spite of formal limits set on fraternization, a crop of several thousand part-Samoan children trace back to the period. After the withdrawal, very large sums were dispensed for years by court process to cover damage claims and displacement from land, e.g., cutting of coconut trees, killing of pigs. A Western Samoan chief gave a kind of benediction when in a speech he said, his eyes alight with memory, "They gave us money and they gave us love"; the palm of his outstretched hand seemed full of piled-up "greenbacks" as he continued, "Se tupe, se tupe, se tupe...," "Money, money, money..."

With United States civilian officials now entirely in charge, on behalf of the Department of the Interior, Samoans have opportunities to gain what are perhaps more representative impressions of modal American behavior. Furthermore, this combines with constantly expanding knowledge of American character gained from a growing number of Samoans returning from travel, schooling, and employment, in Hawaii and the mainland United States. The images and stereotypes are correspondingly becoming more complex, with increasing ambivalances to create tensions.

Samoans are exceedingly appreciative of the prestige and power of the United States, though under civilian control they have not seen Congress dispense "wealth" in the form of the budget subsidies which they expected and some believe had been promised earlier by a representative of the Interior Department. The strength of their loyalties to United States nationality will be shown in later discussions of the question of possible unification of the two territories and the self-government issue, both historically prominent goals of the Western Samoan elite. At the same time there are American

influences which they clearly fear to have loose in Samoa either by
way of Congressional action or through private contacts.

The Samoans are particularly sensitive today to the pressures
of egalitarian tendencies and American initiative. These, they feel,
are threatening not only to the traditional social system but also to
the integrity of the Samoan people in the face of possible aggressive
assertion by white Americans of a right to migrate freely into the
territory, get land, start business enterprises, and otherwise "en-
croach" or "push the Samoan aside, " on the basis of the equal rights
principle. They are well aware of the situation of the Hawaiian in
Hawaii, and fear its repetition in Samoa: "We do not want big busi-
nesses, hotels, tourist resorts, to be developed at the expense of
Samoan rights; we do not want some rich man forcing himself in so
as to get a private estate for his playground. " Samoan leaders are
here aware enough of weaknesses and vulnerabilities among their
own people where large money temptations are concerned. In recent
years there has been a complete rejection by the American Samoan
elite of proposed organic legislation for the territory out of fear that
Congress will not provide protective safeguards, especially as proposals along these lines were deleted from the organic legislation
for Guam passed in 1950 (p. 36). Under Samoan pressures, and
also as an executive policy matter, the Interior Department has
refrained from breaking down the special local legislation developed
under Navy auspices, and indeed traditional in American territorial
policies.

Part of the reason for apparently less historic tension in
interpersonal relations between the Samoan and American elites than
in the corresponding Western Samoa situation could be that there
seems on the whole to be less extreme contrast between Samoan
character and personality modes and those of Americans than in the
case of Samoans as over against New Zealanders. In some respects
at least, the typical American pattern lies somewhere midway between
the New Zealand and the Samoan pattern. Americans enjoy considerable
display dramatics. Social conformity stands higher in proportion to
conscience drive as a motivating force. There is considerably less
repression of emotional reactions and less insistence on puritan
codes in many aspects of the sex roles. Unquestionably frugality
is not a cardinal American virtue; like the Samoan the American
does quite a lavish amount of conspicuous spending and gift-giving.
The writers took part, for example, in the celebration of Christmas
1950 in Pago Pago, and were impressed with the extent to which
American and Samoan patterns were meshed into the Christmas drama.
The round of parties, decorated Christmas trees with gifts heaped

beneath, carol singers and Samoan style dancers, church services, and festivities seemed to involve almost everyone in the area—American, Samoan, and part-Samoan—and to exhaust just about all available bank accounts.

Moreover, with the very great variety of Americans in terms of background—Mexican-Americans, Italian-Americans, Chinese and Japanese Americans, etc.—there is much less rigidity of pattern as to what makes an American. The Samoan can fit in with less self-consciousness of his Samoanness; can find areas in the United States where he fits fairly comfortably with minimal discrimination. In New Zealand he must conform essentially to a well-established Polynesian-white situation developed primarily through relations with the indigenous Maori population.[3] This is not one of serious discrimination but it emphasizes a social separation which is not without its discriminatory edges and it is strongly tinged with Polynesian "cultural nationalism, " and hence reinforces the sense of "Samoanness. " The Samoan does not readily "lose himself" in the New Zealand milieu, as he can to a large extent in the United States, becoming primarily another American. Certainly these seem to be factors in establishing the directions of aspirations and goals to the extent that they differ in the two Samoas. They account considerably for less overt preoccupation with the matter of status equivalence in the American territory, and the willingness to make American citizenship the status goal provided it can coexist with protective legislation for the Samoan population group.

7.   The Part-Samoans

On a racial frontier members of a part-indigenous group play a vital role as mediators. The status afforded to them shapes the kind and content of mediation they provide. Any blockages in their mediator roles which may be thrown up, e.g., as by the use of derogatory names or legal devices, that lower their dignity, restrict their roles, or disguise their relation to the parent stocks, are likely to affect communication processes in marked degree.

The Samoan situation offers a particularly useful case study of this dimension of communication behavior. The status of the part-Samoan group particularly in early days was high, and the de-

---

[3] A source for comparing these latter relations with Samoan—New Zealander relations is Beaglehole, E. Some Modern Maoris.

scendants of legitimate marriages were termed "Europeans." This gave them prestige, but tended to obscure their Samoanness. In Western Samoa, legal restrictions prevented their accession to Samoan titles, and denied them ownership of Samoan lands, leaving them in a confined and increasingly precarious economic condition. In this territory particularly, having the status of a European made the part-Samoan, if not a "foreigner," at least something of an outsider. In consequence it has tended to block the part-Samoan historically from a fully overt role in mediation. In American Samoa, social rather than strict legal definitions have had some-what the same results; though here legislation requires a part-Samoan to have "at least three-quarters Samoan blood" to hold a matai title. own Samoan land, or otherwise exercise Samoan-style rights. [4]

As on many comparable frontiers, mating occurred freely in early days. Individuals of part-Samoan ancestry either merged back into the indigenous milieu, or else identified themselves with the non-Samoan parent groups, especially if formal marriages were sanctioned. Numbers of European settlers married women of elite status, and so they and their children became influential adjuncts of powerful kin groups, notably by way of the feangainga relation-ship, i.e., the tie to a sister and her descendants (p. 51).

In more recent decades the presence of white women and other factors produced a more rounded white social milieu, in which racial attitudes of the home countries have tended to operate at least covertly. "Mixed" marriages now consist mainly of unions between part-Samoans of various proportions of European, Samoan, and Asian ancestry, between part-Samoans and Samoans, and less fre-quently between whites and part-Samoans. More "social distance" tends to have opened out than formerly between part-Samoans and whites, especially of the official groups. To the uncertain economic status of the part-Samoans has therefore been added uncertainty in social status.

---

[4] In Western Samoa, about 5.5 percent of the total land area was purchased by Europeans. This "freehold" land is now held al-most entirely by part-Samoans, and the government has also opened up some blocks of government land for settlement by land-needy part-Samoan families. In American Samoa, such freehold lands are negligible, so that the part-Samoan must make his way through trading, government employment, and other non-farming pursuits.

On the political side, the administrations have always frowned on "interference" by resident Europeans in Samoan affairs, and at crisis points have penalized it.   Robert Louis Stevenson gives vivid accounts of conflicts between officialdom even in the days of the Samoan kings and such settlers as himself.   Today, with the dying off or outmigration of older white residents, and stiff barriers against new white settlement, the "Europeans" are now almost exclusively of part-Samoan ancestry, either as descended from former marriages of European fathers or as "legitimized" to such status by court process.   They are also the most rapidly increasing population element, numbering some 7,000, and heavily weighted to the prereproductive and reproductive age levels.   Their kin ties mesh in with Samoan family lines more or less throughout the whole society. In spite of their differential status, they are likely to be warmly accepted by their Samoan relatives to the fullest extent that they are prepared to exercise social and personal ties.   The official policies relating to European "non-interference" have therefore tended to become an anomaly, even a dangerous blockage in interaction relationships. [5]

Most socially recognized part-Samoans live in the urban settings, and as they come to adulthood try for Western-type jobs in the government and commercial services.   Many have left to make their way in the metropolitan countries.   In Western Samoa, as Europeans, they vote in a European electorate, separate from Samoans, which sends a minority of five members to the Legislative Assembly; in American Samoa, until 1954, they have been able to put themselves on a roll for "persons not living under matai control, " taking part in the election of two members in the Lower House.

A considerable number of part-Samoan families and their outstanding men and women members are in every sense elite in Samoa.   Holding high positions in government or in private plantation and business enterprises, well educated, and highly respected, they comprise an upper stratum of the resident urban community.

---

[5] In Western Samoa, a part-Samoan of European status can participate actively in the Samoan system, with its land and title opportunities, only if he elects to be "naturalized" by court process to Samoan status; very few have done so, presumably because of reluctance to yield the prestige and other associations of the former status, and some of those who have tried it have had their status reversed again.

But the economic status of the group has been on the whole low and
precarious, for want of enough salaried openings, and lack of land
and capital.   Their schooling had until fairly recent years been left
in Western Samoa mainly to the Roman Catholic mission. [6]

Attempts have been made by various observers to define
the cultural milieu and modal character structure of the part-Samoans.
Opinion has ranged from mass stigmatizing of this group, though
usually nowadays in covert talk only, to acknowledgment, grudging
or otherwise, that they are capable of showing special competence and
leadership whenever opportunities are favorable.   The part-Samoan
bears in his person a dual role.   He is in one self a European, with
characteristic drives and aspirations of this heritage.   He is also
a Samoan, with deep feeling for Samoa and things Samoan, nearly
always familiar with the language and custom and keeping active
his kinship connections which often lead by way of a mother into
the Samoan elite.   How far the two may mesh together effectively or
involve clashes, discontinuities, and frustrations in his childhood
and adulthood can produce the range from a well-adjusted leader,
influential in both parental groups, to a disoriented and thoroughly
unhappy personality.   There is therefore a very great range in the
characteristics and degrees of adjustment of part-Samoans.   Taking
into account the fact that, for better or worse, virtually every part-
Samoan of dual heritage becomes something of a linguistic and cultural mediator between the Samoan and Western heritages, it can be
sensed how important are the social and legal definitions pertaining
to them.

The images which other groups have of the part-Samoan, and
the part-Samoans have of other groups and of themselves, appear to
be very complex.   An attempt to tabulate their main characteristics
briefly can be essayed as follows:

1. Whites to part-Samoan. Whites tend to look at part-Samoans
in terms of scientifically inadequate and prejudice-ridden stereotypes,
abroad especially in the English-speaking world, relating to supposed
deleterious effects of miscegenation.   The very term "half-caste"
tends to evoke guilt feelings, to imply inferiority in human terms, to
arouse an expectation of incompetence.   Personalized contacts, together with knowledge of the economic and social record of the part-
Samoan group, can and does overcome this stereotype.   But the battle
has usually to be fought again with each official or other newcomer,

---

[6] The fullest statement of the part-Samoan position treated
historically, is in Keesing, op. cit., chapter XI.

and the misunderstandings and resentments evoked remain as persistent factors to color the relations of whites and part-Samoans.

2. Samoan to part-Samoan. Samoans have no such prejudices in their own sociocultural media. Historically they have accepted the part-Samoan child without significant distinction. But to the extent that the part-Samoan accepts the role of a European he lays himself open to being "tarred with the brush" of foreignism, and any undue pretensions to distinctiveness or superiority on his part will be resented. Furthermore, there has been a recent tendency for white evaluations of the "half-caste" (in Samoan, afakasi) to influence the attitudes of some Samoan leaders. Over against this, as pointed out above, the exercise of kinship ties continues to link most part-Samoans usually quite closely to the Samoan society. A Samoan usually plays his "European status" relatives to the hilt for all they are worth in gifts, loans, and hospitality. As they live by the European economy, and must remain solvent, most of these part-Samoans have had to delimit carefully the extent to which they will participate in the "faaSamoa." Difficult as it is in Samoa, they have to say "no." Inevitably this creates tensions at times, and feelings that the part-Samoan is selfish and stingy—both heinous Samoan sins. The Samoan is frequently both proud of his "European" relatives and sore at them. Increasingly, however, as Samoan elite are seeking to build up islands of personal possessions and wealth in the sea of family ownership that wears them down, Samoans are coming to understand this dilemma. Those part-Samoans who achieve eliteness in Samoan eyes will be seen as exercising a profound influence as well as arousing keen respect.

3. Part-Samoan to white. Part-Samoans who set value on their European role are likely to feel more competent and "at home" than the white outsider, yet still feel a sense of insecurity and frustration that the latter's prejudices generate. Their images of whites are therefore wide-ranging, from extremes of hatred and hostility in relation to some individuals to profound warmth, gratefulness, and friendship where the white person is responsive and prejudice-free. The use or avoidance of the word "half-caste" by a white person is likely to be a particularly crucial matter in fostering bad or good relations.

4. Part-Samoan to Samoan. It is significant that the Samoans are likely to be spoken of by the part-Samoans sometimes with the "we" pronoun and sometimes with the "they." In general the part-Samoans feel themselves to be of higher prestige and greater competence than the full Samoan. Many part-Samoans also appear to have a carry-over of their outside parental prejudices, and to look

down on the Samoan with attitudes that may be the more tension-
charged because of the pressures they themselves are under. Part-
Samoans are likely to see themselves as the "natural leaders" of
the local-born society, and as will be seen some elite individuals
are providing such leadership with effectiveness.

    5. <u>Part-Samoan to part-Samoan</u>. As a population element
the part-Samoans have had little organization or coherence. In
their own internal relations they appear to be particularly sensitive
to status factors. They are broken up into many cliques and have
their own complex social hierarchy from high to low, stemming
from their parental statuses, marital ties, economic achievement,
education, and other definitions of prestige and success. Factionalism has been highly prevalent, e. g., on the self-government
issue they have ranged from complete opposition to complete support and major leadership. On the whole, however, the part-Samoan
group, under the influence of some strong leaders, seems to have
become increasingly conscious of its rather critical collective role
in the construction of the changing Samoa, as will be seen below.

    New Zealand has frequently spelled out an official goal of
"maintaining the purity" of the Samoan heritage, not only in relation
to whites but also to the large number of Chinese laborers formerly
in their territory. This inevitably has reflected upon the worth of
the part-Samoans and added fuel to resentments. The New Zealand
authorities have also had transparent worries about the loyalty of
some of the descendants of the Germans who were in the saddle
until World War I. On the economic side they have tried to subordinate the interests of the white and part-Samoan trader and planter
groups to the "welfare" of the Samoans. Under such pressures it
became almost inevitable that part-Samoans should exercise leverage
against the administration through influence over their Samoan relatives.

    In the <u>Mau</u> movement of the 1920's certain leading local white
and part-Samoan families and personalities were so deeply enmeshed
in its leadership that New Zealand deported several key members of
the group. The outstanding historical figure here was a powerful
part-Samoan leader, the late Mr. O. F. Nelson, head of a major
trading firm, who figured in petitions to the old League of Nations.
He was not only Nelson, the Scandinavian-descended trader with
enterprises throughout Samoa, the only status by which he was rec-
ognised in a legal sense. He was also Taisi, a Samoan elite person,
linked through his mother by the <u>feangainga</u> relation to the "royal"
Satupua line. In this latter role, when he and others felt that private
trading and planting interests were threatened by various forms of

government aid to Samoan enterprises and by the official policy of
repatriating Chinese labor, and when his Satupua kinsmen took stands
against government activities in Samoan spheres, he undertook leadership in developing what became the Mau movement and assuming the
role of a major spokesman for it.   In the process he transformed
himself into the paramount figure of the time, a "patriot" who spent
a fortune and suffered banishment and imprisonment in the antigovernment struggle.   He was one of quite a number of such non-
Samoan and part-Samoan leaders.   The self-government movements
in both territories, indeed, have leaned heavily upon local white and
part-Samoan advisers in formulating their petitions and in other
"braintrusting" activities, though usually behind the scenes.   They
have been the main modernizers of Samoan "nationalism. "

The self-government movement of 1946-47 in Western Samoa,
leading to the investigation by the United Nations Mission, provided
something of a crisis point in the position of the part-Samoan group.
While the self-government petition appears to have been prepared
in co-operation with certain part-Samoans, the deep well of Samoan
feeling on matters of European discrimination had risen so by the
time of the Mission that many part-Samoans felt themselves to be in
considerable jeopardy.   There was talk among the Samoans of "Samoa
for the Samoans, " with clear implications that the part-Samoans were
not included.   Samoans were facing the fact with bitterness that the
advantages of the part-Samoan in educational level, ability in the
English language, general at-home-ness and "know-how" in Western
culture, and freedom from the ties of co-operativeness as defined
by the Samoan system gave the part-Samoans a competitive advantage
in all cross-cultural situations, and would continue to do so for a long
time to come.   Obviously, this new enterprise of self-government
would have to be such a cross-cultural enterprise.   Part-Samoans,
too, realized more clearly than heretofore that as a minority in
Samoa they could be overruled by numbers, and that the current
educational level of these numbers made it a terrifying thought.
Both groups, therefore, were aware of the need for compromise, and
on the whole gladly accepted the arrangements subsequently worked
out.

A recognition by the New Zealand authorities that the part-
Samoans are just as legitimately "residents" of Samoa as the full
Samoans has become a vital factor in the present political situation.
This has been one of the cornerstones of the new policies being de-
veloped since 1947.   As a result, outstanding leaders in the part-
Samoan group have for the first time worked closely with the New
Zealand authorities in promoting the necessary transitional steps
toward fuller self-government, and in influencing Samoan opinion

away from unrealistic goals of immediate autonomy. This has been
notably so with the elected representatives of the European community in the Legislative Assembly, nearly all part-Samoans in recent years. Recently the New Zealand government, supported by
recommendations from U. N. Missions, has been trying to abolish
the legal distinction of European by giving all residents of the territory a common citizenship status (pp. 30-31, 225-26).

    The corresponding problem in American Samoa is whether
any "fraction" of parental derivation should be used to mark off
Samoan rights, as with the historic measure of "three-quarter
Samoan blood. " This has often been discussed by the Samoan leaders
in the legislature, with sentiment at times veering toward an extension of Samoan rights to all persons of part-Samoan ancestry. In
1946, the legislature proposed that anyone with "one drop of Samoan
blood" receive such rights. There is still fear, however, of opening
the door freely to all persons of part-Samoan ancestry, especially
where they may be living, or even have been born, outside Samoa
and so come as strangers and potential exploiters. It is possible
that the solution will lie in requiring a minimum number of years of
local residence as a basis for Samoan status, as is now necessary
to qualify for a matai title; in the latter case, five years. Alterna-
tively, a formula recently accepted by the Legislative Assembly in
Western Samoa may be adopted, namely that in the case of a Samoan
man married to a non-Samoan, the wife and children have unques-
tioned rights, but in the case of a Samoan woman marrying a non-
Samoan man, a personal decision in each case should be made by
the Executive Council. (The latter procedure was established at
the suggestion of the High Commissioner, so as to forestall any new
wave of beachcombing by way of marriage.)

    With a general retreat from official policies defining part-
Samoans as if they were a foreign element, a social atmosphere is
now being fostered in which they are much more free to elect their
own roles in the community. The edges of relationships between
Samoans and part-Samoans are clearly softening. The term "local
born" is replacing the term "half-caste. " The rapidly increasing
crop of younger part-Samoans, several hundred of whom are now
coming to adulthood yearly, may choose, so far as they wish, to
associate themselves with their Samoan kinsmen without feeling that
they lose the prestige of "European" status. Conversely, full Samoans
may elect to move more into the Western way of life without finding
legal barriers to their participation. Differentiation, indeed, is already discernibly lessened from the social point of view. This is
the more so as a number of the elite Samoans have moved strongly
if still selectively in the direction of adopting Western behavior,

and so the differences between them and elite members of the part-Samoan group wear thinner. Some key marriages, too, between Samoan and part-Samoan elite members have added kinship to other social dimensions here. With the new atmosphere, the images which were pictured above as typical of part-Samoan relationships, especially with the Samoans, will undoubtedly be modified. Tensions which have marked the character structure of the part-Samoan group should also lessen. A top Samoan leader pointed the way when he said:

> We look on the part-Samoans as Samoans. We
> want them to come in with us, with their abilities—
> they know more. But they must come as equals
> in our country. If they advocate a superior status,
> or act as exploiting merchants and tax collectors,
> then they must be treated as foreigners.

8. Elite Mediators

To this point the discussion has covered the more general images or stereotypes which bear in upon elite communication across cultural boundaries, seen against the background of the groups concerned and their historic relationships. In closer focus, however, the effectiveness of such intercultural communication depends heavily upon a smaller number of persons who carry the major roles as mediators. Factors arising out of the special statuses and personal characteristics of these mediating individuals may make or mar a "message" or mediation process. Already reference has been made here and there to elite persons who, through strategic position, skill in negotiation, powerful personality, or other characteristics are particularly influential. On such intercultural frontiers the number of persons who carry the brunt of highly significant, top-level interaction is characteristically very small indeed.

In Western Samoa, the two "royal" chiefs who serve as Fautua or "High Advisers" fall into this category—one, Tamasese, is the most powerful and articulate Samoan personality of the present day. This Fautua is well-educated and speaks very good English. He also has an influential, well-educated part-Samoan wife who was brought up in the European community, is well-traveled, widely read, and of a leading mediator family.

Also outstanding as mediating individuals in that territory from the Samoan side are some ten other politically prominent titleholders, several of them of part-European descent though holding Samoan status. Nearly all have been at one time or another in the central legislative and advisory bodies or in administrative employ. Back of these are a considerable range of Samoan government employees such as interpreters, medical practitioners, nurses, school-teachers, and others who carry more specialized mediator roles. On the more isolated island of Savaii two educated younger chiefs not in government service have been leaders in economic experiments in their communities looking towards modernized adaptations of work effort by way of co-operative organization and the introduction of better production techniques. Each such personality deserves a "life history" record to reveal his special characteristics and motivations.

In American Samoa the number of mediator individuals is somewhat larger in proportion to the Samoan population. Outstanding in recent years has been the long-time presiding officer of the House of Representatives, High Talking Chief M. Tuiasosopo, who usually "speaks" for the territory on ceremonious occasions, and commands good English and a wide reading knowledge. In the Manu'a islands High Chief Tufele, for a number of years resident in Los Angeles before he took this title (the senior one since abolition of the "royal" Tuimanu'a title in 1905), is the outstanding mediator.

Further figures, in political and official circles and otherwise, include notably a considerable number of the former naval "Fita Fita" guards and civilian employees who acquired through years of service in the local U.S. Navy establishment a great familiarity with matters American. Numbers of American Samoans of full or part-Samoan ancestry have also lived in Hawaii and some on the United States mainland. Not least familiar with things American are women distributed through the territory with experience as nurses, teachers, and in other roles which brought them into close association with whites.

From the non-Samoan side, the elite communication roles in both territories have been considerably dominated, as indicated in the last section, by persons of European status having part-Samoan ancestry. The writers would count some fifteen part-Samoans in government and private life, including several women, as the outstanding mediators in Western Samoa. A number of them have been active in the legislature and the European Citizens' Committees. Most influential is a business man of American background on his father's side, who has generally been named to take the major leadership vis-à-vis government in recent years on behalf of the European community. In American Samoa members of several outstanding

part-Samoan families have carried the main mediation tasks on
Tutuila and in Manu'a.

The picture is even more sparse when entirely non-Samoan
groups are considered. The small number of private resident
Europeans now left in the two Samoas tend to keep out of overt politics in the interests of their storekeeping, mission work, and other
concerns, and so tend to exercise a backstage role only. The Apia
community in Western Samoa, especially, is large enough for a
number of Europeans to live with surprisingly little direct and effective contact with Samoans other than at the servant level. This
European element, the present counterpart of what has often been
called "the beach" in South Pacific islands, tends to be a main breeding
ground for the stereotype, the "inside story, " the gossip and rumor,
which the visiting journalist or tourist hears about such places.

Too often as well the government official assigned to such
territories from the metropolitan country keeps equally apart from
Samoan contacts, building up an "island" of immigrant life, and
basing his relations with Samoans on these same stereotypes and
rumors. The number of Europeans in either territory who have
commanded effective channels of communication with the Samoan
elite, other than in terms of the limited and formal interaction called
for in their official, mission, or commercial capacities, has been
very small indeed. Most effective, certainly, are some of the older
resident missionary workers, and at times these have been called
on to help in governmental mediation tasks. In Western Samoa, for
a number of years, only one New Zealand official had an intimate
enough knowledge of the Samoan language to be able to communicate
with the Samoan elite in their own cultural context. In turn, this
dubiously informed European group has carried the main weight of
reporting back to the metropolitan countries and to the international
bodies.

This pattern has fortunately been broken to the extent that in
recent years the New Zealand High Commissioner in Western Samoa
has been outstandingly successful in mediation particularly connected
with self-government planning. In American Samoa, too, a chief
judge who is practically the only white civilian to have had any long
tenure in office in the territory has had the confidence of the Samoan
leaders.

The last instances are illustrative of the influence of idiosyncratic factors which together with the chance fall of events can often
play a critical role in situations as sensitive as those in the two
Samoas. It may be said rather categorically that the present peaceful yet highly dynamic situation in Western Samoa represents a

balance of forces negotiated largely by the three highest ranking elite persons, one in each of the groups concerned: Samoan, part-Samoan, and European.

The situation has many other unique variables. For example, the self-government issue between New Zealand and the Samoans, which will be discussed more fully below, has been coming to a head at a time when by chance two of the ordinarily powerful "royal" titles and their adherents have been in obscurity on account of the deaths of their previously influential titleholders and the nonemergence as yet of their young successors as power factors (p. 31). Furthermore, one of the two Fautua (High Advisers) spoken of above, also rather younger, has been willing mostly on the basis of personal and intimate factors to yield the primacy of negotiation leadership to the other older and more experienced Fautua. In other words, the present New Zealand impetus toward self-government is occurring under exceptional circumstances where a unique upset in the balance of elite forces at the "royal" level has enabled one leader to emerge as carrying the main "privilege and dignity" on behalf of the Samoans and with a public front of atypical unity back of him. Events at the recent Constitutional Convention, however, suggest that this may be a temporary situation only (p. 30). Relations among small intimate alignments of top elite persons appear to be particularly open to sudden crises and rapid change.

Samoan elite members were spoken of earlier as having become nimble at shifting from Samoan to European types of communication, as in ceremoniousness, pacing of negotiation, and linguistic modes. Experienced mediators are likely to become adept at escaping the rigidity of the conventional images and stereotypes, and at manipulating the interacting traditions freely in an effort to reach a decision or get an advantage. The skilled European negotiator will use at times the Samoan methods of faamolemole (polite humility), musu (passive opposition), or allusion and metaphor; in turn a Samoan will use a Western-style parliamentary maneuver or written memorandum. A mediator may also deliberately adjust his behavior to the images or stereotypes when this seems to offer best recognition by the other of what is in hand.

Pitfalls lie at hand for the person becoming a skilled mediator. There is a possibility that the elite person will become so enmeshed in the role that he loses touch with opinion in his own group, becomes suspect as being unduly alien, and so loses confidence. Accusations of this kind have even been made against the Fautua, living as they are in European homes in the town. Any metropolitan official who gains knowledge of the local language and so "fraternizes" in ways considered unorthodox by the European group lays himself open to the

same charge.   The part-Samoan mediator alone seems to escape
this charge—or perhaps rather a halfway implication of this kind is
so implicit in his dual heritage that it tends to go without much over
comment.   The likelihood of a mediator losing contact with the group
would appear to be lessened to the extent that communication behavior
is kept public.   This point is consistent with earlier statements on
the greater rigidity of open contexts for negotiation (p. 140).   It is
also in such public settings that mediators tend to adhere to roles
fitting the images and stereotypes current in their group.   To deviate
unduly would open the way to possible misinterpretation and misunderstanding.

A final question here, and one by no means easy to answer
except in the most impressionistic terms, is how far successful
mediators show any tendencies toward common or modally emphasized
characteristics.   This is the more difficult because the kinds of individuals who emerge as mediators tend to be those most affected
by acculturative conditions, and so to show a wide range of characteristics in terms of the varying roles they carry and the stresses
that fall on them.   Several thumbnail-size cases may be given to
indicate their variety:

> Case A: An important titleholder in a rural
> district of Western Samoa; member of the
> Legislative Assembly; son of a pastor and
> formerly a schoolteacher; keeps a local store
> with wife, down-coast from his home village;
> has European-style home along with Samoan
> houses; writer and producer of Samoan-style
> plays; strong feelings of inadequacy in political
> and economic affairs led him to ask the writers
> to send him textbooks; rising rapidly to top
> circle of Samoan mediators.

> Case B: German-Samoan who has changed
> legal status back and forth several times from
> European to Samoan; has oscillated from being
> pro- to antigovernment; prefers to hold minor
> title but has risen to power as "speaker" in
> government affairs for one of the traditionally
> most important districts; has profitable store
> with virtual district monopoly; tense personality;
> feels possessed with power when orating; for
> periods unable to sleep at night without light
> and a kinsman present.

Case C: Leading orator of a traditionally
important village; taken as child to Fiji by
sister married to a European and given
European education; returned as storekeeper
and government interpreter for a period;
maladjusted for official employment by
habits of wearing European clothing and
shoes; has European-style house, operates
store, and acts as district postmaster;
reads overseas magazines; sent children
abroad for good education; is sometimes in
conflict with conservative opinion and Samoan
central leadership.

Case D: a young chief of "royal" descent,
with high title in an outer district; has lived
at Apia and in New Zealand periodically; has
drunk heavily at times; in his rural village runs
store with wife; refuses to participate in
"politics"; used authority to compel extreme
innovations among adherents, including hard
regular work to develop community cocoa
plantations, admission of nontitled people into
village government; swings between extremes of
Samoanism to desire to throw over everything
and go to live abroad; in recent letter to writers
states that he and wife have moved to live away
from the village in a new store in one of their
plantation areas. [7]

Case E: A younger chief from an outer district,
son and successor to one of the few innovating
chiefs of 20 years ago; named to a term as
head of the Fono of Faipule "on the basis of
confidence and ability rather than rank" and

---

[7] He writes as of 1954: "Samoan people still carry on their
old nature; trouble is the nature of everyone in each village over the
islands; they are calling it 'self-government' but they still keep on
the same thing." His wife writes: "We are still in a narrow life,
sometimes happy, sometimes worry. Our country is fine, but
trouble is the nature of our race."

perhaps as not being enmeshed in political
jockeying for power; established producing
and trading co-operative in his district,
admitting untitled as well as titled persons.

A certain helpfulness is afforded here, perhaps, by a list
recently essayed by a research group of what might be called "type"
figures relevant to decision-making under dynamic change and resistance to change, in this case within the setting of "international
politics. "[8] On the basis of this list, applied to elite members of
the three major groups in the Samoan situation, the following is
the spot evaluation of the writers as to their frequency and capacity
as cross-cultural mediators. [9]

Category	Samoans	Part-Samoans	Whites
1. The Communicator (Leader type with special skills in mediation)	Rare; very good	Fairly frequent; very good	Rare; very good
2. The Innovator (Rebel against normative, risk-taker, original thinker)	Rare; good	Frequent; good	Fairly frequent; fair
3. The Traditionalist (Repository of precedent)	Frequent; poor	Rare; poor	Fairly frequent; fair
4. The Literalist (Strict interpreter of rules)	Fairly frequent; poor	Rare; poor	Frequent; poor
5. The Power-Seeker (Upwardly mobile person concerned with own status)	Frequent; fair	Frequent; fair	Fairly rare; poor

[8] Snyder, R. C. , Bruck, H. W. , and Sapin, B. , Decision-
making as an Approach to the Study of International Politics, p. 115.
[9] In each instance the first word-judgment refers to frequency
in the situation, on a rating of "rare, " "fairly rare, " "fairly frequent, " "frequent"; the second word-judgment refers to capacity as
elite mediators, on a rating of "poor, " "fair, " "good, " and "very
good. "

6. The Career Servant (Self-consciously expert, identified with correct role)	Rare; fair	Fairly frequent; fair	Very frequent; fair

In addition, the writers would like to add three other figures who appear frequently in culture-change situations:

Category	Samoans	Part-Samoans	Whites
7. The Reformer (Innovator with dedication to new group goals)	Rare; good	Rare; good	Fairly frequent; fair
8. The Zealot (Fanatical one-track dedication as above)	Rare; poor	Rare; poor	Fairly rare; poor
9. The Reversionist (Dedicated to restoration of real or reformulated older goals)	Fairly frequent; poor	Rare; poor	Fairly rare; poor

The general tenor of such a rough grid of judgments, when scrutinized as a whole, is that in the Samoan group mediators lean to the conservative side, and good mediators are still infrequent; that in the European group the emphasis is on the more formalistic behavioral categories, though the "reformer" type of innovator also comes into the picture, yet the group has generally poor communication; and that the part-Samoans provide the most dynamic element, with the least rigidity and greatest incidence of communication effectiveness lying with this group.

A crucial aspect of mediation in both territories has been the problem of "official" or formal communication through the use of paid specialists as "interpreters." The effectiveness of an interpreter in elite communication appears to correlate with the degree to which his status is that of an elite specialist, with appropriate dignity and prestige.

Since earliest days a shortage of good interpreters has plagued both administrations, particularly that of Western Samoa. In 1930-31 the writers noted that no Samoan interpreter in government employ in that territory had more than stumbling English. Several potentially good interpreters were not officially used because the very cross-cultural experiences which had made them capable of rendering this service had marked them with overt signs of acculturation in dress and other matters which the New Zealand administration officially judged as inconsistent with its efforts to "hold" Samoan culture against Europeanization. The absence of adequate lingual intermediaries and of good channels of communication between the administration and the people was undoubtedly a very important factor in producing and maintaining for years the Mau antigovernment movement. In 1950, with keen hindsight, numbers of Samoan elite leaders remarked independently to the writers that if they had only known what the controversial governor of the time was trying to do for Samoa back at that time they would have been "on his side" and Samoa today might have been so much further along toward goals now widely accepted. A reappraisal of this whole era seemed to be taking place.

As of two decades later, the Western Samoa administration was still not much further ahead in its interpreter problem. The small group of official interpreters and translators were not much better paid or honored, even though much more competent, and were even more burdened down with the increasingly massive operations of English-Samoan verbal and written translation. The reorganized Legislative Assembly quickly found itself being held up for want of adequate interpretive services; the High Commissioner remarked, soon after its sessions began in 1948:

> We are up against this situation increasingly
> every day...we are in need of Interpreters
> and Translaters and believe me they do not
> grow on every tree. [Of the three inter-
> preters] Kalapu has been translating solidly
> for two and a half hours...Papali'i [is at
> Court]...Matatumua [has urgent work in the
> Samoan Affairs office]... There is no doubt
> that though more translators have been taken
> on...there will no doubt be an increasing
> need... I anticipate that it will be weeks before
> a full account of this debate has been passed
> by the Speakers and will give a true picture
> of what has been going on. [10]

[10] Legislative Assembly Debates, Second Session 1948, pp. 91, 93.

The position here was rendered more acute because Samoan members, in the reorganized government setting, insisted that no record or agreement could be recognized as legal unless put into authorized texts in both Samoan and English.

In American Samoa the situation was less acute, and less formal, during the Navy period, as white officials always had on hand, besides civilian employees, members of the former Samoan Navy Corps, the Fita Fita. Many of the latter had long service, a colloquial command of English rare in the neighbor territory, and mobility of assignment to the duties of the moment. Government policies too have not been averse to the use of Westernized Samoans and of part-Samoans. The subsequent Department of Interior administration has had to formalize interpretation and translation services in terms of job posts; but apparently competent personnel has been available within the means of official budgets. In this territory the complaints have taken the turn, further along the pathway of competence in English, that interpreters have imperfect knowledge of the niceties of Samoan, the "deep" meanings in allegory and honorifics.

As is well enough known, linguistic agility and other qualities which make a good interpreter are a rarity in any cross-cultural setting. In the Samoan setting, too, he is unlikely to be aided in the near future with mechanical devices now available to facilitate a record. The implication is that territorial authorities need to give high priority attention to selection and training of interpreters, and also to making interpretation more of an elite service. On the whole, such factors have not been well recognized so far from either the European or the Samoan sides; interpretation tends instead to be treated as just a somewhat higher type of clerkship and paid on that level. Yet the interpreter must have the means and the standing to exercise the role of a neutral in a situation where partisanship has been of the essence. Otherwise he is under constant temptation to intrude his own opinions and interests. This is the more necessary until bilingualism takes wider hold, so that parties to a translation can themselves provide checks on accuracy and the formal interpreter has a lessened role in the cross-cultural picture.

IX: ELITES AND CROSS-CULTURAL COMMUNICATION: GOALS

1. The Importance of "Goals" in Interaction

This chapter will explore the significance for elite communication studies of the "goals" which are valued and being promoted
by the interacting groups. The concept of "goals" is here used in
the sense of strongly motivated, affectively charged objectives and
expectations which are in the forefront of individual and group attention. They are the mental maps of the future.

What do top-level leaders talk about and plan for most in the
Samoa of today? How far are the goals of Samoan and other elites
identical, or at least congruent? how far different, even openly conflicting? How do such goals, in terms of their likenesses and differences, influence communication across ethnic or "national" boundaries? How adequate are the communication tools and techniques
as seen in this study for achieving "total group" or "national" goals,
and what changes are predictable?

A series of broad, if perhaps unduly obvious, propositions
may be advanced ahead of the discussion here:

1. Communication between elites across cultural boundaries
is shaped vitally by the particular goals being promoted in the groups
concerned.

2. Communication tends to be facilitated or retarded according to how far the goals involved are congruent or otherwise.

3. To the extent that the groups concerned use different
communication concepts and techniques, points of interference and
blockage are liable to develop and to retard the consummation of
common goals and the reconciliation of divergent goals, e. g., misunderstandings over the meanings of goal concepts;

4. The interacting elites are therefore likely to be bending
efforts toward improving their communication "tools" as a means
of facilitating mutual goal consummation.

The Samoans demonstrate dramatically a range of goal behavior seen widely in varying racial-cultural settings in the contemporary world. While themselves still struggling to consolidate out
of diversified elements a "national" identity, they wish to maintain
cultural and racial group integrity, conservation, and continuity,
yet at the same time to achieve status "equality" or equivalence
with Westerners. They also want selective advantages from western
technology and education. They are struggling essentially with what
anthropologists as many others would see as probably the most profound problem of twentieth century man: the degree to which in-

tegration into world culture must mean uniformity, or can subsume
the development of the rich variability of human experimentation in
systems of living and of evaluating.

It is characteristic of humans that such goals involve inconsistencies. Goal incompatibilities are notably one of the marks of
acculturation. Already, for example, the fact that the traditional
Samoan house has no room in it for any great accumulation of Western-
style goods is tending to modify house structure, even with those
who highly prize the traditional house style. Much more far-reaching
conflicts are involved in the nonmaterial world of ideas. Yet progress is being made in moving towards these goals and in smoothing
out and compromising their inconsistencies; the decisions are being
made by Samoan and part-Samoan elite persons with awareness of
their difficulties:

> Tofa: I am weighing these two subjects in
> my mind... whether to fill up the technical
> positions of the Government as suggested [by
> putting one hundred Samoans a year through
> high school, etc.] or protect the customs of
> the country... I do not know whether the out-
> come would result in the abolishment of our
> customs in the future.

> Fautua Tamasese: We must swim with the rest
> of the world; we can keep much Samoan custom,
> but have already accepted too much change, as
> in our need for money and goods, to shut our doors
> on the outside world. [1]

A Samoan leader, obviously much troubled by the many possible
alternatives in policies and goals, expressed the problem rather
wryly to the writers in this way:

> We need help to land safely. We need guidance
> of expert navigators to call the waves so we can
> safely make it to shore. For myself there seem
> to be many shores, some with emergency landings.

What responsible Europeans want, and get anxious about,
regarding Samoa, is in many respects congruent with these Samoan
goals. But there are also marked divergences that affect communi-

---

[1] Legislative Assembly Debates, Fourth Session, 1948, p. 12.

cation behavior. On the whole, perhaps, European goals are less clear-cut than those of the Samoan elite.

Governmental personnel is perhaps more sensitive than anything else about how Samoa looks in terms of current international standards of welfare and development. To the older "colonial" goals of peace and order, protection, and what the French call the mission civilizatrice have been added the more positive responsibilities of "trusteeship" and "guardianship. " The New Zealand authorities, particularly, are extremely sensitive to international opinion as represented in the U. N. Trusteeship Council. Policy tends, subject to budgetary possibilities, to be cut to the cloth of health, educational, and other measures considered appropriate to the welfare and development of such areas and peoples. In many respects, the United States programs in American Samoa have been even more ready to push the Samoans along than those of New Zealand, particularly in directions making for "assimilation" into the milieu of the metropolitan country.

In the broader sense such policies have been aligned with the Samoan goals of cultural integrity and of political self-government. But the European is inclined to view the means, and to judge progress, in terms of markedly different standards from those of the Samoans. Furthermore, as with Samoan goals, there tend to be inconsistencies. The goal policy which prods the Samoan more into money earning inevitably results in more migration to the town centers and increasing disruption of traditional family and community life, both of which are officially deplored. A program fostering an "assimilation" tendency may operate cheek-by-jowl with one favoring cultural symbiosis or separatism, as where in Western Samoa scholarships are given to Samoans for education in New Zealand yet separate Samoan and European school systems have been maintained until very recently.

In the sections which follow, the major goals which enter into elite communication today may be viewed. The analyses represent only brief and selective statements of the fields of policy and action involved.

2.   The Goal of Conservation

Elite communication across cultural boundaries is particularly sensitive to factors involving the security and maintenance of the society and cultural traditions of the groups concerned. The safeguarding by Samoans of their heritage against outside encroachment has been most vital to them; for non-Samoans and to some extent even for part-Samoans their Samoan stake is ordinarily only one among alternative stakes to which they have access, e. g., they could always leave and establish a pattern of life elsewhere. For the Samoans especially of the elite group conservation relating to land rights, the social system, village life, and other elements representative of Samoan integrity has been perhaps the most consistent among all goal values, and indeed it is traceable back to the days of first contact with Europeans. It is symbolized in the often repeated slogan, "Samoa for the Samoans," or now more frequently, "Samoa for the local born."

"Conservation" as used here does not mean any dead weight of "conservatism" in the sense of "keeping old Samoa custom." One of the extraordinarily nimble features of Samoan behavior is the speed with which some new element valued by any large number of people can be brought under the tent of what is called the fa'aSamoa, the correct Samoan way. The emphasis is rather on a self-conscious and planned goal of protecting the integrity of Samoanism. It involves a creative, even if defensive, reorganization and reinforcement of what is felt to be basic and most worthwhile in the old—modified as necessary or desired—as a basis for assimilating and adapting the new cultural materials to local needs. As such it appears to be an essential element in an acculturative process. In many comparable settings it has been subsumed under such terms as "cultural nationalism" or "cultural renaissance."

The type European figures of the island frontier, on their sides, have had varied goals here to the extent that their contacts with the Samoan life have been purposive. In general, mission bodies have favored a highly protective policy even while seeking to make over the Samoan way to the Christian theology and ethic. The trader, in his own way, wanted a stable Samoan setting for his transactions even while desiring to stimulate demand for trade goods and willingness to produce for larger markets. The land-hungry settler, considerably in contrast, has usually been ready enough to push the Samoan aside if in his way. Also, in seeking a stable labor supply he tends to resent the preoccupation of Samoans with their own village affairs, which to his thinking makes them "unwilling to work steadily."

Government officials have in general leaned strongly to the protective side. From the early nineteenth century, consuls of the powers ashore and war vessels afloat made efforts to guard such South Pacific peoples from abuses by their nationals as well as to promote the national interest. A ban on land purchases by outsiders, for example, came in 1889 through joint decision by the interested powers. The mood of the early metropolitan administrators, taking account of the Samoan temper of the time, is perhaps most clearly demonstrated in the initial legislative declaration made by the Navy authorities in American Samoa, and incorporated into the Code of American Samoa.

> The customs of the Samoans not in conflict
> with the laws of American Samoa or the laws
> of the United States concerning American Samoa
> shall be preserved. The village, county, and
> district councils consisting of the hereditary
> chiefs and their talking chiefs shall retain their
> own form or forms of meeting together to discuss
> affairs of the village, county, or district according
> to their own Samoan custom...

An essentially similar emphasis on respecting and preserving Samoan custom has permeated New Zealand law and policy.

Inevitably, however, even protective laws designed to foster local integrity have an arbitrary and restrictive character which can arouse resentment, not least of all as implying incompetence as regards self-protection. Furthermore, as governments have moved more positively toward other types of intervention in the interests of modern standards of welfare and development, the sense of pressure increases. As will be seen, political reorganization, economic acceleration, education, and similar government activities all represent pathways beset with the hazards of the unknown to the present generation of Samoans. Recent added fears that the New Zealand and American authorities may permit a new penetration of outside economic interests are also potent factors.

As appears to be typical of such situations, the most self-conscious and aggressive leaders of cultural conservation in the Samoa setting today are frequently individuals among the Samoan elite who have had deep and even long experience in Western living. Most of them have made their way over a period in New Zealand or the United States. The more extensive the experience with the contemporary Western patterns of life, the more certain they have become that the Samoan system as it is evolving has strength and worthwhileness that make it in some ways superior, at least for Samoans and for the Samoa setting, to the Western system. They are likely to be the special leaders in the attempt to adapt Western technology and Western ideas to Samoan values, social structure, and economic organization. In response to a question by one of the writers, some of the advantages as he saw them in the Samoan system were summarized by a top elite leader, who had lived for a considerable time on the United States mainland:

1.   Competition is mainly for the luxuries
of life.

2.   The main rewards are in prestige honors
rather than wealth so that the differences between
rich and poor are not stretched out.

3.   There is an assurance of security and
welfare for all in the family and the community:
all the necessities of food, shelter, companion-
ship, entertainment are there for everyone, and
no family can suffer need without all the community coming to share whatever they have to
share.

4.   There is trusteeship of land for each
generation, so that where the family is small
the matai will allow less land, and where there
are many children there will be a larger share
and more workers to take care of it.

5.   There is a good distribution of responsibilities: the hardest work is for the young
men in their prime of life; the leadership is for
the mature who should no longer do hard physical
work; there is only gentle work for the women;
and for all, work is often made into a pleasure
by working together. And for the children and
the old people there is complete security.

6.   We count the time to be spent for pleasure
and on good times together the most important of
all, instead of always hurrying to get richer.

The task of leadership as seen by such a progressive Samoan leader
therefore would be to preserve these elements in Samoan culture as
far as possible while raising material living levels through the use
of modern technology and increasing total Samoan wealth, while
protecting the country from any "invasion" of outsiders, and while
achieving educational and status equivalence with Westerners. If
it is a dream it is at least a grand dream. In a letter to the authors
dated February 11, 1956, this leader writes:

[There must be] friendly understanding...
between your people and ours, in spite of

the difference in our two worlds of racial ideals
and environment, etc. Such a tie certainly gives
us the will to strive on to gain more cooperation
and better understanding that—we trust—can move
all of us to meet in the middle of the road of human progress and the development of a better world
to live in. ... I believe our own people, this particular time, certainly must have closer and better
understanding and experience about the American
way of doing and accomplishing things—not for
themselves alone but for others.

The sections which follow will bring out major elements in
the current situation which Samoans feel as reinforcing or hostile
to group and cultural conservation: status matters, maintenance
of the social system (including the titleholder hierarchy), urbanization, and economic and educational programs. Above all, perhaps,
the question of "equality" or equivalence with whites is a focal point
of concern in relation to Samoan group and personal security.

3.   The Goal of Status "Equality" or "Equivalence"

The term "equality" is widely used to express the goal of
ending historic distinctions and discriminations as over against the
dominant outsider. But what is usually implied is perhaps status
"equivalence" rather than "equality" with its possible implications
of assimilation. In some respects, indeed, Samoan goals visualize
a preferential status for Samoans in the local setting. As a corollary
of the proposition offered in the discussion of Samoan-style communication it may be stated that just as with status relationships
discussed earlier within the traditional settings of communication,
elite interaction across cultural boundaries is particularly sensitive
to factors indicative of hierarchy or equivalence as between the groups
concerned.
A typical goal of such "colonial" areas, status equivalence is
underlined in Samoa because of the dominant value given in the traditional setting to hierarchy, prestige, privilege. Throughout the
acculturation experience of modern times it has been in the forefront
of concern since feelings of inequality, insecurity, and inadequacy
on the part of elite representatives operate as regards (1) Samoans
in relations with whites, (2) Samoans in relations with part-Samoans,
(3) part-Samoans in relations with whites, and (4) among Samoans,
as in the relations of rural and urban people, uneducated and Western-
educated people. It can be understood why the desire for status

equivalence has been a major driving force of culture change in the modern period, and a focus of elite attention and communication.

In the Pacific setting Samoans are on the whole ahead of other indigenous peoples in their struggle for status equivalence, with the possible exception of the kingdom of Tonga and the French territories. Though "double scales" still operate in many ways in the two Samoas, the battle for equal human rights and dignities regardless of skin color is fully joined, and is recognized officially in principle, and in policies today of education, health, employment, and other fields where tensions have occurred. The elite of each historically lower status group stands vigilant guard in the representative organizations of government to see that these official policies are carried through into practice.

The contemporary preoccupation of elite leadership with the matters of status equality and the elimination of all discrimination may be illustrated by a few excerpts. A Samoan leader who had an active part in Western Samoan self-government movements said in a private discussion:

> We want our Government to be purely Samoan,
> run only by Samoans and no outsiders... No
> Europeans can be brought in to run Samoan
> affairs; it can be run only by pure Samoans
> and [part-Samoans]... if you turn to your
> Samoan side you will be recognized, otherwise
> not. ...the Europeans are draining the life
> blood of Samoa, and the same with you of the
> two bloods. Just as Samoan medicine is not
> good for European illness so European medicine
> is not good for Samoan illness. ...your action
> is the same as some one trying out a piece of
> fruit to see whether or not it is ripe by flicking
> on it.

Illustrations of the sensitivities of Samoan leaders on anything they regard as discriminatory appear frequently in records of official assemblies. The chief medical officer in the Legislative Assembly of Western Samoa in 1949, engaged in the following interchange with a Samoan member:

> Chief Medical Officer: There is no longer any
> discrimination in the hospital with regard to
> race...

> Tofa: But the fact remains that when a Samoan
> is admitted into the European ward he is made
> to pay a certain amount of money in advance...
> This practice does not affect the admission of
> European patients. Sir, it is the marked dis-
> crimination regarding the admission of the two
> classes of patients which hurts... Sir, it is
> things such as this that cause humiliation. [2]

Much the same statements were made in discussion of liquor per-
mits, gun licenses, education, and general salary scales. In relation to a protest about land being taken from a part-Samoan family
of European status for purposes of road widening, a Samoan representative said:

> If the owner of the land now in discussion was
> a Samoan I am sure this land would not be given
> back to him. [3]

As regards a revision of salary scales in the police force, the High
Commissioner pointed out that there could be no satisfactory answer
except as part of a general review of salary scales throughout the
Samoan public service. A part-Samoan "European" representative
insisted that only one solution would be fair: "equal pay for equal
work." The High Commissioner then promised to give it immediate
attention. There continued, however, to be a focus of Samoan interest in this session on details of "discriminatory" practices:

> Is there a difference in the European
> [police] uniforms?
> Do the Samoan police wear sandals?
> Do the European police and the Samoan
> police work the same hours?
> Are the Samoan prisoners on the same
> rations as the European prisoners?
> [No. Different scales based on the normal
> differences in mode of living as established
> by the Medical Department.]

---

[2] Legislative Assembly Debates, Second Session 1949: pp. 6,
10, 69.
[3] Idem., First Session 1949, pp. 39-41. The bill was defeated and road widening went ahead.

> Fonoti: [Says he saw prisoners] eating only
> bananas which were green and only good
> enough for the pigs... It grieves me to
> know that they are not giving sugar and
> other imported goods to the Samoan pris-
> oners, because they are used to this kind
> of food. [High Commissioner points out
> that they do get sugar and tea.]

> Fautua Tamasese: I am sorry to hear remarks
> of the Hon. the Secretary when he mentioned
> the European scale and the Samoan scale...
> Because a local born wears trousers he
> should not get more pay than a Samoan...
> I really feel that if a man is qualified
> enough to handle the job he must be paid
> the same salary and no discrimination
> in scales...

> It is the wish of the Fono of Faipule to
> combine [the Samoan and European higher
> schools in Apia]...that the government
> shall teach all children alike. That no
> discrimination be made of European children
> from Samoan children. Should there be
> any such discrimination the government
> should see that a proper system be adopted
> whereby the Samoan children may benefit
> most as they are the indigenous people of
> this country. [4]

The Hon. Paul, a part-Samoan leader, in commenting on a request
from the Fono of Faipule that there should be a ratio in the new
government high school of fourteen Samoans to one European for
this same purpose of "discrimination in favor of the indigenous
Samoans," said:

> If you want to stamp out discrimination you
> should start with stamping out the idea that
> the local half-caste is not a Samoan. We
> are born and raised in this country and we

---

[4] Idem., Second Session 1948, pp. 104, 162.

> believe that this is our country too...
> Let us be true in purpose and cut out
> discrimination.

The _Fautua_ Tamasese, however, pointed out as regards this request
of the _Fono_ of _Faipule_:

> It is a pity that you are of local-born status
> because if you had been Samoan you would
> have had the same opinion as the Samoans
> for the past sixty years... This matter of
> proportion is a matter of policy. [He points
> out that the local-born Europeans have had
> good schooling for years with seconded New
> Zealand school teachers and that therefore
> unless there is some limiting action they would
> dominate Samoa college completely, and that
> this is not the fault of the Samoans who have not
> had a chance at education.][5]

A key point at which the status equivalence issue enters into
contemporary policy is the question of granting a common status
to all permanent residents of Western Samoa, as advocated in New
Zealand's Development Plan (p. 29). A working committee which
prepared the way for the Constitutional Convention of 1954 finally
put aside the problem, as no agreement was in sight. The convention itself recommended a type of legislature which would keep active
the legal distinction between "Samoans" and "Europeans." The New
Zealand government, in its 1955 reply to the convention's proposals,
expressed the view that "it has a responsibility to encourage further
discussion" of the common-status issue. It therefore welcomed a
proposal that a "Samoan Status Committee" be set up in the Legislative Assembly to "continue the search for a solution equitable to
all sections of the community." This committee has failed so far
to surmount the hurdle as to what percentage if any of Samoan blood
would be required for citizenship status. The High Commissioner,
in a U.N. Trusteeship Council session of 1955, facing attacks by
the Soviet Union and some other countries on what was called "discrimination" in favor of Europeans in status, electoral rights, and
commerce, said in reply:

---

[5] _Idem._, Fourth Session 1948, pp. 121, 128.

> There is discrimination against the Europeans.
> At the moment the Samoan people are not willing
> to grant citizenship to anyone with less than a
> prescribed percentage of Samoan blood. [6]

The anthropologist Stanner, in discussing contemporary Samoan goals, especially in the context of the self-government movements, sums up aptly their orientations in terms of status equivalence:

> The chiefs do not want equality with Europeans
> in a European life context. What they want is
> equality with Europeans in a predominantly
> Samoan life-context in which some good European
> things have a place (op. cit., p. 364).

In American Samoa these problems have been present, but in the face of Navy hierarchical practice have tended in the case of relations with whites to find overt expression in oblique and segmental ways rather than as a total front of opinion. The most consistent thread, perhaps, was a sporadic assertion by the Mau leaders of the 1920's—also in hearings before Congressional committees, and otherwise—that Navy control of a civilian population was "un-American" in the sense of representing military "domination" or "paternalism."

The status "equality" issue is likely to persist in some measure in both territories indefinitely. So long as there are distinctions in law and custom, they can be interpreted by individuals from either side as "discriminative"; even the seating pattern in a movie theater can be assigned such attributes. Shutting of Europeans from land ownership in the interests of safeguarding Samoan economic welfare is "discrimination" to a would-be European settler. It will continue to be one of the most persistently "tender" spots in communication relationships as the groups and individuals involved remain on guard in matters relating to self-esteem.

Under the circumstances, elite leaders in all the groups involved appear to be reasonably alert to the "applied" problems of recognizing and anticipating points of status tension, of avoiding them whenever possible, and of reducing them when they occur. An example of a useful conceptual step has been the recent abolition of the term "native" with its derogatory overtones in such areas, from

---

[6] Reported in Samoa Bulletin, July 22, 1955.

official usage, replacing it with "Samoan." In Western Samoa, the New Zealand government has not only given the Samoans opportunity to choose a flag, but has also taken the symbolic step of permitting it to be flown on a separate flagstaff at an equal height with the New Zealand flag; a separate official seal, "national anthem," and other equivalence symbols have been developed, and a separate currency is contemplated.[7] The many ramified issues involved, however, will need constant public study and discussion if discriminations at the vital levels of personal and private behavior are to be reduced. Understanding by key leaders who influence both general public opinion and the elite communication processes is perhaps the most vital factor of all.

The goals of conservation and status equivalence reviewed to this point are frequently symbolized in the concept, already familiar in discussions of the Samoan setting, of the "honor" or "dignity" of Samoa. In Western Samoa, for example, when the first meeting was held in 1948 of the new Legislative Assembly giving the Samoans a majority representation, the matters most urgently and persistently brought forward by the Samoan members were those concerned with this concept. Foremost was the raising of the hitherto small remuneration, and the adding of other perquisites of prestige value, in relation to the "Honorable Fautua," who were the "Royal Descendants" and bearers of the "dignity of all Samoa." This, of course, involved treading the delicate ground of establishing status relations with the High Commissioner representative of the "dignity" of New Zealand. A Samoan spokesman said:

> I am not trying to lift up the heads of Samoa in
> order to make them level with your excellency...
> There is no intention at all that...the formation
> of the government of Samoa will reduce the prestige...
> of the High Commissioner...representing the
> government of New Zealand, which government is
> looked upon as the father of the government of
> Samoa. I am sure that in your hearts you have the
> same respect for the High Commissioner as you
> have for [the Fautua].[8]

---

[7] A commission of white and Samoan members who have recently recommended this step included in its Report as one of its important reasons that of signalizing Western Samoa's political identity.

[8] Legislative Assembly Debates, First Session 1948, pp. 29-30; Second Session 1948, p. 40.

Harsh penalties were suggested in the legislature for any indignity
to the Samoan flag, and were brought into congruence with international practice only on the insistence of the High Commissioner.

   Clearly the dignity of the <u>Fautua</u> as representing all Samoa,
and symbolizing Samoan status equivalence, was and is a matter of
deep emotional involvement for Samoan elite leaders. The pride
with which ordinary Samoans spoke to the writers of the respect
that was being shown the <u>Fautua</u>, of their official automobiles and
offices, indicated that this emotional investment with the top Samoan
elite is very widespread among Samoans. Even American Samoans
tend to get some reflected glory from it. <u>Identification with the
highest "national" figures in their symbolic role is one element of
a catharsis for the frustrations and feelings of inadequacy and inferiority produced by acculturation experiences.</u>

   It is now possible to appreciate fully why the Samoan leaders,
meeting in July 1955, to consider the reply of the New Zealand
Government to the recommendations of the Constitutional Convention
(p. 31), were particularly unhappy that an indefinite delay was in
prospect in making the two <u>Fautua</u> jointly "Head of State, " and in
appointing a premier and cabinet. For them, the ultimate dignity
as well as the power was at stake, especially as regards the status
of the royal chiefs. This meeting unanimously reaffirmed the recommendations that Samoan leaders be permitted immediately to
assume these key positions of the government. In a further session
with the Minister for Island Affairs, the <u>Fautua</u> Tamasese, who would
in that case become one of the two chiefs serving as joint Head of
State, gave an opening address in which many of the current sensitivities appear:

> It is our opinion, Sir, that we here in Samoa
> can run our own Government with assistance
> and help from New Zealand... As it is at
> present in Samoa the Executive powers are
> solely vested in the High Commissioner, but
> I should like to say this, with our present
> High Commissioner his only qualification is
> that he is a qualified solicitor. When we need
> some advice or information on health we have
> to rely solely on the advice of the Director of
> Health... If advice is required by the Chief
> Executive he has to rely on his Department
> Heads from whom comes the advice...
> [In Tonga] the power is now solely in the hands

of the Tongan people. Power to employ people
is in the hands of the representatives of the
Tongan people...

Selection of political leaders is nowhere in the
British Commonwealth a matter of holding high
degrees or qualifications from a University. I
think the people have the right to choose whoever
they like to represent them without first having to
count certain degrees from the University. What
I mean is that there is no qualification to enter
Parliament that you must have before they will
accept you as a candidate. Therefore, in my
opinion, I think this is the time to run our own
Government—of course with help from New
Zealand from time to time. [9]

4. The Goal of "Self-Government"

Elite communication across political or cultural boundaries
involves great sensitivities where one group resents limits put on
its freedom of action by the other, and so is striving to achieve goals
of "autonomy, " "self-government, " or "independence. " In Samoa,
such goals have already been seen as markedly different in the two
territories. The concept of the Western Samoa elite is of a "self-
governing" or "independent" country under "protection" of the United
Nations and New Zealand. For the American Samoa elite it means
full local autonomy, but continuing as with other constituent States
and Territories of the Union to be an organic part of the United States.

Self-government or "nationalism" is serving to catch into a
recognizable pattern the formerly tangled web of conflicting aspirations and purposes in the different ethnic elites. In this way it is
giving a tremendous impetus toward unity in each territory, and
toward the will to improve communication processes and techniques.
This is well illustrated in the previous discussion of mass media,
and in recent constitutional changes and plans in which Samoans,
part-Samoans, and responsible officials of the governing countries
are collaborating.

---

[9] Papers and Proceedings of a Joint Meeting of the Legislative Assembly and Fono of Faipule with Hon. the Minister of Island
Territories, July 1955, pp. 39-40.

The "self-government" movements of Samoa were seen as having complex elements. They have involved in part the backward look to the past of an "independent" Samoa before European control, and in part the forward look of modern-type "nationalism. "

Supporters of "reversionism, " particularly a goal for the older and non-Westernized leaders, tend to compound out of the traditional polity of old Samoa and of the "king days" an image of a Samoan "Golden Age" of independence. This objective dominated earlier "self-government" strivings in German times: various disturbances during the early 1900's which led the German government to void officially the top ceremonial organization of the Samoan hierarchy, and finally in 1908-9 the so-called "Lauati rebellion" engineered by a powerful orator of that name, which had to be suppressed by a German naval force. The Mau movement of 1927 to 1936, while still evoking these elements, assumed more of the character of modern nationalism, and local Europeans and part-Samoans played an important part in this reformulation. [10]

The Trusteeship Agreement by which New Zealand has exercised its authority over Western Samoa since 1946, gives the following main political directives relating to its inhabitants:

> The Administering Authority undertakes. . .
> to promote. . .their progressive development
> toward self-government or independence as
> may be appropriate to the particular circum-
> stances of [the] territory and its peoples and
> the freely expressed wishes of the peoples
> concerned. . .
> [It] shall promote the development of free
> political institutions suited to Samoa. . .

The top Samoan and part-Samoan leaders are well aware of these statements, reinforcing the wording of Article 76 (b) of the United Nations Charter. In liaison with United Nations Missions, and under pressures of the self-government movement, New Zealand has been directing administrative changes toward the British model of a protected (self-governing) state.

Back of these general positions is a complicated skein of opinions and events in relation to which elite leaders have played vital roles, and which can only be sampled here. The United Nations

---

[10] For these events see Keesing, op. cit., pp. 75-95, 177-91.

Trusteeship system, with its rights of petition and visitation, represented, as a Samoan leader said, an opportunity which could not be bypassed: "If we did not move then, the chance for self-government might not have come again; there is no tomorrow, only today." A Samoan petition of 1947 brought the first United Nations Mission to Western Samoa.

Accounts of the time indicate, however, that "self-government" meant different things to different leaders: e.g., to some more conservative chiefs a reassertion of the political structure of the past (above); to others, exclusion of all whites except those given Samoan permission to enter; to more educated leaders a Samoan body politic in which European technical personnel would be retained until Samoans could be trained to replace them. The Mission had to steer a path in its recommendations between strongly expressed but on the whole still vague Samoan plans for an autonomous country and the existing stage which New Zealand had reached in advancing self-government.

The Report of the Mission puts a finger on certain vital dimensions of Samoan-European relationships. Clearly Samoans were strongly concerned at the time with where the "authority" and the "dignity" were lodged. They felt that the central administrative system at Apia was an imposed pule from New Zealand, hence something intrusive and dominating. A major problem, therefore, was to inaugurate measures which could lay the foundations for Samoans to begin thinking of the administration as "their" government, hence "self-government." Subsequently the New Zealand authorities, in liaison with United Nations Missions, have taken important practical and symbolic steps in this direction: emphasis has been laid on the concept of a "Government of Western Samoa"; the "Administrator" became a "High Commissioner"; the "royal" chiefs as Fautua were given political honors, dignified perquisites, and a voice in practical affairs; Samoans came to have a majority in the Legislative Council; a separate Public (Civil) Service was established; and distinctive "national" symbols were created.[11]

Even so, elite spokesmen for the self-government movement have continued to pepper the New Zealand authorities with criticisms, and to press for great autonomy. The frankness of Samoan criti-

---

[11] Report of the United Nations Mission, 1947, and subsequent United Nations Mission and New Zealand Government reports.

cism shows with particular vigor in records of the Legislative Assembly. [12] The 1953 Development Plan and subsequent Constitutional Convention have represented an attempt by the New Zealand government to find a new ground which would approximate to local self-government for the resident population.   They challenged Samoan leaders to move faster in some respects toward modern "democratic" procedures than they were as yet willing to accept (p. 108).

The atmosphere here is one radically different from that of earlier years of the New Zealand regime in the sense that Samoans are being assigned practical self-government responsibilities and are feeling the weight of them, not always too comfortably.   The writers would judge that, emotionally, the "self-government" drive is providing constructive outlet for the tensions and frustrations of leaders in the face of general acculturation processes.   Former open skepticism on the part of officials and other Europeans as to Samoan capacities to respond rapidly to self-government opportunities has tended to go "underground."

Two quotations from Samoan leaders out of many in the writers' field notes will illustrate the dynamics back of the Western Samoa self-government movements of the last three decades, and their significance for Samoan-European communication.   In 1930 one of the heads of the Mau movement said, of the then current slogan "Samoa for the Samoans":

> [It means] that we want to be broken away from
> the control of Europeans.   We have for many
> years not been shown a proper respect by
> Europeans, who have looked down on the Samoans.
> So the Samoans should be allowed to control
> their own government, but given the pro-
> tection of some European power.   The basis of
> Samoan government shall be the Church; God
> shall be the ruler.

In 1950 a leader in the later "self-government" movement said:

-----

[12] An example is provided by a Samoan leader describing the "inefficiency" of a technical specialist from New Zealand: "He spends most of his time drinking Kava...this gentleman [does] not know his work and has no knowledge of how to approach the Samoan chiefs"—from Legislative Assembly Debates, Second Session 1948, pp. 160-61.   See also pp. 234-36 below.

[The self-government petition of 1946] was
sent for the purpose of having recognized our
birthright and heritage received from God, the
right to look after ourselves. We do not want
to take anything away from any other country or
anyone else. We only claim something that belongs to us as our heritage and birthright. The
Samoans' earnest wish is to run their own government. God will also see that the people of Samoa
will have a good and sound government. In
positions where Samoans do not yet have ability
we can always hire people from countries abroad.

As already demonstrated at a number of points, Samoan
discussions of the New Zealand Development Plan provide a rich
documentation on attitudes and aspirations. A Samoan member of
the Western Samoa Legislative Assembly put the matter of European
control this way:

There is a certain saying that this country of
Samoa is not a country which is waiting for newcomers to come and form up the Government, no,
it is a country which has already been properly
organized and I consider also that Almighty God
has organized this country. Outside ruling administrations [by coming in, have been] creating
ill feeling, war, and uneasiness.[13]

This idealized backward look on Samoan history is also illustrated
by the remark of another Samoan leader in a joint meeting of the
Legislative Assembly and Fono of Faipule:

The leaders of the country of Samoa have been
for several years striving to get back to its
former position. That is to say, in the old days
Samoans had a Government of their own, and
it is only proper that the Samoan people should
strive all they can to have their full voice and
power in managing their own affairs.[14]

---

[13] Legislative Assembly Debates, First Session 1954, p. 157.
[14] Papers and Proceedings of a Joint Meeting of the Legislative Assembly and Fono of Faipule... July 1955, p. 44.

At this same meeting Samoans showed skepticism regarding the powers which New Zealand would give to the proposed new legislature:

> Tualaulelei: We can see that New Zealand is
> not yet prepared to hand over the full
> power to us of self-government... Very
> few changes will come in the legislature
> except in the membership. Very little
> difference in work will be involved...
> All replies are more or less evasive.
> What is the good of switching when the
> powers are the same... [They say that
> there is need for] additional time and
> experience... What time? How much
> longer...?

> To'omata: ... If they keep on postponing we
> may not be here to see the result of our
> efforts. We may be dead by that time.

Samoan leaders are likely to be particularly critical of those areas of government which are still reserved to New Zealand authority. In addition to the issue of top political control (pp. 31, 228), a major point of attack is New Zealand's continuing management of the public service. In view of New Zealand's negative reply to the Constitutional Convention's recommendation that this service be put immediately under control of the Samoan government, the following viewpoints were expressed by members of the Legislative Assembly and Fono of Faipule:

> Fonoti: We all know that the public servants of
> Samoa are paid by the taxpayers in Samoa,
> and as such they should have a voice in the
> control of its own service...

> Tualaulelei: Certain happenings [of alleged
> inefficiency] are sufficient evidence that
> the control should be here...

> Fatialofa: I strongly object [to New Zealand's
> reply]. I feel that New Zealand has no
> concern over us as to the type of system
> that we would like to adopt here for the con-
> trol of our Public Service. The conditions

> in New Zealand are different from the con-
> ditions in Samoa and they do not have to in-
> troduce to us a type of system [foreign to
> Samoa].

> Fautua Tamasese: New Zealand's concern here
> is always based on... [the idea that the
> communal authority would bring abuses]
> or the assumption that the aiga [family]
> system here in Samoa is so strong that it
> might influence the Public Service Com-
> missioner. In this wide world of ours we
> always have the good and the bad... [15]

One Samoan member of the Western Samoa Legislative Assembly has taken many opportunities in recent years to castigate
so-called "inefficiencies" and "mistakes" of the seconded New Zealand officials and of their executive departments, with the implication
that if power was turned over to the local government the situation
would be financially and otherwise improved. He said in a recent
speech addressed directly to the visiting New Zealand Minister for
Island Territories:

> You will find that in spite of what has been
> approved [in the Legislative Assembly] the
> officials concerned just squander the money
> as quickly as they can... We find out the
> losses only at the end of the financial year...
> In most matters the carrying out of the Govern-
> ment is never made known to the various
> Committees and the members of the Legisla-
> tive Assembly who are supposed to hold certain
> executive powers in the Government of Samoa.

Another leader added:

> It is not right for the owner of a business to
> give his employee a free hand to do as he
> wishes without the owner having any say in
> it. That has been the position in Samoa in

---

[15] Papers and Proceedings, Joint Session of the Legislative
Assembly and Fono of Faipule and Meeting with Hon. the Minister of
Island Territories, Apia, July 1955, pp. 20-23. Many passages also
occur in the Legislative Assembly Debates showing Samoan resentment that New Zealand is reserving authority here.

> past years... It is not a fair thing to employ
> a man to look after his affairs and for the
> employee to take full charge without the owner
> having anything to say to him. It is only proper
> that the owner should hold certain powers and
> not let the employee just carry on as he wishes...
> I think this is the proper time for us to manage
> our own affairs with help from New Zealand.
> All we need is the power to carry out the certain
> work of key positions. Once we get that power
> that is the thing we are after. [16]

This quotation expresses about as frankly as can be done widely held attitudes of Samoan leaders toward continuing New Zealand management of government in the territory. The visiting minister reminded the Samoan leaders of its side of the case:

> New Zealand cannot help but have considerable
> responsibility in Samoa for many years to come
> and it is essential that the people of Samoa appreciate
> that New Zealand must retain sufficient power and
> initiative to discharge those responsibilities es-
> pecially during the period when it tries pro-
> gressively to hand over to Samoans the reins of
> government. [17]

What opposition exists to self-government, what is its strength, and how does it enter into the communication setting? Representations to the New Zealand and United Nations authorities by European Citizens' Committees and other organized European groups have expressed fears of letting loose forces of violence and political chaos, and alarm lest the European stake be subordinated or ousted. They have consistently advocated a more or less prolonged period of transition and tutelage to full self-government.

---

[16] Idem, pp. 42-43. A favorite point of attack is on the housing needed for officials from New Zealand. A new Samoan member of the Legislative Assembly, after a committee inspection of such a house, remarked: "When I went in... I thought it was the Palace of Her Majesty Queen Elizabeth II, but this house is... [in Samoa and she is] in England." Legislative Assembly Debates, First Session 1955, p. 110.

[17] Samoa Bulletin, July 8, 1955.

Samoan opposition, to the extent it may exist, is virtually impossible to assess. In the Mau movement of the 1920's the government had the overt support of the "royal" Malietoa titleholder of the time: in other words, a division existed along traditional Samoan lines which symbolized the movement as being primarily an affair of the Satupua royal kin group and its titleholders (p. 24). In the later movement all top leaders stood publicly together, at least until the Mata'afa defection in the Constitutional Convention (p. 31). The writers found, however, that privately a small number of Samoans expressed to them fears of self-government essentially the same as those cited by resident Europeans. "Samoa, " it was said, "would be controlled by a few leaders in their own interests. " An elderly chief, who had a part in resistance against the Germans, said of the relation of mass opinion to the leaders: "In a group one starts to sing, the others join in"; and he added, "It is always the same around the world". Another said: "Such an important matter is not freely discussed or disputed; it is left to the leaders. " Any disturbance, therefore, in the present unusual balance of Samoan political forces, such as the opposition of one strong or traditionally top person under such circumstances could break wide open the public front of unanimity. The anthropologist Stanner stated his conception of the future problem as follows:

> The chiefs rest reasonably content with a
> situation which simulates their autonomy...
> The general drift of Samoan circumstances,
> however, will almost certainly make it less
> and less possible for them to maintain the
> dominant values of the traditional culture...
> The most interesting question concerns the
> leaders' capabilities of averting the reversionary
> cultural movements occurring widely in colonial
> territories. The problem is not necessarily
> insurmountable among so intelligent a people
> (op. cit. , pp. 364-65).

In American Samoa leaders of self-government efforts have been concerned almost wholly with a steady pressure on the United States authorities to put more power in a constitutional sense in the hands of the Samoan central legislative bodies, replacing advisory functions with responsible decision-making functions. Samoan leaders have felt that they faced an uncertain political future from 1951, not knowing what lines of development would be given clear and continuous support by the Department of the Interior in its administrative system (p. 36).   Various "reform" plans have come into the picture through Congressional delegations and other visitors from Washington, D. C. , and through the government personnel among whom a rapid turnover has been occurring.   A Samoan leader, expressing to the writers the tension he feels, said, "We cannot think of other matters until political affairs are straightened out. "

Perusal of the records of the advisory and legislative bodies over the years shows numerous proposals and incidents indicative of the tensions generated in this territory by having an overarching authority outside Samoan control.   Requests are made, for example, to have this or that white official ousted.   Attacks are made on financial policies at many points.   Proposals are made to give Samoan officials leave, retirement, and other perquisities which white officials receive.   Attempts are also made to dislodge appointed Samoan officials who run foul of leaders or of local opinion.   Such stress points tend to follow much the same patterns indeed over the approximately three decades for which the writers have examined advisory and legislative records.

When the Department of the Interior took over, proposals were put forward to reduce the legislature to a smaller unicameral body.   This was at first resisted by Samoan leaders as part of a general rejection of moves initiated from Washington, D. C. , which might open the way to overriding the Samoan protected status.   Later the Samoan legislature itself, considering its own wise moves in the face of such possible pressures, gave support to the idea of reducing the size of the Lower House and aligning elective procedures with modern democratic forms.   It also laid the groundwork for future political development through a constitutional committee (p. 37). It is notable that during more than half a century of American control Samoan identification with United States sovereignty has hardly been questioned, including the personal leadership of the Presidency, the symbolism of the stars-and-stripes flag, and the dollar currency.

"Self-government" has been discussed to this point as a political goal.   But it is also in a real sense a religious issue, as the Christian mission bodies have been concerned for many years with developing local autonomous Samoan churches under their denominational auspices.   Samoan "self-government" progress in church administration is therefore significant.   The different missions have of course varied in the extent to which they have encouraged autonomous church development under Samoan leadership.   The numerically dominant mission in both territories, the London Missionary Society, has almost completely Samoan personnel, with a handful of European administrators and educators carrying certain financial and other cen-

tral responsibilities. One mission worker pointed out that Samoans
are generally unwilling to face as individuals the "inner discipline"
which goes with "accepting real responsibility"; he said of political
self-government:

> If the people wish to put themselves to the
> task and accept all the difficulties, of course
> they could do it; but I question whether they
> will ever do it in our lifetime.

Another stressed the difficulties inherent in the traditional factionalism:

> It crops up in almost everything. One man,
> discontented over something, makes a noise
> about it in the assembly, and expects all his
> relatives to support him whether they believe
> in it or not. So far as church government is
> concerned, self-government could not success-
> fully be worked out. It would be successful to
> a certain extent, but the Samoans are a very
> long way from understanding representative
> government... They represent their constit-
> uency... without any respect for the good of
> the whole. They don't think of themselves as
> representatives of the whole... There is no
> other way than a long course of training in
> self-government.

It may be noted that, in American Samoa, a leading titleholder has
developed an independent Samoan Protestant church, and serves as
the head of this still very small congregation.

The broad goals and high emotional tensions of a political
autonomy movement do not necessarily have strong correlation with
competence to build and carry a modern-style body politic. From
the viewpoints of the governing authorities the various autonomy
movements have been on the whole worryingly unconcerned until recently as to the exact institutional structures which should go to the
making of "self-government." Unity, in the sense of building up a
coherent territory-wide structure of modern government, has been
on the whole a European-supported goal rather than a Samoan goal.
Both in the "king" days of the nineteenth century and under the subsequent Western regimes, it has been primarily the European who
has provided the structural models and legal formulations involved.

It has also been primarily the European who has been made unhappy by "inefficiencies" and "failures" in meeting standards.

In Western Samoa, Samoan spokesmen have been inclined for approximately the last decade to say rather vaguely that the Fautua as "Royal Descendants," with a prime minister and cabinet, and Samoanized forms of the present central institutions, could carry self-government. [18]   To Europeans, aware of the complexities of modern administration, dealing with the public service, public trust, price control, and numerous other technical matters, such suggestions verge on "irresponsibility." A European official said:

> The Samoan village is still amazingly isolated
> and beset with localism and differing local cus-
> toms. In road-building, if we try to take laborers
> into a district from outside, trouble is bound to
> arise, and knives start to swing. The resettle-
> ment of [a certain group in a new district] takes
> interminable consultations.

Another European said:

> The higher Samoan leadership can work together
> when it is against something, and has often com-
> bined to block the Government effectively. But
> it would be hopeless to carry positive, complicated,
> or prolonged responsibilities. Before long the
> various factions would be quarreling, and without
> external law and order there would soon be open
> violence.

The establishment of the reorganized Western Samoa governmental system in 1947 marked a historic turning point in that territory, in that for the first time the tasks of building a realistic and unified body politic began to be shared effectively with the Samoan leadership. Perhaps the most educative factor here was the establishment of working committees in the legislature: top Samoans

---

[18] See statement by the Fautua Tamasese (p. 228); also a general set of proposals put before the U. N. Mission investigating the self-government petition in 1947, quoted in the Report of the Mission to the Trusteeship Council, Annex VII.

found themselves worrying in a responsible way over finance, commerce, public works, the schools, and other practical instrumentalities and policies. Inevitably, the needs of building up the government of Western Samoa, including its economic base in revenues,
became Samoan elite goals as well as European official goals. Furthermore, as indicated particularly in the section on radio, a tremendous
tide of interest has been released among Samoans at all levels in
how "our government" was being run.

Apropos of Samoan leaders taking new responsibilities, a
revealing passage occurs in one of the first meetings of the reorganized Legislative Assembly. A Samoan member asked:

> [As regards] the word 'Government,' does it
> mean that if anything goes wrong it will be to the
> discredit not only of this Assembly but...
> Western Samoa as well? ...[I prefer] the word
> 'Administration.' Should anything go wrong
> the blame would be only on the Heads of the
> Departments and the High Commissioner. [19]

In American Samoa, the Naval authorities were able to develop a much more co-ordinated system of central, regional, and
local government. It has performed with minimum strain the tasks
of integrating official and Samoan authority, the more so as for the
most part American administrative personnel, going on relatively
short-term appointment, have let it settle into its own patterns of
need and convenience. The problems therefore have been less those
of structure-building than of directions of authority, i.e., of re-
versing the early procedures of giving orders from the top down, to
developing self-government responsibilities from the bottom up.

It may be expected that both Samoas will move toward increasingly effective self-government, under present active "tutelage"
policies, at the central, regional, and local levels. The possibility
of new antigovernment movements being generated, however, cannot
be ruled out. Furthermore, because such small territories must
always remain adjuncts of larger states which can provide the overarching services such as those of security and diplomacy, the balance between realistic self-government in internal affairs and levels
of aspiration will not be easily struck. Elite communication in relation to this goal is likely therefore to involve marked tensions for
a long time to come.

---

[19] Legislative Assembly Debates, Second Session 1948, p. 15.

5.   The Goal of Material Advancement

Economic developments in such an area are likely to be
screened through a mesh of often conflicting elite interests.   What
are counted "inequities" are particularly likely to serve as interferences in communication behavior.

The Samoan, part-Samoan, and white groups have shown
marked contrasts in the directions and emphases of economic goals
in both territories, and this has often brought about inconsistencies
and conflicts.   Samoan values, as shown at many points in the study,
are very different from those of the resident European trader or
planter, white or part-Samoan, who is interested in an individualistic
way of life and in stepping up commercial production; or again, of
government officials who want such a territory, along with develop-
mental advances, to become economically self-supporting in terms
of bearing the financial load of administrative costs.   The Samoan
viewpoint is extremely sensitive to any moves which may threaten
the ongoing familiar economic system of the household, kin, and
community groups.   Participation in the commercial economy has
tended for the mass of Samoans to be geared to immediate needs for
outside goods and money: if prices go up at the store for the wanted
goods, the Samoan family concerned will produce more copra, bananas,
wage labor, etc., but if they go down it will produce less; if the pay-
ments go up for what the family produces, it will make less effort;
if down, it will make more effort.   The pacing factors have been
consistently Samoan, little affected by the European standards of
economic "progress."

A report of the European Chamber of Commerce in Western
Samoa as of 1946 gives a good summary of the typical views and goals
of the resident part-Samoan and white community in economic spheres:

> The territory is decidely underdeveloped, and...
> is not making commercial progress.   The
> remedies are obvious enough...   First of all,
> development capital must be attracted, land
> must be made available for opening up, and
> an adequate supply of dependable labour must
> be assured.   Secondly, endeavors should be
> made to induce the Samoans to increase their
> production.   All this is largely a matter for
> adjustment of Government policy.   Until
> these conditions are brought about there can
> be no progress, and the country will continue
> to stagnate.

Samoan leaders understandably fear such goals as threatening to Samoan economic and social integrity. Over the recent period of trade prosperity, too, they have shown a considerable resentment of the fact that European-status persons have reaped what in their perspectives has been a harvest of benefits. [20]

This helps to explain the desire of Samoan leaders, expressed in the self-government negotiations, to have those of non-Samoan status either merge with the Samoans or else leave the territory. When, in 1947, the New Zealand authorities admitted a Dominion furniture firm to utilize Samoan timber, marked opposition developed against the scheme as being a precedent for admitting outside interests on a larger scale and the enterprise was soon withdrawn. The New Zealand government also met Samoan sentiment by turning over for Samoan welfare purposes the income of big, formerly German "Reparations Estates," which it has run profitably since 1914. It plans to turn the estates over soon to the government of Western Samoa. Significantly, too, some combinations of high-ranking Samoan titleholders, and also a number of individual titleholders, have formed trading concerns so as to profit by the boom, and edge in on the business of the established European (white and part-Samoan) commercial firms which generally have a network of stores over the territory. These Samoan trading ventures, usually based on joint-stock or cooperative principles which can fit in with the traditional multiple-rights system of property handling, and in some cases advised and helped by government, have had varying degrees of success and permanence.

The ups and downs of life for the few Samoans, almost exclusively of elite status, who go into trade are vividly shown in an early Legislative Assembly session of Western Samoa. In a discussion of the problem of Samoan traders "swindling brother Samoans," the High Commissioner pointed out the difficulties of getting anyone to make a complaint so legal steps could be taken: "If a man

---

[20] Western Samoa, subject to depressed conditions in the 1930's, has experienced a boom in export products since the start of World War II. Exports in 1953 were valued at £ NZ 1, 954, 698, as compared with £ 248, 605, in 1939; imports values were respectively £ 1, 312, 769 and £ 196, 272. Government revenue in 1953 totaled £ 929, 120 as compared with £ 139, 450 in 1939, and expenditures were respectively £ 1, 054, 320 and £ 139, 070. For more detailed figures see the Annual Reports.

has got to live in a village and particularly if the trader is of high
rank. ... it would be rather difficult if he put the matter in the hands
of the police. " A Samoan leader interested in trade countered by
pointing out that the "poor trader" has to "give a person a tin of
fish as requested because he shows [in this way] his politeness or
respect to that person... [but] he has no way to have this debt ...
recovered by law" as extending credit is legally prohibited. [21]

In American Samoa the commercial superstructure has been
markedly different. Almost no white plantation settlers were established or lands alienated from Samoan hands; the very limited private trading activities were an adjunct of the Samoan economy, the
more so as Navy needs were met through their own logistic system.
Governmental supervision took the form primarily of organizing
through a consolidated Copra Fund the collection and sale of the
copra output by annual competitive tender to some United States
firm, and also the handling of superior handicraft work through a
Department of Samoan Industries. In both these administrative bodies
Samoans are directly represented, and profits are paid to the Samoan
producer by the government. The major source of money income to
1951 was employment in the Navy establishment and in the Government. To a much greater extent than in Western Samoa the ordinary
household came to count goods from the trading store as necessaries
rather than luxuries.

From 1951, with civilian government and the removal of the
Navy installations, the money economy has been in a depressed state,
even though external commerce has increased. [22] Samoans have had
to fall back more on their local subsistence products. This has become for some communities a serious matter in that rapid population
increase combined with land shortages in their nearly always rugged
hinterlands means gardening on steep and marginal terrain, with
consequent transport and erosion problems. In 1954, an American
company was admitted with approval of Samoan leaders to operate
a tuna fishing cannery, using a small fleet of sampans with Japanese

---

[21] See Legislative Assembly Debates, Fourth Session 1948,
p. 55ff.

[22] For American Samoa, the value of exports for 1953-54
totaled $546, 237 as compared with $296, 956 in 1937-38; the corresponding figures for imports were $992, 543 and $194, 138. In
1954, government revenue totaled $524, 970 and expenditures
$1, 627, 324; the territory requires a heavy annual federal subsidy
($1, 388, 629 in 1953). For more detailed figures see the Annual Reports.

fishermen from Japan under an annual contract. The assumption
is that if Samoans will learn the commercial fish-catching methods
they will be able to take over this part of the operation as well as
being employed in the cannery jobs. Fears are deep and widespread
concerning any indiscriminate entry to outside enterprise.

Granting historic differences in economic goals, there is a
discernible tendency in the current atmosphere of open problem discussion for compromises to be reached among the constitutent parties, resident and official. All experience the ever-present tension
of knowing what falling market prices can mean to the economy of
each territory. The special economic problems of the town areas
stand out, including the depressed conditions of many urban Samoans
and part-Samoans trying to live within the commercial economy under
present very low wage structures and ever rising living costs. The
typical "dual salary scales" of such frontier zones for whites and
local people, which are a particular point of resentment by the latter
group, are steadily being brought more into line. [23] The difficult
problem of European land needs, seen as a major area of stress,
is being met partly through government-sponsored resettlement
schemes.

The Samoans, from their side, are on the move at an accelerating pace toward fuller participation in Western technological improvements. Elite spokesmen in the legislative bodies are pressing
for more and better roads, village electric lighting and water systems, and harbor and anchorage facilities, as by coral blasting and
pier building. A number of communities have installed their own
road, lighting, or water systems even without government help.
Village leaders spoke to the writers of needs for refrigeration to
preserve perishable surpluses, and for preservative measures to
combat destruction in house materials. Inventories of goods made
by the writers in sample rural trading stores as of 1930-31 and 1950-
51 show a greatly widened range of Samoan purchases. Such matters
are undoubtedly indicative not only of growing Samoan needs, but al-

---

[23] For example the range of annual salary scales for locally
trained teachers in 1945 was from £ 10 to £ 60. By 1953 the minimum starting salary was £ 100, with the average at about £ 155,
and a few outstanding teachers receiving up to £ 490. A handful of
Samoan teachers holding New Zealand Teachers' Certificates were
paid from £ 385 to £ 710. White teachers from New Zealand received
basic salaries ranging from about £ 750 to £ 1,315, plus special
overseas allowances. (From Beeby, 1954, and Annual Reports.)

so of a belief by Samoan leaders that greater participation in world
technological improvements will give power, knowledge, and dignity
in the face of non-Samoan pressures. On the whole, the elite appear to envisage rising levels of "good living" for the entire kin and
village groups, rather than for themselves alone at the expense of
the non-elite as has been characteristic of so many economic frontiers.

Looking to the economic future, the Samoans and their leaders
are seen as with so many similar peoples to be facing alternatives
in goals: the traditional group-oriented system versus an individualistic way of life; the subsistence emphasis versus the money-
earning emphasis; the rural village setting versus urbanization;
small industries suited to the household versus larger industrial
organization. Fortunately these are not mutually exclusive, but can
be made to a point a matter of choice and preference. The expectation is that increasing numbers of Samoans will elect to become more
self-motivated, to live in town, to earn, and to interest themselves
in larger economic enterprises in and outside Samoa. Over time,
the existing great technological gap between the Samoan and European
will be reduced. For the great majority of residents, however, the
future is likely to continue to be that of villagers combining elements
from the subsistence and commercial economies in highly personalized and co-operative group settings. Tolerant inactivity, if not open
non-co-operation, will be skillfully exercised by Samoan leaders
where the official or trader presses uncongenial economic schemes
or goals on them. As such the situation should continue to involve
many areas of tension and unfulfilled aspiration.

6. The Goal of Education

To a subordinate elite, modern educational instrumentalities
are a special key to the attainment of power and of status equivalence, and notably so, "higher education." Obviously, to the extent
that educational levels between elites become co-ordinate, communication is facilitated.

It might be expected that in such an area as Samoa the goal
of advancing education, as represented particularly in school training for the children, would be clear-cut for both European and Samoan elites. Actually it has been a very complicated one, marked
by uncertainties, ambivalences, inconsistencies, and tensions that

have affected communication processes and obstructed goal achievement. [24]

In Western Samoa the status equivalence issue is a notable factor in the education situation. Samoan leaders have voiced opposition, especially in recent years, to differential curricula as between Samoan and European children, withholding English until the later grades, an emphasis on "technical" as against "academic" subjects, segregation, salary differentials for teachers, and the assignment of European teachers almost wholly to the European school system. Such policies, even when shaped to factors inherent in the cultural matrix, are suspect as seeming to represent a discrimination against Samoans, even a purposive discrimination to withhold the secrets of Western knowledge and power. Samoan elite opinion has also pressed to have high school and university level training for Samoan young people, and some high-ranking families have sent their children abroad for such education at their own expense.

The school situation in Western Samoa has involved a government system and five autonomous mission school systems. Of Samoan children electing to enroll in 1954 (attendance is not compulsory), somewhat over 15,000 went to government schools and 6,500 to the mission schools. Perhaps close to 9,000 were not attending school. Little was done until after World War II to advance schooling beyond the elementary grades, and English instruction was introduced only after several years and in selected institutions. More recently, as a response at least partly to Samoan leadership pressures, these static systems have passed into a dynamic period of educational experiment. Schooling has been desegregated in the Apia area; Samoan teacher training systematized; "acceleration" schools established to bring along the brightest pupils; government and mission high schools opened; scholarships given for young people to study in New Zealand. Samoan communities, touched by the educational magic, have built new schoolhouses, and embarrassed the Samoan treasury with requests for teachers and equipment. [25]

---

[24] See, for example, Keesing, F. M. Education in Pacific Countries and The South Seas in the Modern World; also, in relation more specifically to Samoa, see Keesing, Modern Samoa, and Stanner, The South Seas in Transition; also numerous government survey reports.

[25] For more detail on the school system see the Annual Reports of the Territory; also the special report by Beeby, C. E. Report on Education in Western Samoa.

The pressure by Samoan spokesmen for more and better schooling has been a consistent thread through all the legislative debates in recent years. The territory is now committed by official decisions to (1) the fastest possible training of Samoans and part-Samoans to replace all but a few top echelons of New Zealand official-dom in the territory. (2) Fullest coeducation; indeed recently girls have tended somewhat to outstrip boys in qualifying for scholarships and for placements in "accelerated" schools. (3) The development of the new government high school (Samoa College) to serve all population groups of the territory up to junior university levels. The undoubtedly close relation between the stress on education by Samoan leaders and pressure for self-government is illustrated by the remarks of a Samoan member of the Legislative Assembly:

> It is essential to take the necessary measures
> to get every child into school... In comparing
> the standard of local education with those in
> other parts of the world I feel that our standard
> is lower because of the fact that we have no
> universities here to enable us to further the
> standard of education in the Territory... In
> view of the fact that we are trying to have self-
> government... it is most essential for the people
> of Samoa to be properly educated in all fields
> so that they can personally fill the various official
> posts in such a government. [26]

In American Samoa a government school system had been developed much more rapidly, and mission schools were permitted to continue only if they met the government standards. Compulsory attendance for all children between 7 and 15 years of age, a lack of segregation, an emphasis on Samoan teacher training, reproduction of many features of the "little red schoolhouse" tradition, and in early days an official requirement to use the English language only, in the schoolroom, brought modern-style education along much faster than in the neighboring territory. From the early 1930's partly under Samoan leadership pressures, high school work was started, with standards approaching increasingly those of an American high school. A number of Samoan and part-Samoan young people were

---

[26] Legislative Assembly Debates, First Session 1955, p. 162.

also sent by their families for more advanced education in Hawaii or on the United States mainland. Graduates of the high school have recently been entering American universities annually (approximately 35 between 1950 and 1954), and the first small crop of university-trained graduates has been returning to Samoa. The permeation of the Samoan elite by more advanced education is thus considerably further ahead in the immediate perspective in American Samoa than in Western Samoa.

Granting this general elite stress on the goal of education, many Samoan leaders are likely to have, at least covertly, a fear of education as representing steps into the unknown. They feel a strong sense of threat to the traditional society and custom including the matai system, of losing touch with their children in terms of Western-oriented school behavior, e. g. children stand to speak to a teacher where the Samoan sits or bends over when talking to an elite person, they are not so available for community work, their speech tends to become a pidginized mixture of the two languages. Even leaders most enthusiastic for status equivalence in education may reveal such ambivalent attitudes—as in expressions favoring curtailment of education, reduction of Westernized elements, supervision of textbooks by Samoan leaders, and resistance to giving prestige status in the community to the teacher. There is also a tendency among both Samoans and Europeans to make schooling the "whipping boy" for deterioration in things Samoan, and alleged weaknesses or faults of more educated Samoans, without realizing the extent to which the larger acculturative context, not the school as such, may be responsible for bringing about the changes which they may choose to decry.

Out of the current educational dynamic, it can be expected, will come, in time if not immediately, new integrative influences as well as clearer educational goals, along with some of the disintegrative factors which Samoan elite persons fear. It might be judged, however, that Samoan character, the momentum of nationalist feeling, and the total cultural setting is such that young Samoans are not likely to underevaluate too seriously their Samoan heritage and its own positive values.

Elite communication across ethnic lines in both Samoas will undoubtedly, in the longer-term perspectives, be rendered more facile and congruent through the play of educational factors. The momentum generated in the school systems to date can hardly be checked. It is also a "total front" effort instead of having more advanced schooling limited to the few; of this a New Zealand educational expert says in a survey of 1954:

> I do not think the situation can be met by
> giving a few chosen people a good education
> whilst leaving a proportion...uneducated.
> If there is to be stability in any form of govern-
> ment for Samoa, there must not be too big a
> gap between the leaders and the led. Moreover,
> without a foundation of universal schooling, it
> is impossible to find out who are really bright
> children to be selected for further education. [27]

More Samoans educated abroad will be returning and adding to the
local ferment. Bilingual competence, moderately realized already
in American Samoa, will undoubtedly advance at the pace that needs
demand, and through self-education to the extent that the schools
get out of step with those needs, although semantic deficiencies are
always likely to plague those individuals not given the opportunity
to start the learning process in early childhood. Even so, no complete submerging of the Samoan people and way of life into a larger
white milieu can be foreseen. The survival value of many aspects
of the traditional Samoan culture and society will undoubtedly be
demonstrated in modified forms. As for disorganization, this is
going to continue in any case, so that schooling gives at least the
opportunity for a more controlled transition in meeting newer conditions. Problems of intercommunication between the local resident
elite and the uninformed outsider, while they will persist, should
become relatively unimportant as the level of education of the local
elite rises towards world norms.

10.   Relations Between the Two Territories

A dimension of Samoan elite communication having rather
unique character, though by no means without parallels in other political situations, arises from the division of the Samoan group into
two territories. What is involved, it may be asked, when an ethnic
group has been arbitrarily cut apart, so that elite interaction has to
cross a political boundary? To what extent has "unification" of the
two Samoas become an elite goal?

More than a half century has now elapsed since the arbitary
dissection occurred, essentially to give each of the two participating
powers a strategic harbor. The contemporary interaction in which

---

[27] Beeby, op. cit., p. 21.

the unification question has play involves (1) Samoan leaders in each
territory and the respective American and New Zealand authorities,
and (2) Samoans across the political boundaries, both at the elite
levels and less formally through the continuing exercise by Samoans
at large of kinship and other ties.

The practical issue of unifying the two Samoas, always in
the background of affairs, has been brought considerably into the
open in the last decade, though in a guarded manner. This is partly
because of the rather mobile political situation in both territories.
Some technical consultation has always been carried on between the
two administrations, though this has been primarily conducted at
the level of European top officials rather than of the Samoan leadership.

Apart from customs control, this is one of the easiest of international borders. The lack of organic legislation in American
Samoa leaves this boundary outside the scope of the standard United
States immigration laws, so that entry is controlled by a local rule
which admits Samoans from Western Samoa by a simple permit system. The Western Samoa authorities do not even require an entry
permit for Western Samoa. The frequent launches and occasional
larger vessels carry numerous Samoan and part-Samoan passengers
back and forth across the usually rough 90-mile ocean passage between Apia and Pago Pago for short or long visits, mainly to relatives
(p. 16). Marriages occur; ceremonious property exchanges are
made; jobs are taken. In this sense Samoa continues to be culturally
undivided. Even political fashions tend to be mutually influenced
across the territorial borders. Western Samoa proposes to have an
executive council (a British-type body) and the American Samoa
leaders suggest a similar body for their territory (pp. 27, 33). A
constitutional body is set up in both territories. At the same time,
as has been emphasized, marked differences show in the two territories, notably a considerable Americanization of the way of life
in American Samoa.

There is no doubt whatever that in sheerly sentimental terms
the idea of "Samoan unity" excites strong emotional reactions among
Samoans in both territories. On occasions calling for the enjoyment
of such sentiments, popular Samoan oratory has a field day with the
theme: "We are all one people, " "We are all Samoans, as the fruit
of one great tree, " "We are all brothers and sisters in the true Samoan
family, " and so on. Samoans honor the concept in ceremonial ways.
In 1950, a party of Western Samoan elite representatives, when attending "Flag Day" ceremonies honoring the fiftieth year of United
States sovereignty in American Samoa, presented a symbolic fine

mat which had historical associations of "all Samoa" importance.
At the ceremonies opening the first Legislative Assembly of Western Samoa under the new self-governing administration, an elite
party representing American Samoa was correspondingly present.
Both administrations co-operated in these tributes to Samoan unity.

Even so, weighing the unification issue as a practical goal,
the writers sense that both formal and informal statements by Samoan
leaders show a marked "cross your fingers" attitude. This appeared
to involve much more than caution lest the speaker be counted a political agitator against the respective controlling governments,
though this too is certainly a factor. The following seem to be the
major themes of Samoan elite opinion:

1. Main promoters of the "unity" goal have been the Samoan
leaders of the self-government movement in Western Samoa. They
initiated informal talks on the matter about 1946 with American
Samoan leaders, and desultory discussions have continued subsequently. Their picture involves a unified self-governing Samoa under
protection of a larger power. That power is assumed to be New Zealand, with the United Nations back of it, but undercurrents of opinion
have favored United States protection largely because of the military
might experienced during World War II, when both Samoas were
"occupied" by American military forces.

2. Samoan leaders in American Samoa have given running
consideration to the idea. From the viewpoint of Samoan prestige
and social ties it has been tempting. But the titleholders of Tutuila,
the main island, were minor adjuncts of one district of the present
Western Samoa in the old Samoan title hierarchy, and they appear
completely unwilling to surrender their present great prestige position as top members of the hierarchy in American Samoa to become virtually "nobodies" on the national scene of a united Samoa.
Negotiations with the "royal" titleholders and other top leaders in
Western Samoa have produced no concessions from the old hierarchical
principle toward putting them on or near top rungs of a united Samoa.
Furthermore, the leaders in the Manu'a islands are little interested
in a united Samoa, as their district has stood traditionally apart
from the general Samoan polity (p. 21). The American affiliation
also has held in itself strong attractions to American Samoans in
terms of prestige, certain nationality rights, and other benefits.

Unless, therefore, the governing countries were to initiate
action, or stimulate the Samoan leaders to grapple with the problems
involved, the writers would judge that the Samoan elites in the two
territories are unlikely to reconcile the status factors and other
divergencies in the situation. While still holding unity as a sentimental goal, and continuing to interact both ceremoniously and in

bilateral consultations on technical and other matters, they are likely if anything to keep moving further apart ethnically—the Western Samoans toward a locally autonomous island life under New Zealand protection, the American Samoans toward greater assimilation into the American Pacific sphere. A realistic step as an alternative to unification has been the formal establishment, in January 1955, of an interterritorial committee, comprising the top European officials and Samoan leaders of each jurisdiction, to consult on technical matters of common concern.

On the whole it may be said that the Samoan people are appreciative of having windows and doors open to two of the world's great systems, the one American, the other British. Yet the possibility of a unified Samoa remains on the horizon of practical politics. The issue of transferring American Samoa to New Zealand jurisdiction as part of a united Samoa has even been discussed recently in U.S. Congressional committees. But any move to bring about Samoan unity that merely appeared to be a shuffling off of responsibility by the United States would tend to lower the prestige of this power in Samoa, and perhaps widely in the Pacific area. This is therefore a highly sensitive matter in which the co-operative leadership of the Samoan elite in the two territories would be essential to a successful union. Difficulties in the way of unity might, however, be expected to recede considerably as modern-style constituencies and voting are further developed in Western Samoa.

11.   Elite Communication in the Future

Many factors which have been seen at work in the course of this study suggest that the leadership situation in Samoa can be projected ahead in a number of respects with high predictability.

The historic European controls are turning increasingly from formally hierarchical to co-ordinate relationships. The white specialist official from outside Samoa, though being replaced progressively by Samoans or other local-born persons, will be needed in a number of key government operations for a long time to come. But he will be working more and more alongside rather than over his local colleague. The larger metropolitan countries, the United States and New Zealand, will also need to station indefinitely in such territories their representatives concerned with defense, immegration and naturalization, and other wider national activities.

Within the resident populations, future leadership must continue to lodge strongly with the part-Samoan elite, as "natural" mediators between the Western and Samoan traditions. In Western

Samoa the proposal to create a common resident citizenship, if
implemented, will remove legal barriers between part-Samoans of
European status and those holding Samoan status—each segment
providing leaders today. How far part-Samoans can merge fully into the sociopolitical milieu will then depend on what constitutional
strictures if any may be put in this territory on the right of part-
Samoans to take matai titles with their land and other rights. In
American Samoa any revision of the present requirement of having
"at least three-quarters Samoan blood" to participate in Samoan-
style rights would similarly affect the situation of the part-Samoan
leader group.

The main consideration relating to the future of elite communication, however, is clearly concerned with the Samoan titleholder system and its social matrix. The weight of many factors
considered in the study lies to the side of its general maintenance,
but with internal adaptation to changing circumstances.

For both territories, "preservation of the matai system"
was seen to be a highly self-conscious issue, with great symbolic
value concerned with Samoan integrity and conservation, and of focal
interest to elite leaders. This defensive attitude derives in part
from knowledge that the system is considerably under attack by whites,
and that official emphasis is being put on egalitarian and individualistic
tendencies which supposedly are inconsistent with its hierarchical
and group-responsibility principles. But perhaps even more it is
symptomatic of Samoan-originated changes taking place within the
society iself through which the survival value and adaptability of the
traditional system is being tested ever more pressingly by new circumstances.

The habits of Samoans of looking to the matai leadership have
been seen as highly persistent. The very difficulties of acculturative
problems tend to confirm the matai system. Samoans are fully aware
that as individuals they tend to be weak in the face of Western pressures, but that operating together through their elite leaders, and
choosing leaders who have had training in western ways or can otherwise "pilot the cross-seas of change," they raise their level of competence. The Samoans know that while some of their number can
get along successfully as individuals, the majority are strong only
as they stand together in the modern situation. Without matai trusteeship of family lands, bolstered by prohibitions on the sale of such
lands, a great many Samoans would render themselves landless.
The system is a protection in this way not only against outsiders
buying up land, but also, and today equally important, against its
being accumulated by "rich" Samoans, with a drift of other Samoans
into some type of peonage, as has happened throughout Latin America,

Asia, and many other areas as traditional authority and usehold
rights have been transmuted into private ownership after the coming
of the money economy.   The very high proportion of the adult male
population with a direct personal "vested interest" in maintaining the
system; the very widespread dislike of Samoans of assuming responsibility unnecessarily; the dominating values of "family, " "co-operative enterprise, " and "respect for matai authority": these are but
a few of the additional elements in the situation that to an anthropologist justify a prediction that the matai system will in the main prove
exceedingly persistent within the island milieu.

The proceedings of the legislatures in the two territories
provide a long record of Samoan elite opinion on this matter.   In
Western Samoa it came particularly into focus in the report of the
Commission on District and Village Government (p. 29).   In a Fono
of Faipule meeting during 1952, when the bill to establish this commission was being discussed, an interchange took place which shows
with particular vividness the conceptions held by Samoan leaders of
their continuing authority and role in relation to the people as a
whole:

> Tualaulelei: I ask consideration of the phrase
>   "majority of the people" [which occurred in
>   one of the draft clauses]...because this
>   could be interpreted as the majority of the
>   population including matai, taulele'a, and
>   women.   Would it not be better if it says
>   the majority of the matai?"
>
> New Zealand High Commissioner: At present,
>   to my mind, when it says a majority of
>   the people, the word "people" should be
>   understood to mean all the people—men
>   and women. "
>
> I'iga: Sir, I would like to suggest that the
>   word "people" be deleted and be sub-
>   stituted by the words "chiefs and orators"...
>   In Samoa the only people responsible for
>   administering the authority are the chiefs
>   and orators...
>
> High Commissioner: The future must be
>   based on the welfare of the people as
>   a whole...   One of the purposes of the
>   bill is to develop a strong system of local

> Government backed by law...[so as to]
> help Samoa through the stage where the
> matai system is finding it very difficult
> to control the people and very difficult
> to carry out its functions...

> Peseta (Chairman): It could be assumed that
> it is the unanimous opinion of this Fono
> that "people" be deleted and that the words
> "chiefs and orators" be inserted in its
> place. [28]

The Fautua Tamasese, who with his wife represented Western Samoa at the crowning of the British Queen, said in a 1954
Legislative Assembly debate that the matai customs were as important to Samoa as the coronation ceremony was to the British.
"I could not find, " he remarked, "anyone who said, 'We must abolish
the English coronation customs.'" He added, however, that the
matai authority would "perhaps not be for ever, but this is for a
younger future generation to decide."[29]

In the U.N. Trusteeship Council sessions of 1955 the matai
system and the lack of universal suffrage were major points of attack
by spokesmen for the Soviet Union, India, and some other countries.
The High Commissioner, defending the New Zealand regime, said
that there are many valid features in the Samoan order which New
Zealand wished to retain in the liberalization of the social structure;
he noted that:

> The Administering Authority intends to attain
> its ends by persuasion, discussion and reason...
> It is sound policy to let the Samoan people
> progress in the Samoan way, which is plenty
> of talks and time for consideration and more
> time for talk so that eventually a large measure
> of agreement is arrived at. [30]

In American Samoa, from 1950 on, preservation of the matai
system was a prominent topic in discussions and resolutions on pro-

---

[28] Proceedings of the Fono of Faipule, September 1952,
pp. 28-29.

[29] Legislative Assembly Debates, First Session 1954, p. 48.

[30] Reported in the Samoa Bulletin, July 22, 1955.

tective measures in drafts of proposed organic legislation.   For
example, Resolution No. 6 of the First Session of the legislature
in 1951 on this subject reads in part:

> Whereas the people of Samoa hold in their
> hearts the importance of its matai system,
> which is truly the keynote of the peace and
> happiness of the land, and ...[Whereas] the
> proposed Organic Act... will not, in the
> conviction of Samoa, safeguard their lands
> and customs, and so secure our happiness
> and our way of life...
>
> ...it is the unanimous desire of the Fono
> that the said Organic Act... be withheld until
> The Fono is convinced that the People, Customs
> and Land of Samoa are well protected by such
> Organic Act.

Resolution No. 1 of the Second Session in 1951, continuing to express
the legislature's worry on the matter, reads in part:

> Whereas Samoa is concerned and fearful that
> its lands, customs and traditionally established
> matai system might be inadequately protected
> with the passage of Organic Legislation...

and it is rounded out by the fourth day as follows:

> BE IT RESOLVED that the Congress of the
> United States approve all laws passed by the
> Fono concerning customs and the matai system,
> inasmuch as [the Fono] understands the people
> and their needs, culture and tradition. [31]

How this problem has continued to dominate the minds of Samoan
leaders is shown by a resolution along the same lines passed and

------

[31] Quotations are from the Legislature of American Samoa,
Fono Journal, First Session 1951, p. 130; Second Session 1951,
pp. 4, 10; for the fuller contents of the first resolution, which also
included a request that all limitations on the legislature's powers
be removed.

sent to the governor by the legislature in its January 1956 session
(Resolution 15).   After a preamble stating that the "buying power"
of immigrants who might enter the territory in connection with future economic development could "embody a serious threat... to
the 'age old' Samoan Way of Life" it continues:

> RESOLVED, That the Governor of American
> Samoa enact in the interest of the indigenous
> people of this territory such legislation as
> may be necessary to protect the lands, business
> enterprises, customs, culture, and traditional
> Samoan family organization of persons of Samoan
> ancestry; and providing that no change in the law
> respecting the alienation or transfer of land or
> any interest therein shall be effective unless the
> same be approved by two successive legisla-
> tures by a majority vote of the entire member-
> ship of each house and by the Governor.

This is obviously a Samoan-drafted resolution, and it has additional
interest in revealing not only a persisting uncertainty as to the
powers of the governor and of the legislature, but also a margin
of self-doubt as to whether one elected set of representatives might
yield to pressure or temptation. [32]

The zone in each territory where the authority of the titleholder has tended to lose its grip is, as would be anticipated, the
urban port area.   The government employee or other Samoan towns-
man, more or less wholly dependent on the commercial economy,
and usually maintaining a Western-style nuclear family, can enter
only selectively into the group living system; and he is likely to
have to farm materially more into it than he gets out of it.   By contrast, the rural Samoan would still find it almost impossible to step
outside the system and motivate himself as an individual unless he
moves outside his community.   An apt Samoan saying, matemate
lima, "restrain the hand, " which may be translated freely as "Never
do for yourself what others should do, " still bears the strong sanctions

---

[32] Quotations are from the Legislature of American Samoa,
Fono Journal, First Session 1951, p. 130; Second Session 1951,
pp. 4, 10; and from a list of resolutions passed by the 1956 Regular
Session of the Fourth Legislature, dated January 30, 1956, and
submitted to the governor.

of public opinion. Though in American Samoa an individual could until recently declare himself to be living outside matai control for purposes of voting for his representative in the legislature (p. 33), almost no Samoans cut themselves off so irrevocably from their social group milieu. [33]

Looking to the future, it may be expected that the number of Samoans living permanently in the urban setting more or less outside the matai system will multiply. Increasingly young people will also have a temporary "fling" at town life or at individual enterprises in or out of town. But the rural setting will in the main continue as a sphere of group-oriented living in which the great majority will carry on a round of life under matai, or at least matai-like, leadership. Of the position of the taulele'a or young men, a New Zealand educator writes in 1954:

> I have a strong impression that the need
> [for education] is greatest among the young
> men of the villages. Their status...is not
> high in Samoan society...they have little
> power and inadequate outlet for ambition or
> creative urges. It is the young men who first
> feel the pull of Apia and, beyond it, of New
> Zealand. The reason, I believe, is not just
> the bright lights...but, more deeply, the
> desire for personal freedom, which the
> Samoan Communal System denies, and the
> boredom of village life, which becomes
> apparent as soon as it is touched by...urban
> civilization. I feel that the break will first
> occur with them... A policy of adult educa-
> tion adapted to their needs and interests might
> help to postpone the break, or at least make it
> more disciplined and controlled when it becomes
> inevitable. [34]

An editorial in the Samoa Bulletin for September 2, 1955, presents a European-status editor's view of the problem of the younger

---

[33] Those "outside the matai system" are almost entirely part-Samoans.

[34] Beeby, C. E. op. cit., p. 18.

generation, relating it at the same time to the self-government
issue:

> The attraction which New Zealand holds for
> young Samoans seems to confirm the view that
> the present mode of life within the Territory
> is neither full enough nor interesting enough
> for young people of adventurous spirit who
> have been given a much higher education
> than their forefathers and are therefore
> more keenly aware of the limitations of
> Samoan custom. That should serve as an
> indication that the present basis on which
> Samoa is seeking self-government might
> not be the basis which is acceptable to the
> generation who will have to administer the
> systems founded by their parents. Whether
> the older generation of today recognises the
> fact is one thing; whether it will do anything
> to remedy the position is another!

An interesting discussion has been taking place during 1955
in the Legislative Assembly, the newspaper columns, and elsewhere
as to whether young people could become more reconciled to village
life if it were enriched by sports programs. A proposal that sports
goods such as football gear should have customs duties reduced
received considerable support in the assembly though in the end it
failed to pass. Every village has long had a Samoan-type cricket
pitch on the malae (public "square"), and at times matai can be seen
playing along with the young people. Boxing, wrestling, and in
American Samoa some baseball and volleyball, have their followings.
A notable step in one of the districts near Apia was the start in July
1955 of an intervillage rugby football competition. The integrative
and tension-relieving functions of sports and arts have long been
recognized by students of acculturation, and it will be interesting to
see whether this phase of community life will become considerably
enriched as a voluntary move by the people themselves.

In earlier sections of the study important modifications were
seen as taking place in the matai system which appear to be bringing
it slowly but increasingly toward greater harmony with the patterns
of contemporary world culture, so that a sharp break such as the
two quotations given above seem to suggest may actually not occur. Modifications are under way by which the central government authority

curbs the titleholder's traditional authority.   Titles are being given increasingly by adherent groups to more educated and economically enterprising individuals who can provide practical leadership; untitled persons including women have been extending their freedom of action, presaging a lessening of the power gap between <u>matais</u> and non-<u>matais</u>.   An increasing number of elite outlets for ambitious persons are available outside the <u>matai</u> system: as pastors, schoolteachers, medical practitioners, nurses, and in other fields. It has been noted that some titles are being split among family branches (p. 43), and here and there an unused title is being revived, so that there are more titles available as population increases: in this and in many other ways a titleholder is becoming more synonymous with the headship of a household or local family.   Tendencies also show for the real authority, if not yet the ceremonial status, of <u>matais</u> to become more equalized.

All such adaptations may be incorporated into the Samoan milieu given time and avoidance of undue stress.   In this way the traditional system would align itself much more than now with such hierarchical and authority systems as continue to flourish in Western "democracies."   But a great gulf of conditioning exists, and is likely to be exceedingly persistent, between the group-responsive personality structure of the average Samoan individual with which the <u>matai</u> system marches, and the individually motivated personality structure of the average Westerner.   Meantime elite persons, understandably, will continue to be extremely sensitive in communication behavior on the whole <u>matai</u> question, having as they do such a deep personal investment.

X. CONCLUDING REMARKS

In each territory of Samoa, the resident populations are seen
as developing, within modern structures of government, a working
integration of their historic social and cultural systems. The two
territories are also having to work out various types of arrangements for coexistence and co-operation. More widely, the two
Samoas are having to find their place in relation to the metropolitan
countries, and to the network of political interrelations and ethnic
differences of the larger world milieu.

In these perspectives the behaviors and problems of elite
communication in Samoa become microcosmic examples of the larger
drama of international and cross-cultural relations. In both territories
of Samoa, the general goals are set away from arbitrary external
domination and control toward an autonomy which includes self-motivated modernization. No one cultural system is riding roughshod
over, or trying to assimilate, the other; instead the mutual respect
and tolerance necessary for peaceful coexistence and ethnic conservation are being fostered. It is becoming increasingly realized that
integrations within one country of many cultures and subcultures can
occur, and indeed are typical of democratic countries, and that unity
does not mean uniformity. Steps are being taken to remove fixed
racial definitions of status and to replace them by flexible cultural
terms. Rigidity in custom is being reduced by more elective opportunities for physical movement and for cultural and personal choices.
The Samoan way of life is "backward" in many respects in terms of
modern world standards, yet has many rich and adaptable elements
which will undoubtedly show great survival value.

It will lie particularly with the elite leaders of all the groups
concerned to develop increasingly effective means of intercommunication among ethnic units, and to use these intelligently in the mutual
interest. Perhaps no factor can be as important, or so much needed,
as training outstanding individuals from the local population as specialists in communication and in other leadership and technical fields.
This is particularly important in relation to fields in which, as at
present, outsiders exercise what seems in local eyes a dominating
and arbitrary power.

The question arises as to how far the writers consider the
propositions which were put forward to have more general significance
and predictiveness beyond Samoa, or at least to point the way to
such wider understandings. Wherever a statement is underscored
it indicates a suggested wider applicability.

Some propositions are indicated as likely to have validity in
relation to smaller societies with usually orally transmitted cultures,

and contrasts are indicated in the text to what is familiar in large groupings with major literate traditions. Another group of propositions apply to situations involving international or cross-cultural contacts of elites, especially as characteristic of interaction between ethnic units in which one is a dominant or governing group and the other a subordinate or governed group; most propositions in chapters VIII and IX fall into this category.

Many propositions occur in chapters IV to IX which, at the level of generality used, would certainly apply as much to the international diplomatic scene so far as one of the writers has experienced it as to Samoa. Those in chapter IV relating to the wider context of "symbol, ceremony, and sanction," and stated in very broad generality, might approximate, for what they are worth, to universals. The writers have the impression that they have equivalents even on the simplest levels of leadership organization, and they fit all contexts known to the writers, through field work and personal experience. The same may be true of the very general propositions essayed in chapters VII, VIII, and IX, relating to elite influence over "mass media," and the play of "image" and "goal" factors, so far as the cross-cultural dimensions referred to are inherent in the given situations.

Of central importance is the question as to how far propositions in chapters V and VI, which focus most directly on elite communication behavior, have such wider validity. Placement in the text, as stated in the introduction, is naturally governed by their significance for the Samoan analysis. The writers hope, however, that they can receive careful comparative scrutiny not only by interested anthropologists familiar with field data from other societies, but also by communication specialists working in the larger traditions. It is the impression of the writers that resemblances exist at many points between Samoan elite communication processes and those characteristic of Western society; and indeed that such communication to be effective may always have to take on somewhat the same general character of personalized and intimate interaction among group-responsible individuals which appears in a highly stylized form in the Samoan setting.

Annex I. SOURCE MATERIALS AND METHODS

Samoan culture presents the advantage for research of being well documented. The authors have studied it at first hand, through intermittent visits, starting with an initial year in 1930-31, and including one of three months in 1950-51. Their main research focus has been on culture change. One of the writers served as technical advisor to the special United Nations Mission which visited Western Samoa in 1947 to investigate a self-government petition sent by Samoan leaders to the Trusteeship Council. Of necessity, a visiting scientist must behave as an elite person in such an island setting. Because of that fact and because culture change has been so bound up with the interactions and responses of elite persons, extensive field notes relevant to elite interaction have been accumulated. In the present volume these notes have been supplemented by the standard ethnographic record, by analysis of government documents, particularly legislative proceedings involving verbatim statements by Samoan leaders, and by materials obtained through correspondence with local officials and Samoan friends on particular problems.

Because a main purpose of the study is methodological (i. e., testing the possibilities of a social anthropological approach to the study of communication), attention is paid not only to the "research design" as it relates to field work but also to the problems of analysing and reporting the data.

In this respect the literature of anthropology gives little specific guidance; studies focused problem-wise upon leadership and communication are almost nil. There are plentiful descriptive accounts of hierarchical dimensions of social structure, and of communication media in a linguistic sense. Studies are also becoming available of "national character, " which have significance for "international" or "cross-cultural" relations. But these have not been put into motion, so to speak, so as to show actual processes of negotiation, public opinion formation, decision-making, and other types of communication behavior. At most, scattered materials occur particularly in the "applied" anthropology literature relating to the use of indigenous leaders in "colonial" government settings, as in Africa and Oceania. Perusal of standard bibliographies in the communication field by the writers revealed an almost total absence of anthropological contributors. A separate annex examines in more detail the anthropological sources available for studies in elite communication.

In general, anthropological studies in non-Western settings cannot presume any familiarity on the part of the audience with the

265

cultural context, as is the case with the more familiar communication studies in our own society, based on questionnaires, interviews, and other techniques which can count as implicit a common background of understanding. Anthropology is for this reason a "wordy" discipline. The need for explicit contextual analysis leads always to bulk, much of it given over to descriptive ethnography. The principle has been followed, however, of keeping the study as sparse as possible in terms of ethnographic, historical, and other local detail. A special effort is made to demonstrate the importance of linguistic components for the study of communication contexts; this is done by the analysis of language materials both in the text and in an annex.

The conceptual framework of the study is kept rather rigidly to theory and concepts current in cultural anthropology. The writers were sorely tempted to introduce relevant elements from communication and information theory, from learning and motivation theory, from power structure theory, from social organization theory; but except for an occasional brief discussion, footnote reference, or term, the materials have on the whole been kept free of such conceptual sets. The value of the study, they believe, lies in its straight forward presentation of case data, set within a framework of propositions which could be used in further comparative field studies as well as in theory building. They have also been aware of the fact that the text materials may reach Samoa in time and have tried to keep in mind what a well-educated Samoan familiar with the ethnological approach could read and understand. This is indeed perhaps as good a yardstick as could be used if clarity and coherence are to be among the objectives of a general social science case record.

Necessarily many summary propositions or constructs have to be presented rather boldly in such a study, especially background data relating to the elite and their communicative behavior. The text cannot be broken continually to indicate the validity of each point to the person unfamiliar with the setting or literature of Samoa. In general, where a statement is made in the text relating to the customary setting of Samoan life, without indication of its validity, it may be taken that, to the writers' specialist knowledge, the proposition is supported by the professionally accepted anthropological literature, and that they believe they can validate it on the basis of their own field data. When a statement is made of any critical importance or difficulty in terms of validation, it will have a footnote, quotation from an authority, or other supportive device. In the case of verbatim quotations not identified by footnote as to source, it may be taken that they were said to, or in the presence of, one or other

of the writers, and recorded at the time; where the speaker is not
identified by name in the text it is because of the delicacy of iden-
tifying elite spokesmen by name; the writers stand ready to supply
verifications on a private basis.

Statistical counts and tabulations have been given a very
minor overt place in the study: from the nature of the materials
they are rare in ethnological analysis. Samoan culture has itself
almost no goals or values related to keeping the types of numerical
record which are of interest to social science. Furthermore, quan-
tified records of government go little beyond vital statistics, health,
records, trade figures, government finance, and a few other categories. Yet it may be said here that, even though statistics are
overtly few, the data presented have a considerable basis of quantification.

First, the anthropological field worker, in documenting customs, is constantly trying to establish not only the "pattern" of real
behavior in the sense of frequency or modality, but also the range
of variation, and also the "ideal" and "normative" expectations.
Again, in such an ethnologically well-documented culture as that of
Samoa, frequency of repetition and record by trained observers has
verification value. Where documents have existed, such as verbatim
legislative reports, an abbreviated "content analysis" approach was
used, as in counts relating to participation (p. 153). But time did
not allow adequate coverage in relation to statistical treatment.
Such records, furthermore, have only been kept in the last handful
of years, so they give little significant time-depth.

In the original plan it was hoped to use much more fully than
is actually done a series of specific cases to illustrate general statements: accounts of events and persons in action situations ranging
from folklore materials to happenings as seen by the writers in the
field. The sheer bulk of the developing study ruled out use of such
materials except as passing illustrations other than in the one vital
category of elite mediators in cross-cultural situations (pp. 209-11). It
would be valuable, however, to follow up special categories of such
a study by introducing observed concrete cases—a crisis council
meeting, a successful or unsuccessful instance of mediation, the
fortune or fate of a dissenter.

As indicated above, the format of the study developed directly
out of the materials; no model existed, to the writers' knowledge,
in either the anthropological literature or the general communications literature which could be used as a guide. It is therefore an
empirical case construction, against which an anthropologist or
other social scientist worker could measure his field data and his

own creative efforts at organization. Doubtless if a parallel study were to be made by a field worker in another social and cultural milieu, new questions and zones of problem would emerge, and a different organization would be appropriate.

The writers are frankly doubtful that anything like all the categories and propositions spelled out in the text could have emerged to view from the Samoan materials alone. Inevitably they made comparisons as the study proceeded with their joint field work observations over some three decades in other areas, notably among the near-by Fijians and Tongans, the Polynesian Maoris of New Zealand, the Lepanto, Bontok, and other non-Christian peoples of the northern Philippines, and, much more superficially, certain peoples in New Guinea seen during a field trip in 1951. Furthermore, stimulation of thought came from reviewing personal experiences in the United States and abroad involving governmental, university, and business circles: practical and ceremonious communication behavior at levels approximating to the definition of "eliteness." Being so aware of such comparisons, however, a conscious effort was made at all points to avoid imposing arbitrarily on the Samoan case materials any character or category of analysis which they did not really possess.

Most noteworthy among these comparative materials were data drawn from more than seven years of experience which one of the writers has had in an international diplomatic process. This was referred to in the introduction (p. 2) as providing part of the stimulus for the study. While such a diplomatic setting could not properly be made the subject of detailed and open analysis for reasons of official propriety it has been constantly in mind as a general body of comparative communication experience against which the propositions being developed for Samoa were set, and particularly so those found in chapters IV and V. In the latter case the intellectual process involved a give and take of ideas: from an item of data on Samoa or an insight arising out of these Samoan materials, to the particular international diplomatic setting for a check on likenesses and differences, then back to Samoa; or again, from an item of data on the diplomatic experience, or an insight arising out of this, to the Samoan materials for a check on likenesses and differences. A specific example of the latter could be given, as follows: "In diplomatic behavior, agenda building is of great importance; in deliberation within an orally transmitted culture, is there any equivalent of a written agenda?" The final section of the study gives a brief assessment of the implication of these conscious exercises in comparison.

An analytical examination of the Samoan vocabulary through dictionaries, [1] supplemented by fair personal knowledge of the language, reveals several hundred terms directly associated with communication behavior. These yield, among important impressions, the following:

1. Characteristically there is a very great sensitivity to the nuances of social situations and personal reactions.

2. Terms relating to communication behavior tend to reveal great precision in defining personal characteristics, actions, attitudes and emotions, and detailed attention to the arts of speech and suasion.

3. The vocabulary lays marked emphasis on power, respect, dignity, and other aspects of correct and incorrect behavior relating to eliteness.

4. There is a proliferation of terms relating to divisiveness, conflict, violence, and war, and to the reduction of such tensions.

The following is a representative, though not anything like exhaustive, listing of concepts arranged in convenient communication categories:

1. Assembly, meeting:—aofa'i, to collect together; aofanga, an assembly; alālafanga, a number of people sitting together at night; alofi, the circle of chiefs; faavangavanga, to sit around in a circle, (or to leave a space where the chief is seated); nunu, a gathering of people (in one village); paea'e, to sit together; potopoto, to gather together; potopotenga, an assembly; salemausau, all the world, a great concourse of people; taitetele, a large gathering of people; there are also numerous special names for particular types of assembly or meeting.

2. Speech, speaking:—afionga, a word, a speech (the presence of a high chief); faalangi, to compliment, to call over names and titles; faalangatā, to give the first speech (to give a blow to commence a club match); faamoe, to prepare a speech (also to put to sleep); launga, a speech or sermon; loofono, opening speech; leo,

---

[1] The major source used is the standard Samoan dictionary by Pratt (1861); also used are Downs (1942) and a typed English-Samoan dictionary by Chief Faamausili and W. H. Coulter, Department of Education, American Samoa (1945). Pratt's work is currently undergoing a total revision by Dr. G. B. Milnor of the London School of African and Oriental Studies.

to voice or a voice; longo, to report; muāfofonga, speech (the lips);
ngangana, speech, language; muangangana, a proverb; pango, to
have a command of language and knowledge of titles, etc.; oto'oto,
to speak appropriately; suamua, to be the first in speaking; suamuli,
to be the last in speaking; taitetele, good speakers capable of speechi-
fying at a freat fono; tala, to talk, tell; tala, a narration; tala'i to
tell; tasi, to talk; taulangi, to make an appropriate speech or sing
a song adapted to the dancing; tausi'usi'unga, the end of a speech
(the extremity of a land); tautala, to speak; tautalanga, the speech
of a talking chief; tusi, a letter or book, printed material (also to
print on barkcloth, an indigenous process).

   3. Deliberation, explanation, clarification:—faamatala, in
the sense of "to loosen" (as a knot); faamafolafola, to spread out
(as the fingers); faapupula, to make to shine (as a light); faasa'o,
to make straight; faasino, to show, point to; fili, with the sense of
"being involved," select, represent; iloilo, to investigate, look at;
lafolafo, from lafo, to clear off brushwood or bush; molitino, to tell
plainly; sāunoagna, conversation of chiefs (also games, war); ta'i
to guide, lead, tend as a fire; uinga, to accept a way of going, an
explanation.

   4. Negotiation, exhortation, persuasion:—Some representative terms are: aale, to be prompt, to do things with dispatch;
a'oai, to correct, reprove; ai'oi, to beg, entreat; auitalinga, to be
led away by reports; alai, to be forward in speaking (as a child before elders); alo, to conceal, make excuses; amana'i, to keep in
mind an injury or a favor; apoapoa'i, to exhort; aviti, to give a false
report; faafiafia, to please; ole, to ask, beg, deceive; 'oopa, weak
or ignorant in making a speech; uamuli, to prompt a speaker (also
to assist with food or property exchange); 'uana'i, to urge, compel;
faafete, to make a great show of a little; faafiti, to deny, refuse;
faalaa, to interrupt a speech (to twist, as a rope); faalalo, to intercede; faalepa, to break off a speech for a time (to dam up running
water); faali'a, to insinuate; faalolo'i, to desire earnestly (to be
dark and lowering); faalolongo, to be silent; faaloto malie, to appease,
satisfy; faamā, to put to shame; faamao'i, to be in earnest, to speak
the truth; faamautū, to stand firm; faamālofie, to show off, make a
display; faamāmā, to treat lightly, extenuate; faamāsiasi, to put to
shame; faananinani, to speak indistinctly or childishly; faapalalau,
to put off on others, to be half-hearted; faapāvaina, to talk on one
subject only; faasesē, to mislead (bring in head of a canoe to the
wind so as to leave the sails flapping); faatauanau, to importune,
faatāumanufua, to have no heart in, pay little attention to; faatangā,
to pretend, feign; faatalalē, to disregard; faatamala, to procrastinate;

faatonu, to direct, to instruct; faatanga, to take off the prohibition;
faatuai, to put off, delay; faatumau, to cause to stand fast; fatu'ulu,
to store up grievances; fātua'i, to lay up in the memory; fatufua, to
raise a false report; feavitia'i, to give a different version; fela'ula-
'ua'i, to tell tales; fesanui, to whisper together; fesili, to question;
finauvale, to be obstinate; folafola, to spread out, to promise;
fuafua, to ponder, to weigh (to take aim with a spear); laloma'oa,
to be overshadowed, as in a speech interrupted by another; lapavale,
to make a slip of the tongue, to blunder; lave, to be intricate (to
keep before the wind) also lāvelave, to be intertwined, as in subjects
for discussion; mā'elenga, to be zealous, desirous of; mautaia, to
know with certainty; mapomapo, to exaggerate, make pretensious,
to urge one's opinion in preference to one thought better; masua, to
promise and not perform (to spill over from being full); mutuia, to
be cut short in a speech; na, to conceal, deny; nana, to urge a request; nānunga, to talk nonsense, or in delirium; nganangatā, to be
difficult to persuade; nganangofie, to be easily persuaded; ni'o to
cover up, say something and then try to deny its meaning; nono, to
make a pause in speech, waiting to be prompted; paopaomuli, to
proceed with caution in speaking; papeva, to stumble, make a mis-
take in speaking; salo, to repeat again and again, tell in detail; sapo,
to catch up a word and answer it; sasa, to beat, to reprove in a
speech; sasi, to make a slip of the tongue when speaking (to be delirious); seu, to interrupt a speech (turn the head of a canoe); siita'i,
to exaggerate; sipa, to make an error in speaking (to be awry, or
one-sided); sufi, to choose, select; taa'ina, to be induced or drawn
in; taani'o, to go around about in speaking; taufau, to exhort; taufofō,
to persuade, entreat; taulangilangi, to prompt; ta'uvalea, to be badly
reported; talanoa, to chat, talk inconsequentially; talatalatasi, to
relate each particular; talatala'i, to tell what was hidden; talavale,
to tell a sob story; tali, to answer; tano, to leave a speech unanswered and introduce another subject; tapinga'ese, to act independently; tapoto, to make a telling speech (to strike cleverly with a
club); tavale, to speak without thought (to cut wood without measuring
it); vili, to desire earnestly (also to bore a hole, to writhe in pain—
and, in the modern setting sometimes, to vote).

   5. Opposition, contention, disagreement:—aamu, to whisper
discontents with ridicule; angatele, to use abusive language; alafia,
to be hurt by joining in another's quarrel; ava'avau, to speak out
loud in quarreling or public speaking; ului, to urge on, excite;
faafo'iita, to cause anger to be restrained; faalalo, to stir up, excite;
faalilolio, to do secretly; faamautū, to stand firm; faamafimati, to
use threats; faamafulifuli, to sway from side to side in contempt or

anger; faamemelo, to look at angrily; faamuli'upu, to grumble after
a thing is decided on; faasā, to prohibit; faasalaē, to abuse indirectly,
address one and mean it for another; faasisasisa, to have a misunderstanding; faataufutimisa, to provoke a quarrel; faatala'ese, to
refuse saucily; tautalangia, to be spoken against; faatu'i'ese, or
faalavelave, to object, oppose; faatuituia, to indulge in angry feelings; faatui'u'ala, to refuse angrily; faatuatua, to cherish revenge;
faavevesi, to create a disturbance; faifesia, to dissent, expressed
apologetically; fetau, to upbraid, reproach; fetuatuana'i, to disagree,
to sit with backs to each other; fetuua'a, to accuse falsely one after
another; finau, to contend, dispute; mapomapo, to make pretensions,
to be urgent when others have another opinion; mapumapu, to grumble, to be discontented; masei, to use words giving offense; masesei,
to have a misunderstanding; masuasu, to laugh scornfully; mele, to
refuse, reject; mimio, to be perverse; misa, to quarrel; mula, to
grumble (to singe a pig); pavā, to use bad language, speak evil;
silivale, to grumble, rebel; sisii, to use abusive language in a
haughty manner; sona, to be beset, scolded on all sides (laboring
in a cross sea). taua'i'upu, to fight with words, quarrel with abusive
language; tauanau, to use provoking words after being worsted;
tauiaō, to all talk together, causing confusion, taufutifuti, to continue troublesome after the other party has given up and apologized;
taulaloese, to speak against, or intercede out of turn; tafaifesa, to
speak a word of apology when about to disagree with a speaker;
tafatua'ese'ese, to be divided in opinion; talatalaō, to scold, cackle
(as a hen). tālatō, to relate everything against a speaker so as to
cause him to leave; tangitātūtūvae, to cry and stamp with the feet;
tangitui, to cry and beat the body, tangivale, to fret or beg for more
than one has a right to; tō'u, to scold; vāngātootoo, to quarrel (as
between speakers); vatau, to be at variance (or at war).

6. Agreement, reconciliation:—The following terms appear
representative: ai, probably, very likely, a concession made in
deference to another party; au'aufau, to agree together; āno, to yield
to, listen to; 'une, to grant a request; faalelei, to reconcile, propitiate
(cause to be made good); faalotolotolua, also fetoa'i, to be in two
minds, undecided; faalotomalie, to appease, satisfy; faamolemole,
to smooth down; faatasi, unanimous (to become one, together);
finangalo, the chief's will or desire; langamuli, to gain victory over
an opposing speaker after having been reproved (to gain victory in
war after having been defeated); lelei, to be reconciled (good); liualo,
to be favorable (to turn the belly to); solovi, a word shouted out on
getting the victory; sosoo, to reconcile (join together); tāungata, to
strike hard bargains, be difficult to deal with; tafatuafaatasi, to be
of one mind; toa'i, to do a thing from constraint (or to commit suicide);

toaitiiti, the minority, literally supporters (or warriors)--few; toatele,
the majority, supporters--many; to'ese, to beg pardon, apologise.

7. Decision, announcement, proclamation:—Some significant terms are: ali, to appear, as in faaalia, to cause to appear,
to publish; faaalialia, to make a display; folafolanga, the proclaiming,
promising (from fola to unfold or spread out); i'unga, decision (from
i'u to fulfill); i'ungafono, the decision of a council, a resolution;
faaalinga, a notice; faalāua'itele, to spread abroad a report; manatu,
decision; mau, a conviction, testimony (to be firm); mānuō, to proclaim aloud; māvaenga, a parting command, or promise; molitasi,
to report as the words of one person the sayings of a whole; pasapasa'i,
to spread abroad what was secret; pulenga, a decision or determina-
tion; tala'i, to narrate or proclaim; tala'inga, news, a narration,
talatalanga, information; tali, the answer (also food given to visitors);
talinga, a receiving (the ear); taofi, decision (to hold on to).

8. Hierarchical behavior:—aiuli, ostentatious kindness to a
chief (to give the best of everything); anuilangi, to treat a superior
with great contempt; anusā, to treat a superior with great disrespect;
ataata, to treat with proper respect; usui, to praise undeservedly
(to spear with the hand depressed); faalangi, to compliment, to call
over names and titles; faalangilangi, to be angry on account of disrespect shown; faaleaonga, to treat with disrespect (make of no value);
faaleiila, to be disrespectful (a term of abuse); fāalētala, to treat
with undeserved contempt; faalupe, to compliment; faamalimali, to
talk disrespectfully (with great familiarity); faamā, to shame; faasautu,
to refuse to acknowledge lawful authority; faasulāmuaina, to act or
talk haughtily; faatāla'u'ula, to take unwarrantable freedom; faate-
letelea'i, to act overbearingly; lemingao, disrespectful, rude; lētaualoa,
to be treated with disrespect; lētalatalaē, to despise, treat with contempt; lovi, to be respectful; momoo, to express admiration (or covetous
desires) saufua, to speak hastily without honorifics; so'aitū, to speak
without showing respect; sopovala, to pass over unceremoniously,
to use bad words to a chief; taualoa, to be treated with respect;
tālatū, to boast of power and not have it; vaeane, with all respect to
you (before saying something which may give offense); vii, to praise
(or a song in praise of a chief).

9. Other behavior variants:—aalo, 'ole, etc., to deceive;
angatele, faaleanga, etc., to use abusive language; 'ata'ata, nene'a,
etc., to laugh; aviti, faalata, etc., to lie, give a false report, mislead; faa'ata, to make to laugh; faaaimango, to cheat; faali'a, to insinuate; faalili'a, to frighten; fāaluma, to stigmatize; fe'alo'alofa'i,
to evade, make excuses; masuasu, to laugh scornfully; māvava, to
yawn or express wonder (gape); momoli, to accuse; 'ooa, memee,

mitamita, etc., to boast; pavā, suati, etc., to use bad language; sa'oloto, to have freedom, liberty; siita'i, to exaggerate; sua, ula, to joke, jest (the tacking of a ship); sufi, to choose; tanā, to shame another by telling faults; tauemu, tausua, etc., to mock, jeer at, ridicule; toma, to curse; vangivangi, to talk constantly with lies and jests (a jocular term); vilita'i, to persevere.

10. Behavior characterizations:—Samoans discern and have one or more terms for many personality characteristics. The following is an illustrative selection: aao, proud bearing; aalo, deceitful; aiau, cowardly; alovao, shy, one who gets out of the way of visitors; angafaavalea, acting as a foolish person; angalii, chief-like conduct, well behaved; angapiu, exceedingly ugly or bad; angatele, abusive; angavale, ungrateful (left-handed, empty-handed); atamai, clever, sensible; ava'avau, loud-speaking; itangofie, irritable; o'u, angry, sulky; ulavale, mischievous; upua, wordy; faafefete, puffed up with pride (swollen); faafete, making a great show of a little, threatening; faafiamea, presumptuous, assuming; faalevao, boorish, disrespectful; faamao'i, in earnest, speaking the truth; faamā'ioi, slow, sluggish; faasiasia, haughty, contemptuous; faasulāmuaina, saucily or haughtily; finauvale, obstinate; fongafonga, a great talker and liar; latavale, not afraid of strangers, not shy; latulatu, a man who talks rapidly (like a chattering bird); leofaamama'i, doleful in voice; leoleoā, loud-talking, noisy; leopualii, good voiced; lengaoiā, quiet, mild; lelea'i, puffed up with pride through sudden promotion (carried away by the wind); lili'a, timid; mālele, saying something in a public speech to satisfy the public without intending to carry it out; limasusunu, greedy (burning the hand with haste to get the food); lomu, coward (name of a gelatinous fish); lotoalii, noble-minded; lotooti, courageous; lototaia'e, shallow-brained; lotomaulalo, profound, thoughtful; lototonga, ungrateful, ungenerous; ma'elenga, zealous; mangi, a fearless person; mangomangoa, persistent; masua, promising but not performing (to spill over from being full); matavalea, ignorant-looking (dull-sighted in avoiding a spear); moenoa, inconsiderate; musu, unwilling; nganangata, a difficult person, hard to persuade; nganangofie, an easily persuaded person; ngungutu, a great talker who disregards truth; nonou, cross, surly; papatū, courageous (a standing rock that cannot be moved); sapi, quarrelsome; silivale, grumbling; taungā, pained with words (speared in a mortal part); tapinga'ese, independent (to act differently from others); titipa, careless, negligent; vaongatā, disobedient; vaongofie, obedient; vevesi, confused; vivilu, forward (either the approved learning of a child to talk, etc., or the disapproved overaggressiveness of a person in speech or action).

Annex III. ANTHROPOLOGICAL CONTRIBUTIONS TO ELITE
COMMUNICATION STUDIES—AN EVALUATION

1. General Considerations

What can anthropological case materials, and the anthropological approach more generally, contribute to such a field of study
as "elite communication"? What work has been done to date by
anthropologists, both in other ethnic settings and in the development
of relevant theory?

Perusal of standard bibliographies in the communications
field revealed only an occasional anthropological reference. Yet
anthropologists have been dealing with leadership dimensions of
sociopolitical structure, and with linguistic and other communication media, as part of their standard record from the beginnings
of the science—of course, with almost exclusive emphasis until recently upon nonliterate societies. Any anthropologist could with very
little thought produce a list of field studies in which relevant behavior patterns of leaders are considerably documented. The so-
called "acculturation" literature, particularly, brings out the relation of old and new elites to stability and change in culture, and
the texture of "cross-cultural" interaction.

No inventory has yet mined from this vast body of sources
what would be relevant for communications specialists. It is rather
clear, however, that the products of such an inventory would be
mainly in the form of "raw" case material which would in turn have
to be processed.[1] Anthropologists have rarely taken into the field
the specific problem orientation or conceptual framework which
communications specialists have been developing. Even those few
anthropologists who have written about communications problems
and theory usually do no more than include a few case illustrations
from their past field notes. The comments tried out here might be

---

[1] Very occasionally, as seen in the bibliography, the title of
an anthropological paper points directly to the topics of leadership,
public opinion formation, and decision-making, e.g., a pioneering
paper by Mead on "Some Public Opinion Mechanisms Among Primitive Peoples"; Goldfrank on "Irrigation Agriculture and Navaho Community Leadership"; Firth on "Authority and Public Opinion in Tikopia"; Erasmus on "The Leader vs. Tradition: a Case Study." Almost always, however, such materials appear in longer book or
monograph-length studies for which the titles offer no overt clues.

considered as a preliminary attempt to evaluate the anthropological
literature, and at the same time to suggest a framework for a larger
inventory.

2.   Ethnological Perspectives

Mead has two papers sharply focused on communication problems which could usefully form a starting point for appreciating the
cross-cultural approach of the anthropologist. The first, written
in 1937 (see footnote 1), explores "the relationship between political
function and public opinion." Mead distinguishes three types of
non-Western societies:

1.   Those which depend for impetus or inhibition of community action upon the continuing response of individuals in public
opinion situations. Her examples, comprising the New Guinea
Arapesh, the Andamanese, the Ojibwa, and the Eskimo, show how
"immediately expressed responses of individuals are of maximum
importance."

2.   Those which depend upon the operation of formal alignments of individuals, who react not in terms of their personal
opinions concerning the given issue, but in terms of their defined
position in a formal sociopolitical structure. Her main discussion
is of Iatmul society of north New Guinea, where "emotional allegiance
to a formal group" leads individuals to formulate a common public
opinion.

3.   Those societies which "do not depend for their function-
ing on public opinion at all," but which function by invoking the
purely formal participation in and respect for an impersonal pattern
or code. Here, as in Bali, "each human unit is a cipher" trained
from childhood to fit into a pattern, with his whole safety depending
on its continuance.

Such comparison of divergent social systems, Mead concludes,
"suggests that each of the different types of appeal to public opinion...
which we find in modern society presupposes a different relation between the character formation of the citizen and the political system
of which he is a unit," as in the three typical leads, "How do you
personally feel about this?"; "Every member of X group will of
course support..."; "The proposed change will introduce such and
such discrepancies in the legal structure on which our society is
based."

In a subsequent paper on "Some Cultural Approaches to Communication Problems," Mead presents further case materials from
three of the peoples among whom she has worked, the Arapesh of

New Guinea, the Southern Manus people of the Admiralty Islands, and the Balinese. The stress here is on "the diversity of ways in which the communicator and his audience has been institutionalized."[2]

The Arapesh, marked by values of "warm interdependent responsiveness," lives in hamlets dotted over steep mountain country:

> Any unexpected event is likely to find them
> scattered, and a system of [shouted] calls,
> with linguistic peculiarities, and slit-gong
> beats are used to attract the attention...and
> to convey a little imperfect information...
> [On an important occasion] a furious drumming
> on one hilltop starts off a series of shouted
> queries in a relay system... The point of
> communication is to excite interest and bring
> together human beings who will then respond,
> with emotion to whatever event has occurred.

Mead notes that any individual may set off such a reaction. In another source, she speaks of leadership among the Arapesh:

> The organization of feasts makes one a
> "big man," but the Arapesh conceives this
> as an onerous duty which is forced upon
> him by community recognition of his ability
> to organize and lead... [There is] a native
> dislike for leadership... [The society has]
> no hierarchy of leaders, no competition
> between leaders. It is said that there are
> never enough individuals who will take re-
> sponsibility... There is no way in which
> the big men are ranked, no common de-
> nominator of greatness by means of which
> men within one locality compare themselves.[3]

By contrast, the lagoon-dwelling Manus are a "hardheaded, puritanical, trading people, interested in...continuously purposive behavior";

---

[2] Mead, especially pp. 305-12.
[3] Mead, Cooperation and Competition Among Primitive Peoples, chapter I.

> Action is stimulated... by setting up
> exact instigating situations—a prepay-
> ment, a loan, an advance—to which other
> individuals respond, under penalty of super-
> natural punishment [by ghostly guardians]...
> There are a series of drumbeats [with
> precise intellectual meanings]... The other
> characteristic form of communication... is
> oratory, used in most cases angrily, as a
> stimulus to economic activity... The Manus
> prefer action in a well defined context, under
> the spur of past careful definition reinforced
> by guilt, with anger introduces as [a] stimulus.

Again leadership among the Manus is spoken of in another source:
the prosperity or state of depression of a given community depends
upon the organizing force and ability of leading individuals. Leadership is measured by the amount of ceremonial wealth which such an
individual possesses and which has passed through his hands, particularly in manipulating a traditional structure of kin and marriage
relationships. Mead gives examples of outgoing, aggressive, innovating leaders and also of "reserved, aristocratic, arrogant, un-
communicative ones."[4]

The Balinese community, again in marked contrast, has a
caste system derived from a South Asia background, and a highly
organized leadership, with an elite hierarchy and village council.
The communicator "acts as if the audience were already in a state
of suspended, unemotional attention, and only in need of a small
precise triggering words to set them off into appropriate activity."
To a people trained meticulously in the expected routines, with a
minimum of individual initiative, "the stimuli are as simple as red
and green lights in a well regulated traffic situation, where no policeman is needed." Communications even come from the gods through
possessed persons with all the "impersonality of the voice [in]
telephoning."

These case materials presented by Mead can be immediately
helpful in placing the Samoan data. Clearly Samoa is another variant,
combining some of the characteristics of the Iatmul and of Bali, but
still quite distinctive. And these would by no means begin to exhaust
the range. A person familiar with the standard ethnographic record

---

[4] Idem, chapter VII.

might call to mind such cases as the "military aristocracy" of the Crow Indians, the aggressive "potlatching" in elite interaction among Northwest Coast Indians; the cattle-breeding aristocracies of East and South Africa; the supratribal "league" of the Iroquois; the vast orderly hierarchy of that "original monolithic state, " the Inca Empire.

3. The Potential Range of Comparison

Could any typology be established, it might be asked, which would be of aid in developing comparative or cross-cultural research in such a field as elite communication, especially outside the more familiar range of the "great cultural traditions"? A number of organizing texts in anthropology present what purport to be representative cases in leadership and other dimensions of culture. [5] These usually start, for contrast to our own way of life, with presentations of extreme cases which anthropological research can supply relating to the bands, camps, and hamlets of small migratory or semimigratory peoples: the "strong men" of Eskimo camps or those of Paleoasiatic reindeer hunters and herders; the elder leaders of bands among the African or Southeast Asian Pigmies, or South African Bushmen; the clan elders of Australian Aborigine hunters; the heads of hamlet groups among gardening peoples who use shifting cultivation. These political entities in embryo are shown by anthropologists to have the essential dimensions anticipatory of "the state": a group unified by common loyalties, a recognized territory with resources which they want to use with security and continuity, a system of external relations, and an internal organization of leadership, social control, and common services.

Social structure among such groups, subject to the limits of number, may be highly complex. Even a trained anthropologist finds difficulty in analyzing some of the complicated kinship systems

---

[5] For example, Beals, R. L. , and Hoijer, H. , An Introduction to Anthropology; Coon, C. , A Reader in General Anthropology; Murdock, G. P. , Our Primitive Contemporaries; Forde, C. D. , Habitat Economy and Society (revised edition, 1950). One of the rare organizations of material on political behavior is Thomas, W. I. , Primitive Behavior, chapter XIV, "Primitive Government. " For other selected sources on leadership and the wider contexts of social structure see part V of the bibliography.

of the Australian Aborigines. Religious and ceremonial life is always likely to be highly elaborated. Economic maintenance is everywhere subject to orderly procedures, as with land tenure, work effort, and allotment of what is counted "wealth." Dealings with external groups, though sometimes involving violence, are always subject to negotiation, and quite frequently "international law" turns out to be much elaborated in such miniature settings, in relation to use of resources, trade, intermarriage, religious needs, and other factors of extragroup contact. All such matters require leadership in the 24-hour a day round, with attention to deliberation, group opinion, and the making of decisions.

This is brave talk in terms of research potentials, but actual records of elite communication behavior in such groups are scanty. The literature, for example, on Australian Aborigine peoples has patchy and scattered references. A recent summary relating to the Kariera gives a thumbnail sketch as follows:

> The horde [a group of nuclear families
> related in the paternal line, rarely num-
> bering above 75 individuals] is led by the
> older male members, the fathers and grand-
> fathers... These old men are esteemed for
> their age and experience, as well as for their
> status as elderly relatives. Meeting informally
> they decide when and where the horde is to
> move, conduct negotiations with neighboring
> hordes, and direct other matters affecting the
> horde as a whole. Since the horde is very
> small, order is maintained largely through the
> force of public opinion; the fear of ridicule and
> consequent loss of prestige are ordinarily quite
> sufficient deterrents to antisocial behavior. [6]

It is, nevertheless, a far cry from the elder, the shaman, the strong man, the senior clan descendant, of such a human unit to the Samoan hierarchy of leadership, just as it is from the Samoan to that of a large modern state. The village community, for example, so widely characteristic of sedentary "peasant" societies, gives room and need for differentiations of leadership function as well as

---

[6] Summarized in Beals and Hoijer, An Introduction to Cultural Anthropology, pp. 448-49.

introducing complexities in the communication network beyond those
of the face-to-face band or camp of a few families. One of the most in-
structive case examples here from anthropological literature relates
to so-called "non-Christian" mountain peoples of the northern Philippines. Of two neighboring groups, one, the Ifugao, live in tiny hamlets of kinsmen scattered through their rice terraces; security comes
in this warlike setting through a great elaboration of interhamlet
law and negotiation defining peace and war, visiting, property rights,
trade, ceremonials, interhamlet kindship and marriage arrangements, and other matters of common concern to a group totaling
some 60,000 persons. By contrast, the neighboring Bontok, with
some 50,000 in all, have well-organized villages with up to 2,000
persons; an elaborate internal sociopolitical organization and law
has been needed for the village, but external relations are proportionately much less formulated and more subject to the arbitration
of the leader. [7]

The typology of systems between the migratory camp and
the historically reported city-state and other political consolidations
of the "civilized" world has been handled by anthropologists in broad
terms only. Cleared of the unhappy theoretical brushwood of the
"man of nature," of unilinear social evolution, and of geographic,
economic, psychological, and other determinisms which so often
obscure them, the following seem to be the main patterns:

1. Organizations of peoples living on wild foods which are
sufficient seasonally or permanently to allow groups if they want to
aggregate in larger numbers, e.g., the large temporary summer
camps of North American Plains Indian buffalo hunters, the sedentary
settlements of seed-eating Indians in Western American states, the
villages of the salmon eaters of the Northwest American coast, the
villages of sago-flour eaters in Western Pacific island swamplands.

2. Organizations of herders with migratory animals such
as sheep, goats, horses, donkeys, camels, which usually involve
small local groups, but can have usually loose overarching political
structures, as with the "hordes" of Central Asian herders.

3. Cattle herders, who with this major flesh and dairy produce resource can if they so choose develop sedentary villages and,

---

[7] Eggan, F., "Some Aspects of Culture Change in the Northern
Philippines," pp. 11-18; Jenks, A. E., The Bontoc Igorot; Barton,
R. F., Ifugao Law; Keesing, F. M. and M. M., Taming Philippine
Headhunters: A Study of Government and Culture Change in Northern
Luzon; Keesing, F. M., "Bontok Social Organization," pp. 578-601.

as in Africa, may, in scattering out over the pasturelands, build up
very elaborate political consolidations centered on a "king" or senior
kin line.

   4.   Fishing peoples who can range from migratory boat-
living peoples as in the China seaports to settled villagers.

   5.   Agricultural peoples at varying technological and organizational levels from shifting gardeners to settled farmstead, village,
and small-town cultivators practicing irrigation, fertilization, and
diversified farming and trading.   In this last category it may be noted
that the scattered "farmstead" system characteristic of many rural
Western settings is rare among so-called "primitives," though it
does occur, as in Micronesian islands.

   The significance of such a broad typology is to hint at the
range of choice which a cross-cultural researcher would have in
planning studies in such a field as elite communication.   The Samoa
case clearly involves a greater formalization and social differentiation of leadership and communication than is characteristic of the
migratory herders and shifting gardeners.   But in some respects
it falls short of the centralization and typical elaboration of African
cattle or agricultural kingdoms, or of agricultural-dominant societies
with the plow or at least high-yield grains, as in the Middle American
and Peruvian "civilizations" and those of the Asian lowlands and
their immediate offshore islands.

   Some sense of the likeness and contrasts which would emerge
in such comparative research may be gained by quoting parts of a
brief over-all survey of leadership and social order among nonliterate peoples given by Lowie:

> Many primitive communities are governed by
> public opinion rather than by constituted author-
> ity...   In Queensland [Australia] all the elder
> males made up an informal council that settled
> affairs of state...   The North American Indians
> had "chiefs" but often these were mere advisors
> and virtually never dictators.   Except in emer-
> gencies they had no power over the lives and
> property of their fellows.   Naturally a man of
> strong personality could assert himself but
> his influence was not rooted in office, so that
> it died with himself.   This holds also for many
> South American tribes...   Even among the
> Indians of British Columbia, where caste played
> so important a part, the chief was not a despot...

Religious sanction sometimes gives
absolute power in Polynesia... [The]
African natives have again and again
founded pretentious kingdoms... The
monarchies of Africa present probably
all the variations found in the history
of civilized nations... [In Uganda, for
example,] there is no aristocracy, but
a vast number of officials including the
king's ministers, governors of the 10
provinces, and various grades of chiefs...
The State organization has been worked
out on a clan basis, many clans rendering
special services to the king... As in
Polynesia, the king in [Africa] was sometimes considered divine. [8]

Lowie's references to "constituted authority, " "dictatorship, "
and "despotism, " appear to suggest that he had in mind rather narrow and rigid criteria for leadership behavior. This raises the
question as to what more general interpretations anthropologists have
given of eliteness and its sociopolitical contexts. How far, it may
be asked, have anthropologists developed problem approaches, concepts, hypotheses, relevant to the study of elite communication
whether in the nonliterate setting or in our own?

4. Anthropological Theory Relating to "Eliteness"

The anthropological literature on hierarchical aspects of
social systems is quite penetrating in its structural delineations,
such as those of status and class. But it tends to thin out severely
when the focus is directed toward more specific dimensions of eliteness and elite behavior. Lowie, who was quoted above and who is
perhaps counted the "dean" of modern students of social organization,
has an interpretation of the genesis of eliteness which demonstrates
the level of generality of much of the literature:

———————

[8] Lowie, R. H. An Introduction to Cultural Anthropology,
pp. 292-96; see also his early, classic book, The Origin of the State,
which gives an anthropological critique of then current theories on
the development of political institutions.

"In considering [stratification]...we have
to reckon with several deep-seated drives.
The desire to excel one's fellows, though
repressed by a few peoples...is intense in
most societies. Ability in a direction favored
by a society lends personal eminence, and a
powerful sense of kinship tends to make the
distinction hereditary. The trend has been
found noticeable even in comparatively democratic tribes... Subjugation of one people by
another [sometimes] depressed the conquered...
Stratification is often wholly irrational, i.e.,
from the point of view of the general interest,
sometimes even from that of the upper strata.
At times, as in the Hindu system, it is wholly
capricious... Criss-crossing such developments are widespread human traits—vanity and
power madness, for instance—which are bound
to appear with fair regularity and lead to recurring
manifestations... In [certain] instances, rulers
gained physical means of coercion through the
accession of outsiders whose political ties within the territorial unit were exclusively with the
ruler [Lowie's examples include Fijian and Mongol
cases]... Rude societies are essentially democratic, yet even in them a person believed to be
favored by supernatural beings is able to dominate.
In more sophisticated conditions a chief who aspires
to absolute power claims supernatural descent. [9]

Another illustration of this level of generality would be a chapter by
Lips on "Government" in a standard anthropology text; in his summary he says:

Characteristic of the earlier cultures
is the complexity of legal norms and the low
degree of differentiation in legal concepts.
The pressure from [hostile groups] outside and

---

[9] Lowie, Social Organization, pp. 292-93. Acknowledgments
are due to Mrs. Blodwen Hammond, graduate student in anthropology
at Stanford, for aid in assembling materials on leadership and elite
behavior.

public opinion within the society are the
strongest regulating factors... [In terms
of variety] the individualistic and at the same
time democratic traits of [New World Indians]
stand out in strong contrast against the [more
autocratic] structures of African societies...
For the primitive it is not the individual who
is eternal, but the people, land, and law. [10]

Perhaps the fullest attempt to analyze leadership characteristics so far essayed in the anthropological literature is a discussion
by Chapple and Coon; it is set within a framework of "interaction"
theory characteristic of Chapple's work:

A leader is a man who, when more than
two persons are present, originates action in
a majority of [set] events to which those present responds... Only when an individual has
mastered this technique, and has trained a
group to respond to him continually, has he
developed the basis of leadership... The
well-adjusted leader... is a person who can
also respond in events in which he interacts
with only one other person, and which we
call 'pair events.' He is, in other words
a man who originates action in public, but
who gives his followers the opportunity to
do the same to him in private. Unless he can
do this successfully, the equilibrium of his
followers may be disturbed... [possibly pro-
ducing] new relationships, so that, through the
rise of new leaders, a once homogeneous group
will break up into segments.

The authors have this to say about the political aspect of leadership:

A political institution is a system in which
individuals who are members of different families,

---

[10] Lips, pp. 526-27. The bibliography gives a fairly good
measure of anthropological sources to this time.

and in complex societies other institutions
as well, respond to the origins of a leader...
Every political institution includes a supervisory set, from leader to followers, and
also an external relations set, in which the
leader also originates to outsiders... In
simpler societies political leaders work at
the same tasks as other people... [But in
larger settings] the leader has to spend more
and more time originating in the supervisory
and other sets.[11]

Murdock, in his recent book on Social Structure, fills out
further the context of this picture; he concentrates his discussion
upon the community:

In consequence of its common territory
and of the interdependence of its constituent
families, the community becomes the principal
focus of associate life... Every member...
[has learned] to adapt his behavior to that of
each of his fellows, so that the group is bound
together by a complex network of interpersonal
relationships. Many of these become culturally
patterned, yielding standardized relationships
like those of [kinship, age, sex, clans, and other
associations]...

"Since it is mainly through face-to-face relations that a person's behavior is influenced
through his fellows—motivated, cued, rewarded,
and punished—the community is the primary seat
of social control... United by reciprocal relationships and bound by a common culture, the
members of the community form an "in-group,"
characterized by internal peace, law, order,
and cooperative effort... [But social life also
involves curbs and frustrations, which in turn]
generate aggressive tendencies. The latter
cannot, however, be fully expressed within

_____

[11] Chapple, E. D., and Coon, C. Principles of Anthropology,
pp. 59-60, 330-39, 397-402.

the in-group... Consequently they are
displaced toward the outside and drained off
in the form of antagonistic sentiments and
hostile behavior toward other groups...

Since its members are experienced in
face-to-face cooperation, a community is
ordinarily able to achieve concerted action,
at least in emergencies, whether it does so
under informal leaders or under chiefs and
deliberative bodies with culturally defined
authority and functions... Moreover... it
maintains order and conformity... if not
through formal judicial organs and procedure,
at least through the collective application of
sanctions when public opinion is aroused...
Incidentally, government, as seen in cross-
cultural perspective, has a second primary
function... [It] offers to those in authority
an opportunity to use their power for...
aggrandisement... So long as rulers preserve
law and order, and their exploitive activities
are not disproportionate to the social services
they render, people do not ordinarily begrudge
them their [special privilege and pelf].

Murdock goes on to point out that marriage systems, marketing,
and other factors extending beyond the community tend to counter
the forces of supravillage hostility without discounting war and
feuding. He rightly notes that "the warlikeness and atomism of
simple societies has been grossly exaggerated." Murdock gives
some tabulated materials showing much greater frequency of political autonomy among peoples with small migratory band systems
than those with sedentary communities.[12]
Slotkin, in his Social Anthropology, identifies the "elite" in
society by concentrating attention more upon status and role factors:

Every society arranges the role of its
members into a hierarchy of superiority and
inferiority, which is its status system. A

---

[12] Murdock, pp. 82-87.

> person's status... is based upon the social
> value of his index role... the elite of a society
> are those people who have the highest stand-
> ing...   The term index role [refers to]... that
> role of a person by virtue of which he partici-
> pates in the group's most important activity...
> But not all members of the society have roles
> which permit them to participate directly in
> the important activities. In that case their
> status depends upon the key members of their
> group, i. e. , the one whose index role determines
> the status of some group to which he belongs,
> and the index role of the others is their role as
> members of the group which gives them their
> status.

He goes on to discuss various factors which make for "domination"
and "subordination. " The bases for domination are (1) aptness of
formulated program (by a "formulator"), (2) prestige status, (3) af-
fection derived from admiration, (4) authority role, and (5) coercion
through power. The corresponding bases for subordination are (1)
concurrence, (2) emulation, (3) accedence, (4) deference, and (5)
submission. He gives some brief examples, and then offers several
propositions which might be taken as broad hypotheses on communication, such as the following:

> Where the social acts of the members of
> the group have equivalent effects, the participants
> are equally influential in the determination of
> policy...   In a domination-subordination relation,
> the one who is most influential in determining
> group policy is the leader.

> The customary procedures that are used in
> determining policy vary with the nature of the
> group. In relatively small groups whose culture
> is homogeneous, and especially in the case of
> the primary group, the social interaction is usually
> informal and a decision is reached when consensus
> occurs...   [Even] when no real consensus can be
> achieved, the informal social controls are usually
> strong enough to bring about outward agreement.

> In a secondary group, and particularly if the
> culture is heterogeneous, the social interaction

tends to be ceremonial, and the decision reached
is based upon the program of the dominant segment.

The head is a symbol of the unity of the group,
and like any other symbol he strengthens group
solidarity. [13]

These last statements, stilted as they are, represent the nearest
approximation to general hypotheses relating to elite communication behavior that the writers have turned up in the anthropological
literature on leadership.

The British anthropologist Malinowski, in his functional
studies, was the first theorist to stress the factors of "reciprocity"
inherent in the interrelations of leader and follower. The leader,
in getting honors, must take responsibilities and accept restrictions;
the adherent, in giving service, gets benefits and is freed from self-
responsibility. Even the slave, Malinowski pointed out, has some
rights and his master some duties; as he put it: "You can't have
your slave and eat him, too,"[14] Another British scholar, Firth,
has called these reciprocal relations "basic compensation."[15]

One special facet of public opinion formation and decision-
making stands out here as having been unusually developed in anthropological theory, namely the dimensions relating to law or social
control. Malinowski, Radcliffe-Brown, and Hoebel have been leaders
in showing how both social and supernatural "opinion" rallies to influence the individual to conform to rules, hence fostering social
integration, and presses upon the rule-breaker who upsets the

-----

[13] Slotkin, chapter XIV. He also essays definitions of "democracy," "oligarchy," "the state," and other political concepts.

[14] From personal notes taken in a London seminar, 1933-34;
see also Malinowski, B., "Introduction" to Hogbin, H. I., Law and
Order in Polynesia (1934). It is notable that this influential scholar,
in contributing a section on "Culture" to the Encyclopedia of the
Social Sciences, which is something of a classic in anthropological
theory, has only brief passing references to leadership and political
behavior.

[15] Firth, R., Elements of Social Organization, p. 78. This
is part of a discussion of four principles which this author suggests
are inherent in all social organization in different magnitudes: "co-
ordination," "responsibility," "foresight," and "basic compensation."

equilibrium of group interaction. [16] One of the best studies empha-
sizing this aspect of authority and public opinion is a paper by Firth
combining field work observations from the island of Tikopia with
theoretical considerations. A general statement may be quoted:

> It is a commonplace in modern social
> anthropology that in any authority system
> involving the pre-eminence of individuals,
> the power exercised by these individuals is
> not completely autocratic... In practice it
> is not that this control rests on some ultimate
> acquiescence of their people through virtue of
> some kind of initial covenant, as the earlier
> European philosophers argued. The acquiescence
> may be due to no more than a dull apathy, an in-
> ability to see an alternative mode of government,
> or acceptance by them of some values regarded
> as absolute... But in one way or another the
> people governed impose limitations and modifica-
> tions on the actions of their leaders and rulers.
> In some societies formal institutions such as
> chief's councils or nominated elders help to pro-
> vide checks to authority. In other societies these
> checks come through informal mechanisms such
> as a ruler's gossip with his retainers, the in-
> fluence exercised upon him by his womenfolk, or
> some dramatic event which reveals to him the
> strength of popular feeling. [17]

Murdock, in a quotation given above, stresses the role of
leadership in community settings. Field studies at the community
level have become a major feature of recent anthropological research
in many parts of the world. Such reports not only place leaders in
terms of the sociopolitical structure but may also reveal them in
action situations, e.g., Beaglehole (1941), Goldfrank (1945), Quain
(1948), Tax (1952). Anthropologists have also recorded "life histories" of leaders which can provide case materials in elite com-

---

[16] Malinowski, ibid.; also his Crime and Custom in Savage
Society (1926); Radcliffe-Brown, "Law, primitive" and Taboo; Hoebel,
The Law of Primitive Man: A Study of Comparative Legal Dynamics.

[17] Firth, R. "Authority and Public Opinion in Tikopia, " p. 168.

munication, e. g., Redfield and Rojas, A Village Leader (1934);
Perham's Ten Africans (1936); Barton's Some Philippine Pagans
(1938); Ford's Smoke from Their Fires (1941); Dyk, W., A Navaho
Autobiography (1944); DuBois' People of Alor (1944); Leighton's
Gregorio, The Hand-Trembler (1949); Vogt's Navaho Veterans (1951).
    A facet of anthropological study strongly represented in such
materials is the role of leaders in culturally dynamic situations.
An elite person may exercise influence variously in directions of
stability or of innovation. One of the most extensive bodies of data
here deals with prophets and other leaders of "nativistic" movements. Barnett, in his recent theoretical work on innovation, says:

> It is often taken for granted that a chief, a king,
> a "politician," or a social leader exerts influence
> under any and all circumstances, but...this is
> not true... Prestige ratings of the same person
> ...vary with reference to particular situations,
> particular groups, and particular areas of be-
> havior... Outcasts and marginal men like hoboes
> and criminals without question have paragons
> different from those of the successful merchant...
>   Prestige [cannot be thought of as] the exclusive
> property of the elite...[or as] coextensive with
> authority. Almost never is a leader universally
> admired and looked upon as a model...within the
> domain of his control. There will always be some
> individuals for whom the doings of their headman
> are a matter of indifference or something to be
> scorned, because they do not identify themselves
> with him or with his ambitions...[No one] is so
> versatile that he is a universal exemplar in every
> area of interest.

Barnett notes that radical departures on the part of a leader usually
involve risks of prestige loss: "This is one important reason why
the elite are seldom in the vanguard of culture change."[18] Slotkin

_____

    [18]Barnett, H. B., Innovation; see index for leadership refer-
ences. See also Erasmus. "The Leader Versus Tradition," pp. 168-
78; Mead, Cultural Patterns and Technological Change; and Siegel,
Acculturation Abstracts: North America. For other selected sources
on cultural dynamics see part V of the bibliography.

suggests a type which he called a "formulator," i.e., "one who has an apt program... which seems adequate for organizing and directing the disorganized and random behavior of the group."[19]   Other type-figures have been suggested in the literature of cultural dynamics, as by Gillin, Keesing, Kroeber, Spindler, and others.

Materials on leadership and public opinion are often formulated in an "applied anthropology" context.   One significant body of materials here relates to indigenous leadership behavior in "colonial" or minority situations more or less comparable with Samoa.   Work done by British anthropologists in Africa is particularly voluminous, and has many glimpses of so-called "indirect rule" and other phases of elite behavior in action.   Somewhat more formal, but of generally similar texture, has been the vast accumulation of data by the Dutch on so-called adat or customary law of the Indonesian peoples.   For North American minorities the applied literature on the Indian includes much material on leadership; so, too, do anthropological reports on Japanese evacuees on the West Coast during World War II.[20] Interesting materials are available, for comparison with United States administration in Samoa as examined in the earlier sections, from the former Japanese Pacific islands, now the U.S. Trust Territory of the Pacific Islands, where large numbers of anthropologists have worked since 1945 under governmental and scientific auspices. A number of papers have been published recently by anthropologists taking part in, or advisory to, "technical assistance" operations of national governments and international agencies.   Also becoming available is a small but growing body of studies of leadership within American industry by anthropologists and by scholars under anthropological influence, especially workers in the Warner and Chapple traditions.

---

[19] Slotkin, op. cit., p. 482.

[20] The best known of these "relocation" studies, and an important source documenting American and Japanese leadership behavior under the special conditions involved, is by Leighton, A. H., The Governing of Men (1945).   Among other important references on American minority situations are Kluckhohn, C., "Covert Culture and Administrative Problems" (1943); Thompson, L., Personality and Government (1951); and Spicer, E. H., Human Problems in Technological Change.   Examples of African studies are Barnes, J. A., Politics in a Changing Society... The Fort Jameson Ngoni; Fallers, L., "The Predicament of the Modern African Chief: an Instance from Uganda"; and Gluckman et al, "The Village Headman in British Central Africa."

An applied study tends inevitably to stress both elite structure and opinion formation. The location, influencing, and training of leaders is almost always vital to an action program. So, too, is molding public opinion more generally. The Samoan case materials have illustrated many of the problems likely to be involved: modifications of sociopolitical structure under dynamic conditions; the responsiveness of a group when motivated through its familiar leadership and channels of communication; problems of the abuse of new power by leaders through monopoly and misuse of authority; difficulties of transmuting domination by a group counting itself "superior" into a co-ordinate system of mutual respect and co-operation.

In terms of communication problems, some of the most interesting products of the applied anthropology approach have been suggestions by a number of participating scholars that there are rules, so to speak, to the game of sociocultural manipulation by elites or others. These begin to appear first in writings by the early British anthropologists advising governments in overseas territories. Later some efforts have been made to gather them up and systematize them, particularly in relation to training programs such as those dealing with military government, civilian territorial administration, and the work of the State Department Foreign Service Institute in Washington, D. C. A recent formulation, tried out by one of the writers in connection with a discussion of overseas economic operations included a series of principles of which the following are examples of the propositional statements:

> Peoples... tend to hold tenaciously to basic culture and personality elements laid down in childhood training, carried in language and other symbols, relating to individual and group survival, expressing deep-seated values and interpretations of life.

> Voluntary or self-motivated choice [provides] the most favorable conditions of response to new experience [i. e., a principle of self-determination].

> So far as possible the people themselves should be allowed to set the pace of readaptation to new experience [i. e., a principle of proper timing].

> When expurgation of a custom becomes necessary... the attempt should be made to

provide some satisfying alternative which can
fill as far as possible the resulting functional void
[i. e., a principle of substitution].

Where an outside element has to be imposed
arbitrarily... the new usage should be made as far
as possible congruent with, and integrated into,
the familiar culture and personality system of the
people concerned [i. e., a principle of indigeniza-
tion].

New experience appears far less arbitrary if
it can be reasonably explained and justified in the
people's own terms [i. e., a principle of adequate
communication]. [21]

Propositions of this type, which imply broad predictions and are
becoming increasingly refined, undoubtedly have importance in elite
communication situations involving cross-cultural interaction.

At this point an inventory of anthropological contributions
to theory bearing on eliteness could with some justification move
out into other more general fields: the study of values, of personality development, and of national character. All have selective
bearing on elite roles in communication, particularly where ethnic
boundaries are crossed, as the Samoan study shows. They also
provide understanding of general contexts in which communication
behavior occurs. Such a venture, however, would involve extension
both of this appendix and the bibliography beyond the available space.

The materials given here represent a sampling of the various
approaches which anthropologists have made to elite behavior. Their
greatest strengths appears to lie in (1) analyses of leadership and of
opinion formation and social control in smaller face-to-face groups,
under conditions both of great cultural homogeneity and of accelerated
culture change, and (2) expositions of the total cultural contexts in
which elite behavior occurs. On the whole the treatment of leader-

---

[21] From an unpublished paper, Keesing, F. M., "Social
Anthropology and Overseas Business Enterprises." See also Mead,
Cultural Patterns and Technological Change; this includes a useful
bibliography. For a general review of "applied anthropology" see
pertinent papers in Kroeber, A. L. (ed.), Anthropology Today (1953).
For other selected references see part V of the bibliography.

ship, and in fact political behavior in general, is by no means one of the strongly focused points in anthropological literature. No marked controversy or other stimulation of problem has come from political scientists, historians, or others interested in political behavior to orient anthropological work in this field toward their interests comparably, say, to the interaction of sociologists, psychologists, psychiatrists, educators, or even in recent years economists, with anthropologists.

The internal preoccupations of the anthropological profession, moreover, have been surprisingly impervious to the political atmosphere of the times, except for an occasional sortie in the interests of human rights and scientific freedoms.[22] The World War II setting stimulated a few essays by anthropologists on dictatorship versus democracy, internationalism, and other political issues of the time. Research, military-sponsored and otherwise, on morale, psychological warfare, and international relations, also included study of leadership factors in particular societies.[23] But, all in all, a major-scale attack to align the political science and anthropological approaches appears overdue.

5. Anthropological Theory Relating to "Communication"

Anthropology has long had an important stake in studies of "communication" in the broad sense of research on symbol systems, especially language. Specialists in "anthropological linguistics,"

---

[22] Anthropologists have consistently attacked "racist" philosophies. They also participated in recent formulations on the scientific concept of race by UNESCO. A postwar attempt by an anthropological group to develop a "Statement on Human Rights" (see American Anthropologist, volume 49, 1947, pp. 543-45) aroused considerable subsequent controversy as to its accuracy and scientific propriety.

[23] See, for example, Malinowski, B., Freedom and Civilization; Mead, M., And Keep Your Powder Dry; Benedict, R., The Chrysanthemum and the Sword; also papers by Arensberg, C., and Chapple, E. D., on "World Equilibrium" in Proceedings American Academy of Science, 75 (1942), 29-37; Bateson, G., "Morale and National Character," in Watson, G., (ed.), Civilian Morale, pp. 71-91; Mead, M., "The...Purposive Cultivation of Democratic Values," Conference on Science, Philosophy and Religion: Second Symposium, pp. 56-69; other sources can easily be located.

following up pioneer work by Sapir and later by Whorf and Lee, have been carefully probing the relationships of language to the larger cultural milieu.

What is now often called "metalinguistics" deals with the understandings developed, and the limitations imposed, through the particular conceptualizations of "reality" and "world view" represented in a given language medium. Hoijer has recently summarized this point of view in offering a constructive critique of the work done to date:

> Peoples with different languages may be said to
> live in different "worlds of reality, " in the
> sense that the languages they speak affect, to
> a considerable degree, both their sensory per-
> ceptions and their habitual modes of thought. . .
> Language plays a unique role in the total net-
> work of cultural patterns, since, for one thing,
> it apparently functions together with most, if
> not all, cultural behavior. [24]

The Samoan linguistic materials cited in this study demonstrate how forms and meanings of language enter into both intragroup and cross-cultural relationships, and especially in the latter case may involve interferences and misunderstandings. An over-all view of the relations of language to culture is presented in the proceedings of a conference on this topic held in 1954 at the University of Chicago. [25]

Numbers of special phases of linguistic and ethnolinguistic study can be pertinent to communications research. Workers in overseas zones, for example, will do well to familiarize themselves with technical methods of linguistic recording, including standard orthographic systems for transcribing local languages. Again, the study of language stability and change in relation to wider con-

---

[24] Hoijer, H. , "The Relation of Language to Culture, " in Kroeber, A. L. (ed.), Anthropology Today, pp. 554-73; a very good bibliography is included.

[25] Hoijer, H. (ed.), Language in Culture. A careful analysis of the problem, with reference to key studies, is given by Kluckhohn, "Culture and Behavior"; see also Trager and Hall, "Culture and Communication. "

texts of cultural dynamics is particularly significant in relation to problems of transmitting messages and of controlling and directing opinion, both within a culture and across cultural boundaries. [26]

Going beyond the spoken and written word, anthropological studies of gesture, mnemonic devices, conventionalized art forms, and other symbolic systems may assume importance. [27] In this respect the recent formulation by Birdwhistell and associates, growing out of work at the Foreign Service Institute, of a field which he calls "kinesics," or the study of body motion, has significance. His Introduction to Kinesics (1952) offers a detailed annotation system for gestures and other bodily motions.

A much wider sweep still is being tried out by Bateson, who is seeking to bridge between the anthropological approaches, cybernetics, and other systems of communication and information theory. His earlier concepts of "schismogenesis" and "deuterolearning," together with later formulations arising particularly out of collaborative studies with psychiatrists, are brought together in Communication: The Social Matrix of Psychiatry (1951). Since 1952 Bateson has been engaged in a research program, using a small staff, on paradoxes of communication in the psychiatric interview and the nature of play, with specific reference to schizophrenic behavior. [28] Somewhat comparable interests are being followed by Henry in the field of child learning and play. [29]

As with records in leadership and government, however, communication studies by anthropologists thin out when the more specific focus of elite communication is applied. Materials exist relative to honorific and other formally symbolic aspects of language pertaining to eliteness. In some linguistic records, leaders may be the speakers and informants, so that for any zone involving unfamiliar languages the availability of any linguistic texts might well be checked with the linguistic specialists. But usable case materials rarely have sharp definition in terms of the problems of communications research, and so would probably be of broad con-

---

[26] See Keesing, F. M., Culture Change, An Analysis and Bibliography of Anthropological Sources to 1952, especially p. 92.

[27] See notably LaBarre, W., "The Cultural Basis of Emotions and Gestures"; again, Kluckhohn offers a summary and critique, idem.

[28] This program, supported initially by the Rockefeller Foundation and subsequently by the Macy Foundation, is centered at Stanford University and the Palo Alto Veterans' Hospital.

[29] Henry, J., "Anthropology, Education and Communications Theory."

textual value only. Fortunately interaction between specialists in linguistic anthropology and communications research is currently on the increase, and should prove mutually beneficial in relation to this and other problem fields. [30]

---

[30] The values of such interdisciplinary discussion, as well as the limits of anthropological attention to date, were demonstrated in a "mass communications seminar" held in 1951 under the auspices of the Wenner-Gren Foundation for Anthropological Research—see Powdermaker's Mass Communication Seminar.

GLOSSARY OF SAMOAN TERMS

ainga	family
ali'i	chief
ali'i ma faipule	organization of chiefs and orators
aualuma	organization of unattached women and unmarried girls
'aumanga	organization of untitled men and youths
'ava	"kava"--the ceremonial drink
fa'alupenga	ceremonial "Who's who"
fa'aSamoa	Samoan custom
Faifeau	Christian pastor
Faipule	District Representative (Western Samoa)
fale	house
faletua ma tausi	organization of wives of chiefs and orators
Fautua	High Adviser (Western Samoa)
feangainga	relationship between brother and sister sides in kinship
filifili	select, represent, voice
fono	council, meeting
Fono of Faipule	Advisory Council of Representatives (Western Samoa)
ifonga	ceremonial humbling or apology
lavalava	waistcloth
malae	ceremonial open area or "square" of village
malanga	journey
Malo	party in power, Government
mamalu	dignity
manaia	chief's son and "heir apparent"
matai	titleholder
Mau	"opinion," name of antigovernment movements

papalangi	European
pule	authority, power
Pulenu'u	Village "Mayor"
Samalietoa, Satupua	great "royal" kin groups
Savali	Government publication (Western Samoa)
siapo	"tapa" -- bark cloth
taule'ale'a (plural taulele'a)	untitled man or youth
taupou	ceremonial maiden
tulafale	orator, talking chief
Tumua and Pule	two ceremonial orator groups, spokesmen for "all Samoa"

Note: The Samoan phonemic unit spelled ng throughout this study is pronounced approximately as the ng in "singing." Early mission orthographers chose to spell this as g, and this has persisted in official writing of the language, e.g., Pago Pago, pronounced "Pango Pango."

SELECTED BIBLIOGRAPHY

I. Elite Communication

Center for International Studies, Massachusetts Institute of Technology, 1953, Research in International Communication: an Advisory Report of the Planning Committee. Cambridge, Massachusetts. Also Progress Reports, Research Program in International Communication.

Deutsch, K. 1953 Political Community at the International Level: Problems of Definition and Measurement. Foreign Policy Analysis Series 2. Organizational Behavior Section, Princeton University.

Lasswell, H. D., Lerner, D., and Rothwell, C. E. 1952 The Comparative Study of Elites, an Introduction and Bibliography. Stanford.

Selznick, P. 1948 Foundations of the theory of organization, American Sociological Review, 13: 25-35.

Snyder, R. C., Bruck, H. W., and Sapin, B. 1954 Decision-Making as an Approach to the Study of International Politics. Foreign Policy Analysis Series 3. Organizational Behavior Section, Princeton University.

These references cover cited sources only. For other works, standard sources on communications research should be consulted.

II. Official Sources

A. Western Samoa

New Zealand Government, Annual Reports on the Trust Territory of Western Samoa to the United Nations Trusteeship Council.

United Nations Trusteeship Council, documentation on Western Samoa, including Reports of Visiting Missions, notably that of 1947 investigating a "self-government" petition from Samoan leaders.

O le Savali (monthly official journal); Government Gazette.

Legislative Assembly of Western Samoa, Debates of Sessions since 1948 (mimeographed).

Fono of Faipule, Proceedings (mimeographed).

The Samoa Act, 1921, with subsequent Amendments and implementing Ordinances.

Various reports of government commissions, notably the recent Commission on District and Village Government, 1950 (mimeographed).

Department reports and other publications, including the Education Department Samoan School Journal and textbooks; note especially "Samoan Proverbs, Phrases, and Similes, " by A. McKenzie, Director of Education (mimeographed).

Beeby, E. C. 1954 A Survey of Education in Western Samoa. Department of Island Territories.

B. American Samoa

Annual Reports, mimeographed until 1948, then printed for submission by U. S. Government to the United Nations.

Congressional and other hearings and investigations since 1900, including Report of a Special Subcommittee on Territorial and Insular Affairs, House of Representatives: American Samoa. Washington, D. C., November 1954.

Code of American Samoa (laws, regulations, and orders codified in 1949), with subsequent amendments.

Legislature of American Samoa, Fono Journal.

O le Fa'atonu (Government newspaper).

Departmental reports and other materials, including school texts; notable is a Teachers' Guide on Samoan custom and government, in nine booklets (mimeographed, 1945-47).

U. S. Department of the Navy, 1952, Administration of the Government of American Samoa, 1900-1951. Washington, D. C. Prepared by Captain T. F. Darden, USN (ret.), last Naval Governor.

Other official sources are cited in footnotes.

III.   Anthropological and Related Sources.

Buck, P. H. (Te Rangi Hiroa), 1930 Samoan Material Culture. B. P. Bishop Museum Bulletin 75. Honolulu.

Churchill, W. 1916 "Samoan kava custom, " Holmes Anniversary Volume: Anthropological Essays. Washington, D. C.

Cook, P. H. 1942 "The application of the Rorschach test to a Samoan group, " Rorschach Research Exchange, 6, 2: 51-60.

Copp, J. D. 1950 The Samoan Dance of Life: an Anthropological Narrative. Boston.

Downs, E. A. 1942 Everyday Samoan. Auckland, N. Z.

Downs, E. A. 1944 Daughters of the Islands. London.

Ella, S. 1895 "The ancient Samoan government, " Australasian Association for the Advancement of Science, Reports, 6: 596-603.

Freeman, J. D. 1947 "The tradition of Sanalala. Some notes on Samoan folklore, " Polynesian Society, Journal, 56: 295-317.

Grattan, F. J. H. 1948 An Introduction to Samoan Custom. Malua (Western Samoa).

Keesing, F. M. 1932 "Language change in relation to native education in Samoa, " Mid-Pacific Magazine, 44: 303-313.

Keesing, F. M. 1934 Modern Samoa. London, Stanford.

Keesing, F. M. 1937 "The taupo system of Samoa, " Oceania, 8: 1-14.

Krämer, A. 1902-1903 Die Samoa—Inseln (2 vols.) Stuttgart.

Krämer, A. 1923 Salamasina: Bilder aus altsamoanischer Kultur und Geschichte. Stuttgart.

Lewis, A. M. 1938 They Call Them Savages. London.

London Missionary Society 1946 O le tusi fa'alupega o Samoa. Malua (Western Samoa).

Mead, M. 1928 a Coming of Age in Samoa. New York, London.

Mead, M. 1928 b "The role of the individual in Samoan culture, " Royal Anthropological Institute, Journal, 58: 481-96.

Mead, M. 1930 Social Organization of Manua. B. P. Bishop Museum Bulletin 76. Honolulu.

Mead, M. 1937 "Samoans, " Cooperation and competition among primitive peoples: 282-312. New York.

Pratt, G. 1861 Grammar and Dictionary of the Samoan Language. (various editions). Western Samoa.

Pratt, G. 1890 "Genealogy of kings and princes of Samoa, " Australasian Association for the Advancement of Science, Reports, 2: 655-63.

Reinecke, F. 1902 Samoa. Berlin.

Schultz-Ewerth, E. von 1911 "The most important princi- ples of Samoan family law..., " Polynesian Society, Journal, 20: 43-53.

Schultz-Ewerth, E. von 1949-50 "Proverbial expressions of the Samoans" (translated by Brother Herman), Polynesian Society, Journal, 58, 4: 139-84; 59, 1: 35-62, 2: 112-34.

Stair, J. B. 1897 Old Samoa. London.

Stanner, W. E. H. 1953 The South Seas in Transition (Part III). Sydney, London.

Tregear, E. 1895 "Ceremonial language (Samoa), " New Zealand Institute, Transactions, 27: 593-97.

Turner, G. 1884 Samoa a Hundred Years Ago and Long Before. London.

Williamson, R. W. 1924 The Social and Political Systems
of Central Polynesia. Vols. 1-3. Cambridge.
For a more comprehensive bibliography see Keesing, F. M.
Social Anthropology in Polynesia. Melbourne, 1953.

IV.   Other Sources

Barstow Memorial Foundation, 1932 ff. Typescript reports
and other papers relating to education in American
Samoa.
Beaglehole, E. 1947 "Trusteeship and New Zealand's Pacific
dependencies," Polynesian Society, Journal, 56: 128-
157.
Brookes, J. I. 1941 International Rivalry in the Pacific
Islands. Berkeley.
Brown, G. G. 1936 "Education in American Samoa; the na-
tive teacher in Samoa," Papers of the Seminar-
Conference on Education in Pacific Countries, Uni-
versity of Hawaii (mimeographed).
Chamber of Commerce, Western Samoa, 1900 ff. Annual
Reports. Apia.
Churchill, L. P. 1902 Samoa 'Uma. New York.
Churchward, W. B. 1887 My Consulate in Samoa. London.
Davidson, J. W. 1948 "Political development in Western
Samoa," Pacific Affairs, 20: 136-49.
Furnas, J. C. 1946 Anatomy of Paradise. New York.
Green, W. 1924 "Social traits of Samoans," Applied Sociology,
Journal, November.
McKay, C. G. R. 1937 A Chronology of Western Samoa.
Apia.
Mander, L. A. 1954 Some Dependent Peoples of the South
Pacific. II: Western Samoa. New York.
Masterman, S. 1934 The Origins of International Rivalry in
Samoa. London.
Nelson, O. F. 1928 The Truth About Samoa. Auckland,
N. Z.
Pritchard, W. T. 1866 Polynesian Reminiscences. London.
Rowe, N. A. 1930 Samoa Under the Sailing Gods. London.
Ryden, G. H. 1933 The Foreign Policy of the United States
in Relation to Samoa. New Haven.
Schultz-Ewerth, E. von 1926 Erinnerungen an Samoa.
Berlin.
Solf, W. H. 1919 Colonial Policies, My Political Testament.
Berlin (author was first German Governor).

Stace, V. D. 1955 Economic Survey of Western Samoa.
    South Pacific Commission, Noumea.
Stevenson, R. L. 1892 A Footnote to History. New York.
Stevenson, R. L. 1895 Vailima Letters. Chicago.
Tennent, H. C. 1926 "Samoa: old and new, " Hawaiian His-
    torical Society, Annual Report, 35: 17-31.
Tuvale, T. 1918 "History of modern Samoa" (unpublished
    manuscript translated from Samoan by E. Riddel,
    Office of Samoan Affairs, Apia).
United Nations, Department of Social Affairs 1948 The
    Population of Western Samoa. Lake Success.
Watson, R. W. 1918 History of Samoa. Wellington, N. Z.
Westbrook, G. E. L. 1935 Gods Who Die. New York.

V.   Selected General Anthropological References

Barnes, J. A. 1954 Politics in a Changing Society... The
    Fort Jameson Ngoni. New York.
Barnett, H. G. 1953 Innovation: the Basis of Cultural
    Change. New York.
Bateson, G. 1935 "Culture contact and schismogenesis, "
    Man, 35: 178-83. (See also under Ruesch.)
Bateson, G., and Mead, M. 1941 "Principles of morale
    building, " Journal of Educational Sociology, 15: 206-
    220.
Beaglehole, E. and P. 1941 Pangai, a Village in Tonga.
    Wellington, N. Z.
Beaglehole, E. 1946 Some Modern Maoris. Wellington, N. Z.
Beals, R. L. 1951 "Urbanism, urbanization and accultura-
    tion, " American Anthropologist, 53: 1-10.
Beals, R. L., and Hoijer, H. 1953 An Introduction to Cul-
    tural Anthropology. New York.
Benedict, R. 1946 The Chrysanthemum and the Sword. New
    York.
Birdwhistell, R. 1955 "Kinesics, " Explorations, 4. Toronto.
Chapple, E. E. and Coon, C. 1942 Principles of Anthropology.
    New York.
Dozier, E. P. 1951 "Resistance to acculturation and assimila-
    tion in an Indian pueblo, " American Anthropologist,
    53: 56-66.
Erasmus, C. J. 1952 "The leader vs. tradition: a case
    study, " American Anthropologist, 54: 168-78.
Erasmus, C. J. 1954 "An anthropologist views technical
    assistance, " Scientific Monthly, 78: 147-58.

Fallers, L. "The predicament of the modern African chief: an instance from Uganda, " American Anthropologist, 57: 290-305. 1955.

Firth, R. 1949 "Authority and public opinion in Tikopia, " in Fortes, M. (ed.) Social Structure: Studies Presented to A. R. Radcliffe-Brown: 168-88. London.

Ford, C. S. 1941 Smoke from Their Fires: the Life of a Kwakiutl Chief. New Haven.

Fortes, M. (ed.) 1949 Social Structure: Studies Presented to A. R. Radcliffe-Brown. London.

Fortes, M., and Evans-Pritchard, E. E. 1950 African Political Systems. London.

Geddes, W. R. 1946 Deuba, a Study of a Fijian Village. Wellington, N. Z.

Gluckman, M., Mitchell, J. C., and Barnes, J. A. 1949 "The village headman in British Central Africa, " Africa, 19: 89-106.

Goldfrank, E. S. 1945 "Irrigation agriculture and Navaho community leadership, " American Anthropologist, 47: 262-77.

Hallowell, A. I. 1950 "Values, acculturation and mental health, " American Journal of Orthopsychiatry, 20: 732-43.

Henry, J. 1955 "Anthropology, education and communications theory, " Spindler, G. D. (ed.) Education and Anthropology. Stanford.

Herskovits, M. J. 1943 "Education and cultural dynamics, " American Journal of Sociology, 48: 737-49.

Herskovits, M. J. 1944 "Native self-government, " Foreign Affairs, 22: 413-23.

Hoebel, E. A. 1940 The Political Organization and Law-Ways of the Comanche Indians. American Anthropological Association, Memoir 54.

Hoebel, E. A. 1954 The Law of Primitive Man: a Study of Comparative Legal Dynamics. Cambridge, Mass.

Hogbin, H. I. 1934 Law and Order in Polynesia. London.

Hogbin, H. I. 1946 "Local government for New Guinea, " Oceania, 17: 38-66.

Hoijer, H. (ed.) 1954 Language in Culture: Conference on the Interrelations of Language and Other Aspects of Culture. Chicago.

Keesing, F. M. 1941 The South Seas in the Modern World. New York.

Keesing, F. M. 1953 Culture Change: an Analysis and Bibliography of Anthropological Sources to 1952. Stanford.

Keesing, F. M. 1953 "Cultural dynamics and administration, " Seventh Pacific Science Congress, Proceedings. New Zealand.

Kennard, E. 1948 "Anthropology and the foreign service, " The American Foreign Service Journal, November. Washington, D. C.

Kluckhohn, C. 1943 "Covert culture and administrative problems, " American Anthropologist, 45: 213-27.

Kluckhohn, C. 1944 "Anthropological research and world peace, " Conference on Science, Philosophy and Religion, Fourth Symposium, Approaches to World Peace: 143-52. New York.

Kluckhohn, C. 1949 Mirror for Man, New York.

Kluckhohn, C. 1954 "Culture and behavior, " Lindzey, G. (ed.) Handbook of Social Psychology. Cambridge, Mass.

Kluckhohn, C. and Kluckhohn, F. R. 1947 "American culture: generalized orientations and class patterns, " Conference on Science, Philosophy and Religion, Seventh Symposium, Conflicts of Power in Modern Culture: 106-28. New York.

Kroeber, A. L. (ed.) 1953 Anthropology Today. Chicago.

LaBarre, W. 1947 "The cultural basis of emotions and gestures, " Journal of Personality, 16: 49-68.

Leighton, A. H. 1945 The Governing of Men. Princeton.

Leighton, A. H. 1949 Human Relations in a Changing World. New York.

Leighton, A. H. , and Opler, M. E. 1955 "Psychiatry and applied anthropology in psychological warfare against Japan, " Schramm, W. (ed.) The Process and Effects of Mass Communication. Urbana, Ill.

Linton, R. (ed.) 1945 The Science of Man in the World Crisis. New York.

Lips, J. 1938 "Government, " in Boas, F. General Anthropology. New York.

Lowie, R. H. 1924 The Origin of the State. New York.

Lowie, R. H. 1948 Social Organization. New York.

Malinowski, B. 1926 Crime and Custom in Savage Society. London.

Malinowski, B. 1944 Freedom and Civilization. New York.

Mead, M. (ed.) 1937 Cooperation and Competition Among Primitive Peoples. New York.

Mead, M. 1937 "Some public opinion mechanisms among primitive peoples, " Public Opinion Quarterly, 1: 5-16.

Mead, M. 1940 "Education and cultural surrogates, " Journal of Educational Sociology, 14: 92-109.

Mead, M. 1942 "The comparative study of culture and the
purposive cultivation of democratic values. Comments
by Benedict, Kluckhohn and others. " Conference on
Science, Philosophy and Religion, Second Symposium:
56-69. New York.

Mead, M. 1943 And Keep Your Powder Dry. New York.

Mead, M. 1943 "The role of small South Sea cultures in the
postwar world, " American Anthropologist, 45: 193-
95.

Mead, M. 1947 "The application of anthropological techniques
to cross-national communication, " New York Academy
of Sciences, Transactions, Series II, 94: 133-52.

Mead, M. 1948 "Some cultural approaches to communication
problems, " Bryson, L. (ed.), The Communication of
Ideas, Institute for Religious and Social Studies, New
York; also quoted in Schramm, W. (ed.), Mass Communications. Urbana (1949).

Mead, M. 1951 Soviet Attitudes Toward Authority. New York.

Mead, M. 1953 Cultural Patterns and Technological Change.
Paris.

Miller, W. B. 1955 "Two concepts of authority, " American
Anthropologist, 57: 271-89.

Mühlmann, W. E. 1950 "Soziale Mechanismen der ethnischen
Assimilation, " Abhandlungen des 14 Internat. Sozio-
logenkongresses, 2: 1-47. Rome.

Murdock, G. P. 1949 Social Structure. New York.

Murdock, G. P. 1949 Social Organization and Government
in Micronesia. Pacific Science Board, Washington,
D. C.

Oliver, D. L. 1948 "Personnel management in overseas
business enterprises. " Applied Anthropology, 7:
18-23.

Oliver, D. L. 1955 A Solomon Island Society. Kinship and
Leadership among the Siuai of Bougainville. Cambridge, Mass.

Powdermaker, H. 1950 Hollywood, the Dream Factory.
Boston.

Powdermaker, H. (ed.) 1953 Mass Communications Seminar.
Wenner-Gren Foundation for Anthropological Research.
New York. (This included brief comments by Kroeber,
Linton, and a number of other anthropologists, re-
vealing anthropological approaches to communications
problems.)

Quain, B. 1948 Fijian Village. New York.

Radcliffe-Brown, A. R. 1931 "Law, primitive" in Encyclopaedia of the Social Sciences.

Radcliffe-Brown, A. R. 1939 Taboo. Frazer lecture, Cambridge University Press.

Redfield, R. 1953 The Primitive World and Its Transformations. Ithaca.

Ruesch, J., and Bateson, G. 1949 "Structure and process in social relations," Psychiatry, 12: 105-24.

Ruesch, J., and Bateson, G. 1951 Communication: the Social Matrix of Psychiatry. New York.

Siegel, B. J. 1949 "Anthropological analysis of shared respect," Southwestern Journal of Anthropology, 5: pp. 351-68.

Siegel, B. J. (ed.) 1955 Acculturation: Critical Abstracts, North America. Stanford.

Slotkin, J. S. 1950 Social Anthropology, especially chapters XII (Communication) and XIV (Politics). New York.

Spicer, E. H. (ed.) 1952 Human Problems in Technological Change. New York.

Tax, S. 1952 Penny Capitalism: a Guatemalan Village Economy. Washington, D. C.

Thomas, W. I. 1937 "Primitive government," chapter 14, Primitive behavior. New York.

Thompson, L. 1950 Culture in Crisis: a Study of the Hopi Indians. New York.

Thompson, L. 1951 Personality and Government. Ediciones des Instituto Indigenista Interamericano. Mexico, D. F.

Thurnwald, R. 1952 "The role of political organization in the development of man," International Congress of Americanists, Proceedings, 29; 1: 280-84.

Trager, G. and Hall, E. 1955 "Culture and communication," Explorations, 4. Toronto.

Turney-High, H. H. 1942 The Practice of Primitive War. Missoula, Montana.

Useem, J. 1946 "Americans as governors of natives in the Pacific," Journal of Social Issues, 2: 39-49.

Van Baal, J. 1953 "National movements and the problem of acculturation," Seventh Pacific Science Congress, Proceedings, New Zealand.

Vogt, E. Z. 1951 Navaho Veterans: a Study of Changing Values. Cambridge, Mass.

Warner, W. L. and Lunt, P. S. 1942 The Status System of a Modern Community. New Haven.

Wilson, G. and M. 1945 The Analysis of Social Change, Based on Observations in Central Africa. Cambridge, England.